THE

FALL

OF

LANGUAGE

IN THE

AGE

OF

ENGLISH

THE
FALL
OF
LANGUAGE
IN THE
AGE
OF
ENGLISH

MINAE MIZUMURA

TRANSLATED BY MARI YOSHIHARA AND JULIET WINTERS CARPENTER

COLUMBIA UNIVERSITY PRESS
New York

COLUMBIA UNIVERSITY PRESS

Publishers Since 1893

NEW YORK   CHICHESTER, WEST SUSSEX

cup.columbia.edu

Library of Congress Cataloging-in-Publication Data
Mizumura, Minae
[Nihongo ga horobiru toki. English]
The fall of language in the age of English / Minae Mizumura ; Translated by
Mari Yoshihara and Juliet Winters Carpenter.
p. cm.
First published in Japan in 2008 by Chikumashobo Ltd., Tokyo.
entitled "Nihongo ga horobiru toki: Eigo no seiki no naka de."
Includes bibliographical references and index.
ISBN 978-0-231-16302-6 (cloth : alk. paper)
ISBN 978-0-231-53854-1 (e-book)
1. Japanese language—Social aspects.   2. English language—Influence on Japan.
I. Yoshihara, Mari, 1968– translator.   II. Carpenter, Juliet Winters, translator.   III. Title.
PL523.5.M5813 2015
495.609'051—dc23

Cover design: Evan Gaffney

PUBLICATION of the ENGLISH EDITION
IS SUPPORTED by a GRANT from
FIGURE FOUNDATION

CONTENTS

PREFACE TO THE ENGLISH EDITION

T HE DOMINANCE OF ENGLISH IS A SUBJECT OFTEN DISCUSSED IN THE MASS MEDIA AND BY SCHOLARS IN THE WEST. WHEN Professor Mari Yoshihara approached me with the idea of rendering this book into English, I was simply thankful and did not envision the difficulty that would be involved. I flattered myself in thinking that the book might contribute to the ongoing debate by adding a theoretical and historical perspective that has not been sufficiently explored. I also hoped the book would help readers become acquainted, however tangentially, with a magical written language only a few of them are likely ever to know.

Naturally some adjustments were expected from the start. Written for the general reader in Japan, the book is overflowing with concepts, proper nouns, and historical facts that would mean little to readers unfamiliar with that country. A straightforward translation would end up appealing only to Japanese specialists, who can always read the book in the original if they so wish. I wanted to make the book open to a wider readership, realizing that once the translation came out, my ideas could reach not just readers in the English-speaking world but readers everywhere in this age of English. Professor Juliet Winters Carpenter agreed to collaborate with me in revising the book for this purpose, adding explanations here, shortening or eliminating there, and recasting the discussion as necessary for a new readership.

The true nature of the challenge became apparent to me only after she and I set to work. The book's original title, rendered in English, was "When the Japanese Language Falls: In the Age of English." That title was changed for the translation, but even so the thread running throughout the work is the same: my sense of crisis over the current state of the written language in Japan. My dismay and frustration are first expressed at the end of the first chapter, where I declare that, rude though it may sound, I find much of contemporary Japanese literature "just juvenile." In the original, I then conclude with the following words, which have been deleted from the translation because they are specifically addressed to Japanese readers:

> This book was written for those who, in moments of solitude, quietly worry about the future of Japanese literature and the Japanese language. It is for those who think that what is being written in Japanese today is ultimately of little relevance but who wish, with mingled despair and resignation, that at the very least more people would read Japanese literature written in those years when it was deserving of the name.[1]

I limited prospective readers of the original to those sharing my sense of crisis, thereby freeing myself from the need to justify my ungracious claim about contemporary Japanese literature. The sentiment that the Japanese language is "falling" is in fact so widely shared by lovers of modern Japanese literature that it seemed to me to require no explanation.

The problem is that this sentiment will not be evident to—cannot possibly be grasped by—anyone reading this book in translation. For readers unfamiliar with Japan, my distress is likely to sound no different from the lament voiced by those involved with literature and the humanities the world over; the lament of librarians, schoolteachers, and middle-class parents; the lament that such people have always made and that now in the age of the Internet has only increased in harping intensity: "Young people don't read real literature!"

Yet I would say that as a Japanese observing the folly of her country, my frustration is of a different order—it borders on disbelief. But little of this sentiment, I fear, can easily be understood by readers of this book in translation.

Worse, because the book is founded on that frustration of mine, it may end up sounding overly patriotic. Every ethnic group cherishes its language and takes pride in its literature. Some readers may protest that this book gives pride of place to Japanese, which is merely one language among many, and trumpets the brilliance of modern Japanese literature, which is merely one literature among many. But my aim is not to congratulate my fellow Japanese for whatever our ancestors may have accomplished. The important point to remember is that Japanese is a non-Western language, and the first blossoming of Japanese modern literature, written in this non-Western language, took place some century and a half ago after a long and tortuous course dating back to the seventh century, when the country first acquired a written language. I wanted Japanese readers to understand how truly miraculous that blossoming was, to have them see what a treasure we share, and to make the case that we are now on the verge of letting that treasure slip through our fingers.

I attempted at first to use this preface to the English translation to explain my dismay and frustration but soon abandoned the attempt. Explaining would have required me to go into considerable detail, taking up many pages and taxing the reader's patience. Instead, I decided to substantially rewrite the final chapter to describe the current linguistic and cultural mess we Japanese find ourselves in and to sketch in terms relevant to foreign readers how we might yet escape from it.

When Mari Yoshihara volunteered to translate the book into English, I assumed that it would be years before anything happened, knowing how busy she is with her other work. But to my astonishment, she finished the first six chapters in just six months. I myself, slowed in part by fragile health, took six *years* to write the book, so her quickness floored me. Then, in the blink of an eye, she found me a distinguished publisher: Columbia University Press. Her power of action, and her total commitment to seeing the book into print, far exceeded my expectations. I was tied up with other projects, however, and unable to begin revising the manuscript for English readers right away. Once I got started, as mentioned, I sought the assistance of Juliet Winters Carpenter, who had just recently rendered my novel *A True Novel* into English. When her fingers touch the keyboard, a dizzying variety of English phrases appear as if by magic. I am struck by her utter mastery of her craft.

I am deeply grateful to both of my translators.

THE

FALL

OF

LANGUAGE

IN THE

AGE

OF

ENGLISH

INTRODUCTION

MARI YOSHIHARA AND JULIET WINTERS CARPENTER

*T*HE FALL OF LANGUAGE IN THE AGE OF ENGLISH (*NI-HONGO GA HOROBIRU TOKI: EIGO NO SEIKI NO NAKA DE*) BY Minae Mizumura caused a sensation when it came out in Japan in 2008. Not only did the book achieve high critical acclaim, winning the Kobayashi Hideo Award for the year's outstanding work of nonfiction, but also it was a surprising commercial success: soon after being published, it ranked number one on Amazon Japan, an almost unheard-of feat for a work of such intellectual substance. As of April 2014, sixty-five thousand hardcover copies had been sold.

Controversy spurred the book's success. An influential author and blogger flatly declared *The Fall of Language* a "must-read for all Japanese," sparking an Internet flame war fanned by irate people who had either not read or misread the book and equally irate people who had read it and disliked it. Legions of others joined in, equally vociferous in the book's defense. Thanks to this initial controversy, other media picked up the book and it went on to reach readers far beyond literary and academic circles.

Though originally written for Japanese readers, Mizumura's book has the power to extend its reach. The broader themes of language and literature the author addresses will lead those who come across the book in translation to ask themselves about the missions of their own language and literature in a world where English functions as the universal language. Mizumura's analysis is breathtakingly innovative and will appeal not only to those interested in Japanese studies or the humanities but to all who care about the written word.

MINAE MIZUMURA, NOVELIST

In Japan, the book made a special impact partly because of its author, the acclaimed novelist Minae Mizumura.

Born in Tokyo in the 1950s, Mizumura moved with her family to Long Island, New York, at the age of twelve. Even though she lived in the United States for the next two decades, she never came to feel quite at ease there, and she spent her teenage years yearning for home while absorbed in stories from a sixty-three-volume collection of modern Japanese literature—an experience that forever shaped her sensibilities about language and literature. She studied French literature and literary criticism at Yale, both in college and in graduate school, during its heyday as the center of literary theory; her first publication was a much-praised critical essay in English on the central and controversial theorist Paul de Man.[1] Yet she never considered a career in academia, and she returned to Japan to devote herself to doing what she had always wanted to do—write fiction in her native language.

From the first, Mizumura has played with ideas of language, literature, and translation in her fiction, returning repeatedly to the question: What does it mean to read and write in the Japanese language—or any language other than English—in the world today? In her debut novel, *Zoku meian* (Light and dark, continued, 1990), she daringly and mischievously completed the final, unfinished work of Natsume Sōseki, the titan of the modern Japanese novel, perfectly capturing his idiosyncratic style. Her second novel, *Shishōsetsu from left to right* (An I-novel from left to right, 1995), was equally but differently audacious. Written as a fictionalized autobiography, a long-cherished genre in Japan, the text is interwoven with English and printed horizontally—marking the first time that a work of Japanese literature was printed in this way, "from left to right." Her third novel, *A True Novel* (*Honkaku shōsetsu*, 2002)—available in English—is an imaginative tour de force, a complex, multilayered retelling of Emily Brontë's *Wuthering Heights*. In it, she follows in the footsteps of earlier Japanese writers by basing her work on a Western classic while bringing the extraordinary romance home for Japanese readers. Translations have been published in French, Spanish, Chinese, and Korean as well as English. Mizumura's most recent novel, *Haha no isan—shinbun shōsetsu* (Inheritance from mother: A newspaper novel, 2011), was, as indicated by the title, originally serialized weekly in a major newspaper. Narrating the saga of three generations of Japanese women, the first of whom tragicomically identifies herself with a heroine in a newspaper novel, the work highlights the role that such novels played in the formation of the modern Japanese language and psyche. Each of Mizumura's novels has won a distinguished literary prize: *Zoku meian* won the Minister of Education Award for New Artists; *Shishōsetsu from left to right*, the Noma New Author Award; *A True Novel*, the Yomiuri Prize for Literature; and *Haha no isan—shinbun shōsetsu*, the Osaragi Jirō Award.

Precisely because Mizumura keeps returning to the question of what it means to read and write in the Japanese language, examining the traditional in highly unconventional ways, her novels have a unique attraction for Japanese readers while posing unique challenges for the translator. For instance, the intermingling of English and Japanese in her fictional autobiography cannot possibly have the same effect in languages using the Roman alphabet. That novel also inserts vertical printing amid the horizontal text and mixes different typefaces and modes of notation, new and old, for different effects. The difficulty—or impossibility—of translating her novels is undeniable; yet, resisting any temptation to write in a more transparent style, she has continued to stimulate and amuse her readers (and herself) by producing works of literature that evoke the path that written Japanese has traveled. Why she does so will become clear in *The Fall of Language in the Age of English*.

THE FALL OF LANGUAGE IN THE AGE OF ENGLISH

In this, her first nonfiction book, Mizumura discusses the same issues she has grappled with as a novelist. She takes a critical look at the phenomenon of the English language functioning as the singular universal language today, in the digital era, and what this means for national languages and literatures of the world. The effects of English supremacy, though vaguely acknowledged, have nowhere been so lucidly and mercilessly examined as in this book. The fact of English supremacy is something most native speakers of English unknowingly suppress, all the while enjoying the privileges that come with it. Many non-English-speaking populations, however, cannot afford to suppress that fact but are forced to face it in one way or another, though their writers generally turn their backs on the linguistic asymmetry lest they end up too discouraged to write, overwhelmed by the unfairness of it all.

Mizumura opens with an engaging account of her experience in the International Writing Program at the University of Iowa in 2003. Through sometimes humorous, often touching encounters with authors from around the world, she begins to consider the meaning of "national literature," especially literature being written in non-English languages. She next turns her attention to French, a language she herself spent years studying. She reflects on her own relationship with Japanese, English, and French to shed light on a recent historical shift by which French, once the world's reigning language, was reduced to being merely one among many. At the core of this section is a talk she gave in French in Paris, slyly urging the French audience to confront the deplorable downfall of their language. It is a delightful read—unless you happen to be French.

From there, Mizumura traces the development of the hierarchy of languages using three core concepts—universal language, local language, and national language. Building on Benedict Anderson's now-classic *Imagined Communities* (1983), and revealing a critical blind spot in his analysis, she provides insight into what a universal language truly is. The highlight of her analysis rests on her focus on the role of translation—an endeavor little understood or appreciated in the modern era. According to Mizumura, it was the very act of translation from the universal language into various vernaculars that gave birth to national languages and literatures.

Then she contemplates a miracle: nineteenth-century Japan's production of an extraordinary corpus of modern novels shortly after opening its doors to the West, despite geographical, cultural, and linguistic constraints. In aggregate, these novels are now counted among the major literatures of the world. Mizumura devotes an entire chapter to a groundbreaking analysis of Sōseki's bildungsroman, *Sanshirō* (1908).

Next her examination of English as today's universal language challenges the naïve celebration of the Internet as the conveyer of global knowledge. She cautions that the act of acquiring knowledge is wholly dependent on the language one knows. The less English one knows, the less access one has to global knowledge. This leads more and more people in the non-English-speaking world, especially those whom she calls "seekers of knowledge," to be drawn into the "universal" world of English, possibly leading to the impoverishment of their own language—an outcome that would, in turn, assuredly lead to the impoverishment of the entire human race.

In the final chapter, Mizumura begins by reflecting on the possible future of various languages, Western and non-Western alike. She then takes the reader to a specific period in Japanese history, the years following the defeat in World War II, and the detrimental effect that period had on Japanese language and literature. Her account of how the war and the American occupation affected the nation's written language will surely come as a surprise to many readers, as will her description of the current sorry state of language arts education in Japan. The book closes with suggestions for major policy changes in the nation's education system.

THE AFTERMATH

The impact of *The Fall of Language* in Japan has been tremendous. As we have seen, the book's initial commercial success owed much to controversy that erupted on the Internet. That flame war was fueled in part by the book's provocative original title, which means literally "when the Japanese language falls: in the age of English." Some took the title as a warning that the Japanese language is at imminent risk of perishing under the dominance of English. Yet Mizumura makes no such claim. She clearly indicates that the long history of the Japanese language, the large population of its users, and the nation's relative economic stability and cultural autonomy make it highly improbable that Japanese will disappear in any foreseeable future. She is concerned about the quality of written Japanese and about whether Japanese modern literature— that is, those works worthy of being passed on for generations to come—will continue to attract readers.

The power of the Internet to ignite diatribes aside, the ferocity with which the book was initially attacked—antagonistic readers resorted to deleting favorable Amazon reviews, which a major newspaper found newsworthy—deserves some attention. The book broke taboos, especially in the final chapter. That Mizumura is a woman in a society where men still basically control intellectual debate must have contributed to the vitriol. None of her suggestions for improvements in the education system is drastic in and of itself, but the accumulation may have worked to exasperate people, evoking reactions like these:

Mizumura says we must defend the Japanese language. She must be a jingoist who ignores Japan's imperial past and the way we imposed our language on other Asians.

She says children must read classics of modern Japanese literature. She must be a hopeless reactionary.

No, she must be an elitist.

She says to give special English education to a cadre of chosen people? Then she is *definitely* an elitist.

She talks down about contemporary Japanese literature, when even Americans say it's great!

Really, who does she think she is, a privileged bilingual preaching to the rest of us Japanese!

Then, on November 26, 2008, while the controversy was still in full swing, a review came out in the literary arts column of the newspaper *Asahi Shimbun* in which, after conceding that the book "is large in scope and inspiring," the columnist voiced comments closely echoing the attacks circulating on the Internet: the book was "virtually indistinguishable from nationalist cries," "an affirmation of elitism," and even, said this woman, "just all too macho." (*Asahi Shimbun*, it should be noted, is Japan's closest equivalent to the *New York Times* or *Le Monde*.)

As the initial buzz subsided and the book reached wider readership, however, *The Fall of Language* indeed became a must-read among the well-educated segment of Japanese society. A flood of reviews, essays, roundtables, and interviews appeared in well over a hundred newspapers, magazines, and other national print media. It seems as if everyone from novelists, poets, translators, linguists, and literary scholars to journalists, schoolteachers, diplomats, businesspeople, physicists, and neuroscientists has written or spoken publicly about the book. This surge of attention attests to the urgency with which the Japanese reading public was waiting for a book like this, one that gives voice to their angst about the linguistic future of their country. Eventually related books began appearing; one has even called for the Japanese language to be protected by law.

That said, it is our opinion that the book will be even better served when read outside Japan. Japanese readers have been traumatized by years of senseless language and literature education in both English and Japanese; as a result, they tend to focus all their attention on the final chapter, where Mizumura talks about the need for pedagogical changes. The ideas presented in earlier chapters often get lost in the shuffle. Yet what makes this book a genuinely worthwhile read is its theoretical and historical analysis of written language, literature, and translation, a contribution that has significance far beyond the rise and fall of any one language. May readers around the world engage in a fruitful dialogue with the ideas presented in this fascinating book.

NOTE ON NAMES AND BOOK TITLES

Except for the names of the author and the translator Mari Yoshihara, who have established identities in English, Japanese names are rendered family name first, as custom dictates in Japan. For authors writing at the dawn of modernity who are better known by a pen name, that name is used, after their name is first introduced in full. For instance, Natsume Sōseki is referred to as "Sōseki." For Japanese books that have been translated, the title is given in English first, with the original title in parentheses; for untranslated books, the Japanese title is used, with an English gloss.

THE FALL OF LANGUAGE

IN THE AGE OF ENGLISH

1. UNDER THE BLUE SKY OF IOWA

THOSE WHO WRITE IN THEIR OWN LANGUAGE

S EPTEMBER MORNINGS IN IOWA CITY GET PRETTY CHILLY.

Stepping out of the hotel, I saw a scattering of writers waiting for the mini-buses, standing stooped with mugs of steamy Starbucks coffee in hand. Writers tend to be stooped specimens to begin with, and these looked particularly so in the cold morning air. At their feet was a variety of luggage in all shapes and sizes.

Before I left Japan, I had gone to the Web site of the International Writing Program, or IWP, and printed out the list of writers participating in this Fall Residency. Intent on familiarizing myself with their faces, names, and brief biographies during my flight to Iowa, I made a point of putting the printout in my carry-on bag. Yet even now, the morning when we were about to set out together on a four-day trip to Minneapolis, I still hadn't studied the list. My physical ailments and the medication that I had been taking left me groggy, unable to muster the energy to browse through it. Besides, nearly all the names on the list were foreign ones I could hardly pronounce.

Today was going to be the day I would meet most of the other writers for the first time. Some were engaged in a friendly chat, while others stood apart, looking all the more aloof in the cold morning air. They had already been in Iowa for a month or so, whereas I had arrived just a few days before. Not only that, I had arrived with a hidden vow to keep my participation to a minimum. Still, as I stood there alone with my overnight bag, not knowing what to do with myself, I felt that as a newcomer I should at least introduce myself to some of the others. But this morning, as on so many other mornings, I was feeling lethargic, and so I only kept eyeing them.

Two minibuses soon arrived. Most of the Westerners headed toward one, and shortly afterward, Asians with uniformly black hair began trooping toward the other. The group seemed to split naturally into two as for one reason or another the Westerners stuck together, leaving the Asians behind. I see, this is how it goes, I told myself. I then headed toward the second bus, the one with mostly Asian passengers.

Seated at the back of the bus were several buff East Asian men at the peak of their manhood, Chinese or Korean or both. In the middle of the bus was a woman with the air of a girl. The line from cheekbone to chin, as keen as if carved with a knife, reminded me of the women in the film *The Scent of Green Papaya*, which I had seen about ten years earlier. She must be Vietnamese, I thought, or some other Southeast Asian nationality. Toward the front of the bus was a man who looked just like a Japanese, with plump cheeks and small eyes slanting downward. He seemed close to sixty, not exactly the peak of manhood. I wondered what nationality he was, knowing that I was the sole Japanese participant. There were three whites on the bus, among them the program director, Chris, to whom I had already introduced myself the day before; he was doing double duty as our driver. I was the last one to board the bus through the front door, so I ended up sitting in the passenger seat beside him. A journalist and a poet, Chris was a handsome man whose blond-bearded face still looked a bit boyish.

Soon after Chris started us on our journey, I turned around to greet the man sitting diagonally behind me, the one with typical Japanese features, only to find him looking vacantly out the window. Rather curiously, I thought, he occupied the aisle seat, leaving the window seat next to him empty. Across the aisle from him was a young white man who likewise occupied the aisle seat, leaving the window seat next to him empty, and he too was looking vacantly out the window.

Once we left the college town behind, tall buildings disappeared and modest, two-story houses typical of the American countryside took their place, lit by the white morning light. The view was not particularly beautiful. There was none of the poetry one sees in scenes of the countryside in American films. There was neither order nor coherence, much as in life itself.

Turning to Chris, I roused myself and said exactly what an American might say at such a moment: "Beautiful day!" Chris responded, "Yes, very beautiful!" as one would expect of an American constitutionally blessed, as most Americans are, with an admirably positive outlook on life. And with that began something of a conversation. When I engage an American in conversation, typically the exchange follows a pattern: I try to come up with a question, and the almost always talkative American responds with a lengthy answer. On this day, I had no trouble coming up with one question after another, for, having arrived late and missed the orientation week, I knew next to nothing about the IWP.

While effortlessly steering the wheel, Chris, who has an astonishingly orderly brain—a trait common among American intellectuals but rare among speakers of Japanese, a language that doesn't even require a clear distinction between "and" and "but"—gave me a succinct summary of the IWP, including its history and its current financial situation. He was relaxed enough to turn toward me and show me his blond-bearded smile as he spoke. He was, of course, constantly checking the rearview mirror. He also reached out an arm from time to time to find a radio station that played classical music or to adjust the volume. I myself am a bad driver who hardly ever took the wheel and ended up losing my license by forgetting to renew it; as I listened with an occasional "Oh, yes?" or "Really?" I was in secret awe of Chris for being able to talk coherently while simultaneously driving and doing so many other things.

Meanwhile, I felt the presence of the Asian writers in the bus weighing on me, especially the middle-aged man sitting right behind me, the one who looked so Japanese.

Fifteen minutes or so passed. When Chris paused, I made an overt gesture this time to turn myself around, feeling I should at least introduce myself. In such a situation, the longer you wait, the harder it is to begin a conversation. The man was still looking vacantly out the window, but this time he noticed me. I put on the brightest smile I could and said, "Hi! I am from Japan."

The man had a gentle face. It also seemed full of wisdom. I wondered if he might be Korean or Chinese. Mentally I combed through my meager knowledge of expressions from classical Chinese, searching for one that might describe him, and came up with *shunpū taitō* (serene as the spring breeze).

Where was he from, I asked.

"I am from Mongolia." A smile filled his gentle face.

Mongolia? Quickly I spread out the world map in my head. At the same time, a vague memory came to me that on the list of IWP participants there was indeed a leader of the Mongolian democratic movement, a one-time presidential candidate. Now that I looked at him armed with this knowledge, he suddenly acquired an aura peculiar to a great man—an aura we can hardly expect from Japanese politicians today. Perhaps when a nation goes through a period of upheaval, those who should become politicians, do. Mongolian sumo wrestlers are a familiar sight on Japanese television, but this was only the second time in my life that I had met a Mongolian in person. The first time was about twenty-five years ago, when I encountered a girl in Paris who claimed to be one. Her ancestors had left Mongolia in the seventeenth century and taken three more centuries to make their leisurely way to Paris. "I know this sounds incredible, but it's true," the slim, tall, and strikingly beautiful girl said in perfect Parisian French. A picture unfolded before my eyes, as if on wide-screen CinemaScope, of clusters of the round tents called "ger" moving ever westward across the Eurasian continent at a timeless pace.

The man on the bus was a bona fide Mongolian, born and raised in Mongolia. To me, the word "Mongolia" itself sounds as if it transcends the worldly. Hearing it, I felt a rush of fresh wind from the steppes sweep through my mind, clearing away the clouds that had been ever-present since my first illness a couple of years before. I may have looked too inquisitively at his gentle face when I asked, "Are you a novelist or a poet?"

"I'm a poet."

"Is this your first time in America?" I asked, assuming that of course it was.

"Yes, it is my first time." The Mongolian poet then motioned to the young white man sitting across the aisle. "He's from Lithuania."

Really? Was there someone from Lithuania in the program? I couldn't remember a Lithuanian youth on the list of participants. And because as a child, instead of learning anything useful, all I ever did was read novels, now when I tried to check the world map in my head I could not begin to locate Lithuania. I knew that it must be somewhere near Russia, but as to what sort of country it was, what the capital was, or whether there were any Lithuanian historical figures I should have heard of, I was clueless.

Like many young men around the globe, he had an edgy style, with spiky hair and piercing in one ear. I asked him, "Are you a novelist?"

"No, I'm a poet."

"I see. I'm a novelist."

Thus ended our conversation that sounded like an excerpt from an English textbook for beginners. Both the Mongolian poet and the Lithuanian poet had what looked like a smile playing around the mouth, but they said nothing further. I too smiled, then faced front again, relieved that I had now made my obligatory greetings as a newcomer and so let others know that I am not excessively antisocial. It was a shame that I had nothing to say about either

Mongolia or Lithuania, but the conversation ended not only because of my ignorance: their half-smiles eloquently conveyed their discomfort in speaking English.

On both sides of the road were cornfields spreading endlessly flat under what was now a blue sky. Only later did I learn that cornfields are symbols of industrial agriculture, which is destructive of nature. At the time, as I looked at the long stretches of cornfields, all I vaguely felt was that the sort of poetic country scene that appears in American films was now finally here before me. As the sun rose higher in the sky, it became as bright as midsummer. Several minutes passed before the Lithuanian poet leaned forward and asked me a question.

"Do you know bonsai?"

Bonsai? He was obviously trying to find a topic he could talk about with a Japanese person, I thought. Turning back, I answered, not hiding my sense of being at a loss, "I know what bonsai is, but I really don't know anything about it."

That there were bonsai fans in the United States, I knew. But it had never occurred to me that the pastime of elderly Japanese bending over to trim dwarf pine trees had reached all the way to the youth of a country I couldn't even locate on a map. He actually seemed interested in bonsai. Apparently he was trying to ask something about a particular kind of tree; he mumbled incoherently while drawing the shape of a tree in the air with his finger. I could not understand what he was trying to ask, let alone visualize what tree he had in mind. When it comes to tree names, I hardly know any even in Japanese.

Pine? No. Plum? No. Cherry? No, no, much smaller. But all bonsai trees are small, aren't they? Mmm, yes, but much smaller. As this exchange went on, the Mongolian poet volunteered to help by leaning in and saying something to the Lithuanian.

I gasped.

He was speaking in Russian. I could tell immediately because of all the Soviet films I had seen screened on campus when I was a student. In the same fluent Russian I'd heard in those films, he was asking something of the young Lithuanian poet. I knew that on the Eurasian continent there are people who look perfectly Japanese and speak fluent Russian, yet this was the first time that I had actually seen one. Had I known the first thing about the modern history of Mongolia, this would have come as no surprise. But at the time, I *was* surprised. Bonsai dropped from my mind.

"You speak Russian?"

"Yes, I studied in Moscow."

The Lithuanian poet interjected, "His Russian is much better than mine."

Hearing this, the Mongolian poet laughed heartily. I then understood: these two men did not just happen to be sitting across the aisle from each other. This unlikely pair had become friends through the medium of the Russian language. I see, I said to myself. One could be born in Mongolia, study in Moscow, learn Russian, and later in life be invited to an American university and use the Russian learned in Moscow to become friends with a young Lithuanian with a pierced ear. "The fall of the Berlin Wall in 1989 ended the Cold War and handed the United States a single-handed victory"—similar words had been said over and over in the intervening years. It felt as if that history was laid before me, in front of my very eyes. Little did I imagine that barely six months later, the U.S. invasion of Iraq would usher in a new era of instability.

The two of them went on talking in Russian. Soon a white middle-aged woman sitting one row behind the Mongolian, in the window seat, joined in. I later learned that she was a novelist from Ukraine with the name of a princess in Greek mythology, Yevgeniya.

From farther back in the bus, I heard the Chinese and Korean languages being spoken.

The minibus kept driving through cornfields, carrying onboard the history of the vast Eurasian continent. After a lunch break, we crossed the Iowa–Minnesota border and kept on. By the time we got to the hotel in Minneapolis, it was close to evening and the air was beginning to feel chilly again.

Perhaps because I had been locked inside an enclosed space with other foreigners all day, when we got off the minibus and entered the hotel, I had the visceral sensation of being thrown back into mid-America. Americans grown tall and stout on too many hamburgers and French fries were talking loudly. American English emerged from the full movement of chins and lips, both consonants and vowels pronounced with force. The white columns and walls of the atrium lobby were made to resemble a Mediterranean villa—not as horrific as Japanese imitations, but still fake looking—and every corner smacked of America. In this very American lobby, we multinational writers gathered with our luggage of all shapes and sizes, our tired faces on full display.

From Asian countries, besides me, the lone Japanese, there were two Chinese, three Koreans, a Vietnamese, a Burmese, and a Mongolian. From Africa, there was a Botswanan. From the Middle East, an Israeli. From eastern Europe, two Poles, a Romanian, a Hungarian, a Ukrainian, a Lithuanian, and a Bosnian; from western Europe, an Englishman, an Irishman, and a German. From northern Europe, there was a Norwegian, and from South America, a Chilean and an Argentinean. In total, there were twenty-some writers. After a few days in Minneapolis, we drove back together through the cornfields, and then for a month, the duration of my stay, we all lived on the same hotel floor in Iowa City.

THE PALM READER'S PREDICTION

My invitation to participate in the International Writing Program hosted by the University of Iowa had come earlier that year, in the spring. The IWP is a fine program that brings together novelists and poets from around the world. Participants are free to keep on writing while getting a taste of life in an American university. Round-trip transportation, accommodation at the university-owned hotel, and a daily stipend are provided, as well as some extra money to buy books during the stay.

As is always the case when I am invited abroad, I felt conflicted. My upbringing was not typical for a Japanese. When I was twelve, my family moved to New York because of my father's business, and I lived in the United States for the next twenty years. Even so, I never felt comfortable with either American life or the English language. As a teenager, I immersed myself in classic Japanese novels of the modern era, a set of books that my great uncle gave my mother for her daughters—my sister and me—to read lest we forget our own language. In college and then in graduate school, I even took the trouble of majoring in French literature as a way to continue avoiding English. I was the prisoner of an intense longing for home—a kind of longing perhaps unimaginable in the age of the Internet, which allows one never to leave home, wherever one's body may be. A confluence of circumstances forced me to go on living this incomprehensible life. And the kind of life I lived so affects everything about me that I can scarcely write a word without addressing it.

After reaching thirty, I finally went back to Japan. One day, as I was about to walk down a bustling street in Tokyo's Shibuya, I caught sight of a palm reader—an exotic sight for me at the time. He was wearing a Chinese-style hat and had auspiciously full cheeks. In my mind, he even ended up with a drooping mandarin moustache. When I held out my palms, he took one look and said, "I see you have a strong tie to foreign countries."

I was shocked. I told him that I had been living abroad but now intended to stay put in Japan.

"Oh, no, your tie with foreign countries will last all your life." He sounded oddly confident.

By then Japan was a rich country, and one did not have to be particularly privileged to travel abroad. It was thus unlikely that the palm reader had said this just to please me. Of course, he wouldn't have said it just to upset me, either. But I had only recently returned to Japan, at long last, with dozens of cardboard boxes in tow. That I was finally back in my home country had apparently not quite sunk into my psyche, for I still had dreams in which I was dismayed to find myself living in the United States—What's going on? When will I ever get back to Japan?—and I would let out a sigh of relief when I woke up and saw the low ceiling of my small Tokyo apartment. During those first months, when the voices of screaming children on their way to school came through the window, in my half sleep it would eventually register that the screams were not in English but in Japanese, and I would repeat to myself, "Yes, those are the screams of Japanese children. The same as I heard when I was a little girl going to elementary school myself. Those are Japanese children, and I am in Japan." And as I went from being half awake to awake, the awareness that I had finally returned to my homeland would fill me to overflowing.

The palm reader's words were carved into my memory, along with the accompanying shock.

Whether one's palms can show a "tie to foreign countries" remains a mystery to me, although it's true that sometime thereafter an unexpected development took me back to the United States. It's also true that, contrary to what I had dreamed for years, I ended up writing my first novel there. Many flights across the sea then followed. Of course, there are people who constantly crisscross the globe on business or pleasure. I am certainly not in their league. Still, for someone who expected to stay in Japan for the remainder of her life, rooted like a tree, I was making more than my share of trips abroad, though seldom willingly. And now, having passed my prime, to put it mildly, I was finding transoceanic flights an increasing burden, one that took a toll not only on my nerves but also on my never-very-robust health.

Meanwhile, airfare dropped dramatically, a phenomenon giving rise in recent years to more and more events with the word "international" somewhere in the title. Writers too are now frequently invited to foreign countries for one reason or another, though typically to a university. Universities are usually modestly funded—university literature departments in particular. I have no doubt that Nobel laureates are treated differently, but someone like me has to fly economy as a matter of course. I do not have the money to pay out of pocket to upgrade to business class. Consequently, if I accept an invitation, I have to squeeze myself into a seat so cramped that it feels like I'm being transported by a prison security van or cattle truck, eat meals served as unceremoniously as if they were fodder, and, unless I am going to Korea or China, remain stuck in my seat for well over ten hours. It is on these occasions that I curse my fate in being Japanese and living in what is literally the "Far" East. When I finally reach my destination, rarely is there someone to pick me up; most of the time, I nervously get into a taxi alone. Of course, my stay is filled with tiring events, and what with strain and lack of sleep and the cold I always catch, after I get back to Japan I am as depleted as if I'd been through a major illness. And I make a firm promise to myself that I'll never travel abroad again.

Then some time later, there is another invitation. My immediate reaction is always, "No, thank you, I've had enough." Foreigners, even those who teach Japanese literature at a university, cannot read novels written in Japanese with any ease. More than likely I am invited not because the host read and liked my novels, but because I conveniently speak English. I feel a bit like I am being cheaply used. Besides, what difference could it possibly make if a novelist goes to a foreign country and speaks about her work or reads out passages from it in front of a small audience who might not even know who she is? And yet, though I mumble and grumble, every so often I do accept an invitation—in part because it is gratifying to be invited, after all, but also in part because the palm reader's oddly confident prediction remains engraved in my mind. It could well be that some higher power is at work, unbeknownst to me, and if so I figure it can't hurt to do its bidding every once in a while.

The invitation from the IWP came at a rather tricky time. That is, it came only two years after my health abruptly fell apart.

Life is a tiring business indeed.

Soy sauce runs out. Milk runs out. Dishwashing detergent runs out. Even Lancôme lipsticks—I thought I had stockpiled several years' worth—run out. Dust underneath the dining table becomes dust balls. Newspapers and magazines pile up, and so does laundry. E-mail and junk mail keep coming. When occasion demands, I make myself presentable and I present myself. I listen to my sister's same old complaints on the phone. I withdraw money for my elderly mother, whose tongue works fine but whose body is a mess. I contact her caseworker. And now I have reached a stage in life when my own health is prone to betray me.

On top of all this, I had just suffered the stress of writing an inordinately long novel and having it serialized in a monthly literary journal. Every single minute of that time, my mind was obsessed with the panic-stricken idea that if I wasted even one day a month I would be publishing something one-thirtieth poorer in quality. For days on end, I was at my desk before even brushing my teeth in the morning and remained virtually nailed there until I collapsed into bed at night.

It happened one summer night when I sat in a restaurant for hours with my neck exposed to air-conditioning. The occasion being a festive one, I was wearing a dress cut rather low in the back, which only made matters worse. I began to feel strange and then increasingly awful; finally it was all I could do to leave the table, stumble to the ladies' room, and squat down in my high heels—but by then it was too late. My cheeks were like ice; my blood was not circulating.

Beginning that summer, I had something called "autonomic dysfunction." I could no longer drink tap water because it tasted too cold. I shivered just opening the refrigerator. I had to avoid air-conditioned subways, buses, and taxis. Merely looking at brightly lit convenience stores from the outside, knowing how freezing they are kept to lure customers, made me sick. A year later, after somehow managing to finish the inordinately long novel, I finally visited a psychosomatic clinic and received a prescription for medications to release my built-up tension: an antidepressant, an antianxiety drug, sleeping pills. It was about a year after this that the invitation from the IWP reached me through an American scholar of Japanese literature, also a well-known translator.

One thing I learned from having my health fail so miserably is that having no physical energy makes socializing a burden unimaginable to a healthy person. Just the idea of seeing someone caused pain and tension to spread through my back, as if blackish liquid lead had been injected down my spine. While I was actually meeting with someone, I often found myself reaching for the medication in my handbag, like a drug addict. When finally home and alone, I would throw myself on the bed, close my eyes, and sleep with my jaw sloppily open like an old woman. Being transported on a plane like a prisoner or a cow I might somehow tolerate, but a program like the IWP would entail extended interaction with other writers, I thought. I was not sure I would be able to survive the obligation. My hesitation was exacerbated by the feeling that I was at an age when I had little to gain from new encounters.

At the same time, the invitation did offer one attraction: I could go someplace for a change of air and get some truly needed rest—health resort therapy, if you will. The fantasy of health resort therapy had haunted me as I anxiously worked to finish my novel amid my ailments. My fantasy resembled something from a foreign film set in a lushly bucolic location, or an advertisement in a high-end women's magazine portraying vacationers sipping aperitifs. With my novel finally out in two volumes, I would have just received my royalties, conveniently double the usual amount. I could leave Japan, stay for a month or two in a small, quaint hotel overlooking some wonderfully soothing scenery—perhaps a Swiss lake—and spend my days reading and walking, free from daily chores, letting my exhausted mind and body unwind in the tranquil flow of time. I pictured myself in a tweed skirt that fell just below the knees and low pumps—things I never actually wear—looking (apart from my decidedly Japanese features) like a behind-the-times middle-aged English lady. This particular element of the fantasy must have arisen from my habit after finishing my novel of lying down and mindlessly listening to Agatha Christie audiobooks. The images in my mind were illusory, but my desire to be free from the tedium of daily life, to live in a magically beautiful setting, and to enjoy an entire life's worth of rest was quite real. The fantasy kept haunting me, but I did not have the energy to decide on a destination, let alone take any action. According to the IWP brochure, participants had merely to continue their work, and they would each be provided a room by the Iowa River in which to do so. True, "Iowa River" did not have quite the same appeal as "Swiss lake," but given that scenery with flowing water would be nearby, it was a compromise worth considering. Should I decline because the burden of international exchange would be too much? Or should I succumb to the temptations of a health resort idyll?

As I debated in my mind, the palm reader's words about my fated tie to foreign countries kept coming back to me, and that sealed the deal. Officially participants were obligated to stay for three months, but I could not imagine leaving my elderly mother alone that long; I could not imagine that my own health would sustain itself for that long either. The host kindly agreed to reduce my stay to one month, and before I left, as I have mentioned, I had secretly made up my mind to hold my participation to a minimum without being ungracious.

THE INTERNATIONAL WRITING PROGRAM

This was my first visit to the real American Midwest.

The American Midwest, particularly the state of Iowa, is a symbol of rural America, known for its endless stretches of cornfields. Iowa City, located right in the middle of those cornfields, is a college town centered on the state university, the University of Iowa. Of the city's population of seventy thousand, nearly half are students. What became clear to me as I stayed there, however, was that Iowa City is not exactly your typical rural college town. Streets both on and off campus are lined with fine establishments—libraries, museums, theaters, and an array of restaurants representing all kinds of cuisine. Particularly unusual in the middle of rural America is the thriving presence of small, independently run bookstores and coffee shops that would look at home in Manhattan's Greenwich Village. It all started from the university's creative writing program, called Iowa Writers' Workshop, or IWW, which shaped the town into what it is today—a lively literary community distinct from any other rural college town in the United States.

IWW, founded in 1936, was the first workshop of its kind in the country and is still considered to be the best. If teaching there is an honor, studying there is an honor no less. Every year about fifty students—aspiring novelists, poets, and a few translators—are admitted into the two-year program. Like many writers, I had never seen much significance in creative-writing programs beyond providing those who already know how to write a means to make a living; however, seeing those earnest students changed my mind. They live a life in which they write every day for at least two years. To be sure, not all graduates will succeed in earning their living by writing, but they all make it their goal to make use of their training at some point in their lives. Students with such commendable aspirations gather from all over the United States in this little place. (In 2008 Iowa City was designated as a UNESCO City of Literature, the only one in the United States.)

In 1966, when the respected poet Paul Engle stepped down from his twenty-five-year tenure as the director of IWW, his future wife, Nieh Hualing, a Chinese writer in her own right, suggested to him the idea of creating a program that would bring writers from across the nations to Iowa City. Together they founded the IWP. Since its inception in 1967, the program has invited over 1,400 writers from more than 140 countries. While IWW is widely known in the United States, its offspring, the IWP, is not as well recognized. Outside the United States its name recognition seems to vary: virtually unknown in some countries, it is an important stepping-stone in a writer's career in others.

The faculty of the imagination is indeed cruel. My dream of a restful sojourn at a resort dissipated into thin air the minute the airport taxi pulled up in front of the university-owned hotel. For me, the sine qua non of my fantasy was not just that I would be freed from daily chores but that, even if not exactly wallowing in luxury, I would at least lead an *aesthetic* life. From outside, the hotel was nothing more than a plain concrete apartment building. Inside, what could nominally be called an entrance and lobby greeted me. I knew by then that the room I was being escorted to would be nothing like what I had envisioned. The IWP brochure had implied that we would each be given a suite overlooking the Iowa River. What I got was not a suite but a room, and not even a very spacious room at that, considering this was the American Midwest and not Tokyo. Furnishings included a double bed, an office desk and chair, a chest of drawers with mirror, a television, a tea table, and an arm-chair. "Modern" would have been a generous adjective to describe the decor, consisting of a set of standard furniture manufactured with no other goal than durability, the sort one finds in any basic accommodation in the United States. The Venetian blinds covering the windows had dented ends and fell below standard. As for the Iowa River, all I could see from my window was the back of what looked like an annex. I could hardly see the sky. Perhaps because I arrived late, I may have been given the last remaining room; but if this room was for rent, I thought, it would certainly be among the cheapest anywhere.

Within a few hours of my arrival, I was also dismayed to find that what the brochure claimed was a "restaurant" inside the hotel was more like a cafeteria in the middle of nowhere. Not only did we have to serve ourselves, but the menu was shockingly limited and the food plainly unappealing, especially to someone coming from a gastronomically sophisticated country like Japan. After a moment's hesitation, I turned my back on the so-called restaurant and ended up buying my first meal in the basement of the student union next door. There I found an impressive range of offerings: fresh fruit, veg-etable sticks, a variety of hot soups, and, to my pleasant surprise, sushi rolls sky-delivered daily from California—but after all, they were meals meant to be eaten out of plastic containers with a plastic fork. It was a "feast" not very different from those I remembered from my too-long graduate school years in my too-long life in the United States.

The program, however, was designed to give foreign writers a taste of uni-versity life in America; I had no right to complain like a spoiled child. For a younger writer, or one whose opportunities were limited, the IWP might well be a godsend. By the next morning, resigned to forgoing the aesthetic life that had seemed an absolute prerequisite for my therapy, I just looked forward to securing a good rest away from home. In the afternoon, I took a walk by the Iowa River, which runs through the campus. Though the narrow waterway did not remotely resemble the Swiss lake of my imagining, I would surely be able to take daily walks by it and rest my mind: as nightfall of the second day approached, my dream had already shrunk to these humble proportions.

And yet not even that humble dream was to materialize. It just so happened that I had joined the IWP at a critical juncture. Several years before, the university had decided to terminate the program because of financial difficulties. Unexpectedly, students and citizens rose to demonstrate against the decision and the IWP was miraculously saved. When I arrived, the entire staff under Chris Merrill, the new director, was frantically working to rebuild what once lay in shambles—or so I understood. The turmoil and excitement necessarily affected all the participating writers.

In the United States even cultural enterprises must be results oriented, and in order for the IWP to raise its operating funds, which come from State Department grants and private donations, it needed to publicize its contributions to society. For those writers who had some command of the English language, talking about their work, their language, and their country's literature in university classes and public libraries, at social gatherings and bookstore events, or even on radio and television became an important part of their routine during the residency. Given my inadequate English, I ended up spending a ridiculous amount of time drafting my talks, though since writers' presentations usually lasted no more than twenty minutes, I'm sure the people who hosted these initiatives had no idea. I could have declined, but that would have seemed like refusing to do my share in rebuilding the IWP, and when I thought about all the people working untiringly under Chris, I didn't have the heart. Thus to audiences who had never seen or heard the Japanese language, I explained that though Japanese people use Chinese characters in their writing, the two languages come from entirely different linguistic families; that written Japanese combines Chinese characters with two kinds of phonetic signs the Japanese themselves developed, *katakana* and *hiragana*; and that, as unbelievable as this may sound to the users of Western languages, Japanese sentences do not require a grammatical subject. Even when strolling along the banks of the Iowa River, I kept thinking about what to say. Remarkably, my health didn't break down completely. To keep myself going, I took stronger doses of medication that left me uncomfortably bloated.

THE WRITERS

Life unfolds in strange ways.

I was not granted the aesthetic and relaxing health resort therapy I'd been hoping for. Instead I was granted a new, keener awareness as a Japanese writer from an unexpected source—from the very thing I had secretly tried to avoid: international exchange with writers. It might be an overstatement to call what took place an "exchange," for few of my fellow participants had sufficient command of English, and even with those who did, I seldom got to engage in real conversation. Still, the eventual impetus to write this book was indeed occasioned by my mingling with writers from diverse countries. Reflecting back, I can only feel grateful to the IWP for providing me with what turned out to be an invaluable experience.

The new and keener awareness I gained as a Japanese writer had very little to do with the IWP participants as individuals. If truth be told—and if I may be allowed a little impertinence—these writers, myself included, were not particularly outstanding individuals. At least we did not give any such impression. To start with, our appearance was unprepossessing. The American Midwest has an overwhelmingly white majority. Many residents are of German or Scandinavian descent, the kind of people who would once have been called "Aryan." Having grown up in the New York metropolitan area, where all kinds of ethnic groups coexist, as I looked around at the University of Iowa students I was stunned by how many blond, blue-eyed people there are on Earth. They were also amazingly tall and dazzlingly young. People who I secretly thought would look perfect in Nazi propaganda films as members of the Hitler Jugend—though they might not like the comparison—were walking all over campus with majestic long strides.

Among such people, we writers cut a poor figure. Of course, many of us were not white, and even among the whites, many were of eastern European or Mediterranean descent—neither blond nor blue-eyed. We also were not tall. We were not young. And because many of us came from poor countries, and because writers are the way they are, we were not well dressed. Everywhere we went in this small college town that appreciates literature, we were always treated warmly and respectfully. But when we moved around in a group, we could have easily been mistaken for a band of recent immigrants or refugees. If our connection to the IWP weren't known, some might have found our presence a bit disturbing.

Despite our unimpressive exteriors, perhaps our souls were aglow with inner light, you may kindly suggest. Well, sadly, that didn't seem to be the case either. Ancient tales tell of people who look like beggars, lunatics, or imbeciles but are in fact a company of saints in the eyes of God. Those tales did not seem to apply to us writers. Interacting with the others on a daily basis, I didn't get the sense that this was a group of people blessed with particularly high spirituality, generous hearts, or noble aspirations. I didn't even get the sense that this was a group of people with particularly fine minds, as writers are generally credited with having—though I am sure this was mostly because so many of us did not speak English well. In fact, I kept thinking that if anything we were a bunch of hard-to-please curmudgeons. I often pondered the stress Chris and the other organizers must be going through.

And yet, as I kept spending more and more time with the other writers, a sense of wonderment began to wash over me.

IN EVERY CORNER OF THE GLOBE, WRITERS ARE WRITING. IN every corner of the globe, different writers under different conditions are giving all they've got to their writing. To be sure, more than 99.9 percent of the seven billion inhabitants on Earth will end their lives not knowing that these writers ever existed or that their novels, short stories, or poems were ever written. Still, in every corner of the globe, while they work, raise their children, or care for their elderly parents, writers are finding the time to hunch in front of a computer or scribble in a notebook, trying their best to write. They are probably shortening their lives a bit by doing so, but they are trying their best to write nonetheless.

I began to spend more time with a world map from the campus bookstore spread out on my desk.

Yes, people were writing in Mongolia, too. The Mongolian poet I mentioned had the family name of Dashnyam. He was the only person whom everyone addressed by his family name, his first name being too long to remember, let alone pronounce. Dashnyam's presence was a constant reminder that people were writing in Mongolia, too, in that distant, almost mythical land. The bits and pieces of his life that he shared with me using his limited English only deepened my sense of wonder.

Dashnyam, a big man, was prone to feeling lonely. "I'm lonely," he would say as he came into my room. "I miss Mongolia." Despite his hearty appearance, maybe he was sensitive to the cold like me. Or maybe he simply liked warm drinks. I would offer him one of the lukewarm canned beers stacked in the corner of my fridgeless room; he would drink it while warming it even more in his big hands. And he would tell me stories. His father, I learned, was a hunter. The big family lived in a big tent, or ger, in the steppe. He grew up eating mutton stew cooked in a pot in the middle of the ger. The stew was not a feast for special occasions, he said. Day after day, they ate the same mutton stew. They also had lamb cheese and sheep's milk; they drank liquor made of sheep's milk, too. It sounded like ovine torture to me, but Dashnyam, warming the canned beer in his hands, repeated longingly: "I miss Mongolia."

Dashnyam's study in the Soviet Union happened by chance. With the aim of solidifying its empire, the former Soviet government took the policy of urging satellite nations to send their brightest boys and girls to the Soviet Union so that they could experience several years of boarding school, receive intensive training in the Russian language and Marxist-Leninist thought, and then go back to their home countries to become new leaders. One-party rule always incubates corruption. Each nation's high government officials naturally packed off their own children to the program. Frustrated with all the lazy idiots arriving year after year, the Soviet government decided to change its policy: it would return to the true principle of Communism and bring in the commonest of all children, the children of hunters, farmers, and fishers. Sons of a hunter, Dashnyam and his younger brother were selected. The two boys must have excelled in their local school; perhaps their father was also a leading figure in their village—though this is pure speculation. Quite predictably, things again did not turn out as hoped. The commoners' children proved to be, if anything, even more incompetent than those of the elites. The government abandoned its new policy after only a few years, but by then Dashnyam and his brother had begun studying in the Soviet Union. Or at least that's how I understood his story. He later returned to the Soviet Union to earn his doctorate and then, once back in Mongolia for good, became involved in the independence movement. The Soviets' laudable policy of letting in the children of commoners ended up coming home to roost.

Dashnyam also wrote poems with romantic refrains like "I think of you." He told me that there was a young Russian woman he was in love with back in his student days in Moscow, a woman who was blonde and beautiful. Yet when they finally reunited a few years ago, after the Soviet Union fell, she had gained weight—"like this," he said, using both hands to suggest a belly even bigger than his own. When a man talks this way about a woman he once loved, it usually comes off as a cheap shot. Dashnyam's tone and manner, however, suggested that life's all-too-predictable course left him nonplussed, or richly amused, or both. He did not sound vulgar at all.

"You are a very important person," I said to him on some occasion.

"Everybody is important," he amended instantly. He was the kind of person who immediately came up with a response like that despite his rudimentary English. Apparently, one's true worth shows through regardless of how well or how poorly one speaks a language; everyone trusted Dashnyam as a man of character.

Gintaris was the name of Dashnyam's young Lithuanian poet friend. He liked to fish, and he often went to fish in the Iowa River. Like bonsai, fishing happens to be another hobby often associated in Japan with stoop-shouldered retirees. I don't know how it sounds in the Lithuanian language for a young man with spiky hair and pierced ear to count bonsai and fishing among his hobbies. I do know that connotations differ according to the language, so it must not sound as funny as it does in Japanese. One day he caught a big fish and, not knowing what to do with it, let it swim in his bathtub all week. Dashnyam finally stepped in and cooked the fish. Once you caught something, you ate it—that was the philosophy embraced by Dashnyam, the hunter's son. "But it didn't look very good, so I didn't eat it myself," he added, laughing.

Historically Mongolia had a much longer relationship with China than with the Soviets, but I never saw Dashnyam talk with either of the two male Chinese novelists, to whom I took the liberty of mentally attaching nicknames. The one who wore jeans and sat with his legs wide apart was "the country dude," and the one who looked smart in a white suit, almost as smart as the fabulous male impersonators in the all-female Takarazuka Revue, was "the city dude." The country dude's real name was Yu Hua. On the alphabetical list of IWP participants, his name came last, and I had not gone far enough down the list to find out who he was. He himself did not understand a word of English, and when we saw each other in the hallway, he would rush into his room with a smile as if he wanted to vanish into thin air. Initially I didn't give him much thought, but soon I began to hear his name associated with a film. When I became curious enough to actually go through the list, I learned that the acclaimed director Zhang Yimou had made a film based on Yu's novel *To Live* that won the Grand Jury Prize at the Cannes Film Festival in 1994. We had a celebrity among us! (He later became a frequent *New York Times* contributor.)

From South Korea, there were three male writers. In descending order of fluency in English, the first was a poet who had earned his doctorate in English literature at the University of Iowa. He owned a car, so he would invite me on rides, saying, "C'mon, Minae!" and motioning his head toward his car like an American. He would take me and the other Koreans to a Korean or Japanese restaurant. As the four of us busily moved our chopsticks, I sensed as I always did the tender ways in which East Asians living in the United States relate to one another, creating a momentary safe haven, as it were.

The second Korean was a young novelist who had an easy laugh and kept taking photographs. Unsurprisingly, the two men were both surnamed Kim. The one who had lived longer in the United States put his surname last and called himself Ethan Kim. The other one, a direct import from Korea, called himself Kim Young-ha. I kept getting their names confused. Kim Young-ha liked to visit hot springs in Japan. I'm not sure if his fondness for hot springs had anything to do with it, but he later kindly played a role in getting my inordinately long novel translated into Korean. Only when I visited Seoul did I learn that he is a prominent novelist in Korea.

The third Korean, Jeong Han Yong, who had the least command of English, was a poet with a singularly serious expression, like many Japanese of a past generation. Once when he appeared before an audience, he stroked his short hair, smiled bashfully, and said, "I got a haircut," acknowledging what he had done for that day's presentation. That one sentence made the audience howl with laughter, delighted to find out that this man who had until then barely opened his mouth had a charmingly self-mocking sense of humor.

A novelist from Argentina named Leopoldo also volunteered to help get my long novel translated into Spanish. He and I were not particularly close during my residency. In fact, we hardly spoke. His kindness was unexpected—puzzling, even. But life is nothing but a series of inexplicable events anyway, so I decided to simply feel grateful for his generosity. When I ran into him at night in the hotel hallway, he would swiftly edge his compact body against the wall and walk past me with a smile. He had a sharp face and always walked barefoot, his feet full of life, the nerves reaching to the very tips of his energetic toes. As I watched his agile body glide by, I could not help thinking of a wild leopard. After the program, I didn't hear from him for several years, but by the time the Spanish translation—my first in a Western language—was due to come out in Buenos Aires we had begun to exchange frequent e-mails, and I even learned to close mine with an affectionate *Abrazo!*

Whereas Leopoldo the Latin American exuded a touch of animal wildness, Matthias from Germany predictably, almost comically, reeked of civilization. It may be because his tall body was topped by a perfectly shaped cranium that looked for all the world like a specimen of the *Homo sapiens* brain that had reached its evolutionary goal. It stood out even more because he completely shaved his head. As days went by, I took to calling him by a nickname, too. "Hi, Perfect Cranium!" I would greet him. At first, Matthias laughed off my greeting with an "Oh, no!" I'm sure he was aware I was teasing about the Nazis' eugenicist claim to be the most advanced race. Later he half-admitted that he shaved his head to showcase its superb shape. Men with fine appearance seem too resplendent. The more I lose my youth, the more resplendent they seem.

Shimon from Israel was a vegetarian. Marcin from Poland, who spoke no English, seemed to spend all his time drinking hard liquor in a philosophical silence. Barolong from Botswana was as enormous as a sumo wrestler. Young Gregory from England had rosy cheeks that would have nicely matched one of those curly silver wigs you see in eighteenth-century portraits. Paddy the Irishman spoke with a wonderful Irish lilt.

Writers are writing in every corner of the globe.

WRITERS ARE WRITING, MOREOVER, IN RICH COUNTRIES AND poor countries alike.

Traveling in a foreign country for even a week makes you painfully aware of the economic status of your own country. Living in a foreign country for an entire month with people from a wide spectrum of rich countries to poor sharpens your awareness even more. The dollar had heartbreakingly different meanings for writers from different countries. Thanks to Iowa's low cost of living and the accommodation provided by the IWP, I found the modest daily stipend more than enough to cover my everyday expenses. With it, I not only splurged on ready-made food at the student union but also dined out and occasionally even satisfied my morning craving for French toast and sausages by walking into the center of town, braving the still-chilly air. I bought amenities like toothpaste and shampoo at the co-op without looking at the price. I went to the movies. I went to coffee shops. Being from Japan, I wasn't tempted to save the daily stipend to take back home. I also felt comfortable in knowing that if I ever ran out of money, I could exchange some of the Japanese currency I had brought along. Despite Japan's recession, the yen provided me with as great a sense of security as if I had bullion gold bars to fall back on.

Things were different for writers from poor countries. If they economized on their daily stipend and took the extra dollars home, they could live on that amount for a while. They could help their aging parents or their children in college. Since cutting down on accommodations was not an option, they cut down mostly on food. The common room that served as both kitchen and dining room had only a microwave, but this did not deter some writers from cooking nearly every meal on their own. When we went on excursions on the minibus and stopped for a meal en route, writers from poor countries stood around munching on the snacks sold at the counter while the rest of us sat at a table in a diner. And whenever there was an event with a free meal, even those who were always holed up in their rooms would somehow get wind of it and appear. Free alcohol was consumed with stupefying fervor. If one carelessly left a bottle of Jack Daniel's in the common room, it would be empty by morning with absurd certainty.

I was particularly sensitive to the want of money among other female writers in the group. Take, for instance, Yevgeniya from Ukraine, who was on the same minibus to Minneapolis. In spite of her august name, she was a genial, down-to-earth woman who told one obscene joke after another and shook her small, slightly rotund body as she laughed. One day, on another of our excursions, during a pit stop at a gas station I saw Yevgeniya holding some gloves inside the adjoining convenience store. She was contemplating whether to buy them for her sons, as if she had all the time in the world to make the decision.

She turned her serious gaze toward me as I stood nearby and asked, "What do you think of these?"

I could not very well respond, "They look cheap. I wouldn't buy them." The thickness of the gloves told of the severe winters in Ukraine.

One evening, as the two of us were walking back to the hotel, she looked at the streetlights, sighed, and said, "Kiev is a sad town. It's dark. And miserable."

But the times when I became distressingly aware of my own good fortune were not when I was with someone like Yevgeniya, who heartily shook her body as she laughed. They were when I was with someone like Ligia, a writer from Poland. Ligia is the name of the beautiful daughter of a deceased king in the famous novel *Quo Vadis*—written in 1895 by the Polish writer Henryk Sienkiewicz—that I'd read as a girl; I secretly gave her this name because she had all the makings of a princess. She was a philosopher who never showed up without perfect makeup, looking rather regal among us. On that day of my first excursion with the other writers, as we arrived at the hotel in Minneapolis, we were told that we were to share rooms, and I learned that Ligia was to be my roommate. I went pale. I had enough difficulty sleeping by myself, and now I had to sleep alongside a stranger? And a foreigner at that? At my age? If only I could discreetly tell Chris that I would pay out of pocket for a single room! But I feared creating a reputation as a spoiled Japanese. Matter-of-factly, I took the card key and put on a smile toward Ligia, who also smiled back at me. What did she think of sharing a room with me, I wondered.

I was unpacking in the bedroom when I heard Ligia cry out as she opened the closet near the entrance.

"Look! Look! Someone's left a robe here!" One can always tell a woman's voice of envy when she finds something beautiful.

As I approached, Ligia touched the sleeve with one hand and whispered, "It's silk."

"Oh, that's mine," I said awkwardly.

It was an ash-gray coat that I had bought after much hesitation nearly ten years earlier and had cherished ever since. Both the exterior and the lining were silk, and it had heavenly light down padding. It stained easily, however, and I always tried to take off the stain with benzene only to end up spreading it even more, whereupon I would rush to the cleaners—something I'm usually too lazy to do. When part of the lining wore out, I took it to the store where I'd bought it, and though they no longer had the exact same fabric, I had them mend it nonetheless. It was easy to wear, and despite its simple cut, it had a rather grand appearance. That Ligia called it a "robe" rather than a "coat" seemed somehow appropriate. In anticipation of the colder Minneapolis climate, I had packed the coat in my overnight bag, and as soon as I entered the room I'd hung it up to get rid of the wrinkles.

On its own, not draped around the mid-size (here in the United States, the child-size) body of a middle-aged woman, the silk coat had regained its aura and hung in the closet looking elegant and dignified.

Ligia was a pretty woman. By some trick of the genes, white people tend to age faster than Asians, and though still at the peak of womanhood in her mid-thirties, she already showed a flower's subtle signs of fading. But even that added to her charm, and she exuded the characteristic self-awareness of an attractive woman. Of the two of us, she would have been the more appropriate owner of the "robe." I could not help feeling that she must be thinking the same thing as she murmured, "So beautiful!"

The dreaded night came quickly.

With a glass of water and all kinds of sleeping aids at my bedside, I waited primly in bed, wearing my pajamas. For a long time, I heard water hitting the washroom sink. Then Ligia emerged. To my astonishment, the regal lady was wearing a babydoll—a fluffy, translucent mini nightgown. She also had a big, white bath towel wrapped around her head, like those beauties in American soap commercials I used to admire as a child, back in the golden years of babydolls. It seemed too much for someone who had only been washing her face. (Couldn't she have just put on a shower cap, I wondered. Or used a hair band?) Oblivious of my bewilderment, Ligia then went straight to the dresser, sat on the chair in front of the mirror, and started putting gobs of cream on her face. Her face immediately began to shine. I watched, mesmerized: in this day and age, is there a cream that you slather on like that after washing your face? I thought of my own tiny jar of expensive "night cream," which I use only sparingly. Was it possible that the historical development of eastern European women's makeup was still stalled at the stage of "cold cream"?

It was amusing, after all, sharing a room with a stranger.

As Ligia got into the bed next to mine, we started to talk, a bit out of courtesy. The one Polish person I knew was a poor and alcoholic former Solidarity member named Henryk whom my sister used to date in New York. I told Ligia that my sister, now also back in Japan, was still in touch with him and that both my mother and I, along with my sister, sent him some money when he lost his job and was on the verge of having his electricity cut off. At this point in the story, Ligia suddenly sat up. "So typical!" she cried out. "That's why I hate Polish men. They grow up completely spoiled by their mothers and sisters, and they come to believe they're some kind of geniuses, and yet in the end, they can't even manage to make a living. It's terrible!" She directed her fury at the ceiling, glaring up and menacing it with clenched fists. "Oh, how embarrassing! I'm so ashamed!" It was as if a disgrace of the entire Polish nation had been exposed halfway around the world. I was shocked myself. My sister's boyfriend Henryk indeed grew up completely spoiled by his mother and sister and had come to believe he was a genius poet. But how could she have guessed all that?

Ligia had a brilliant mind, as a philosopher should, and an outstanding command of English, having grown up speaking it at home because of her grandfather, who was a great Anglophile and once a man of property. Either he or his wife was half-Jewish, and the family seems to have gone through layers of trouble to avoid the concentration camps during the Nazi occupation. Born after the war, Ligia only heard about this family history. What she does know firsthand is the Soviet oppression that followed. "In the sense that it lasted much longer, it was worse than the Nazis," she reflected, her shining face still turned toward the ceiling, though she now lay quietly, flat in bed. She and her family were made to share with strangers a stately manor her grandfather had built long ago. Ligia was someone who could have and would have appreciated all the luxuries money can buy, but instead, tossed about by the vicissitudes of Poland's destiny, she did not even own a coat that befitted her.

As our parting approached, she looked gloomier, the shadows under her eyes turning darker. "When I go back to Poland, I have to teach at the university again. You won't believe how low our salary is." She lived with her cat in a Warsaw apartment.

The one I ended up becoming closest to was a female writer from Norway named Brit. Soon after we met, we started having drinks together, enjoying the breeze at restaurants with tables set out on the sidewalk to make the most of the fading summer light. We also went to the theater together. Red-haired and freckled, Brit was exceptionally personable, and for someone who was a writer, she had refreshing common sense. On top of being a Scandinavian, she was a translator, and so she spoke very good English too. But those were not the only reasons I became friends with her. We both came from rich countries, making it easy for us to do things together. Many writers did not allow themselves even the small luxury of going out for a cup of coffee; we two could drink beer, munch on tacos, and confess our sins of frivolous spending as the sun went down, turning the blue sky purple-red. We could also talk about whatever film was showing. Just about then, *Lost in Translation*, set in Japan, was playing in town.

AND THEN, THERE WERE THE DIVERSE POLITICAL SITUATIONS.

Living with other writers, I saw for the first time what I had only known abstractly before: people write not just in rich and poor countries but also in various political climates. Being able to participate in a program like the IWP meant in itself that you came from a country that was functioning, at least minimally. In a totally dysfunctional society, the profession of a writer would not exist. Still, not all writers enjoyed the kind of peace I took for granted, almost indolently, as a Japanese.

For many writers, the freedom of speech, first of all, was not a given. Take, for instance, the Romanian poet Denisa. Probably because of Romania's linguistic and cultural proximity to France, when she threw out "Bah!" in a dismissive tone, or shrugged her shoulders with both hands raised, she somehow looked French. Besides, she was a stylish woman who didn't look anything like my image of someone from a former Eastern Bloc country. Yet her mind remained obsessed by her memory of where she and others had to draw a line in "dealing with state power." Under Soviet rule, the state censored not only literary content but also form, and even toward the end of the twentieth century, there still remained such absurdities as not being able to publish free verse. Should one compromise with the state in order to make a living and so lose one's dignity as a writer (and as a human being)? Or should one refuse even if it meant going hungry? Having had to make such choices still haunted Denisa, and it was as if she could not *not* talk about it, either in public or in private.

And, of course, there were writers currently facing state suppression. What I gradually came to understand, for example, is that the Chinese "city dude" who looked so smart in his white suit was actually a warrior fighting for freedom of speech. Having relocated himself to New York, he was editing works that writers dared not publish in mainland China, distributing them for the Chinese readership spread around the world. His English was still quite basic, and we didn't go beyond greeting each other in the hallway, but when he found out that I was leaving earlier than everyone else, the night before my departure he slipped under my door a short story that he had written which someone had translated into English. Reading it on the airplane, I felt I was getting to know him for the first time.

The story has a tragicomic plot. The protagonist's grandfather is raised poor, but after the Cultural Revolution breaks out, the authorities discover that his ancestors had owned some land. Labeled as having "landowner's blood," he is imprisoned and tortured and spends the rest of his life half deranged. Eventually, he suffers from septic poisoning, upon which he receives a series of blood transfusions. His body is now infused with "peasant's blood." He is overjoyed. Yet he is also full of regret. If there was such a convenient method, why didn't he think of replacing his "landowner's blood" with "peasant's blood" before? Cursing his own ignorance, he begs his son and grandson to go through the same procedure as soon as possible. On his deathbed, he feels comforted in the thought that his blood is now entirely cleansed; he has nothing to fear in the afterlife and can die in peace, and so he does. The second half of the story takes place after the grandson arrives in New York, whereupon it turns into a fantasy. Failing after all to ride the wave of capitalism, one day the young man has an idea: why not transfuse Coca-Cola into his arm! Suddenly everything begins to go smoothly. The story is a critique of both Communism and capitalism; I found the first half both sadder and funnier.

And there was also a writer from Myanmar—a country under military rule—who actually defected to the United States during his residency. Wearing sandals and a colorful sarong, this man, well past middle age, was always

walking quietly but briskly down the hallway of our hotel, spreading a tropical aura in the fluorescent-lit space. To my pleasant surprise, he was a Ja-
panophile and told me he quite liked *Harp of Burma*, the Japanese children's
story about a World War II soldier who turns pacifist and becomes a monk in
Burma. Whenever we met, he would greet me with a full smile and a cheery
"*Banzai!*" Perhaps he had been taught to say it as a child in a Japanese-run
school. In foreign countries, *banzai* is often interpreted as a Japanese war cry;
in Chinese films, evil Japanese soldiers shout it while stabbing tied-up Chinese with bamboo spears. It would have been too bizarre for me to respond
to his greeting in kind, so I hid my discomfort and responded with a cheerful
American "Hi!" He also knew polite Japanese greetings like *ohayō gozaimasu*
(good morning) and *sayonara* (good-bye), which he said he'd learned in elementary school. One time he even sang a Japanese children's song for me. His
hoarse voice echoed under the blue Iowa sky, reminding me of a time when
Asian children were made to sing Japanese songs under the tropical sun; the
recent, yet already distant, history of the Japanese Empire came back with
unexpected vividness. He seemed to read English but did not speak it much,
so everyone only thought of him as a quiet, harmless man. Then rumor began
to circulate that he had made a request to the U.S. State Department seeking
political asylum; we soon found out that his request was granted. Since the
State Department grants political asylum only when there is a demonstrable
probability that the applicant will actually be imprisoned upon his return,
this writer was apparently perceived by his government as a danger to his
country. We all found it hard to believe; we speculated that probably, having
abandoned his country, he would never get to see his family again. But he
didn't seem particularly sad. He continued to briskly walk down the hotel's
hallway in his traditional attire, spreading a tropical aura.

Indeed, writers who came from countries with a tradition of freedom of
speech were in the minority. Those from countries where there had been
uninterrupted peace for more than half a century—countries where World
War II inflicted the last major scar—were also in the minority. Barolong from
Botswana was born when his homeland was still a part of the British Empire;
Shimon from Israel lived in what could suddenly turn into a combat zone;
the participant from Bosnia, the group's only Muslim, had bullet fragments in
his knee; the girl-like writer from Vietnam was born in the year her country's
long war finally ended. Latin American writers had lived through military
rule or civil war or both. Even the writers from South Korea did not take

peace for granted; with their country always preparing for war, men have mandatory military service that is notoriously fraught with horror. One of them told me that he still had nightmares about the hazing he endured: "I'm still in the barracks!" he would cry as he jumped up in bed in fear.

That all these writers just kept on writing, whatever their circumstances, never ceased to amaze me.

WRITERS WRITING IN THEIR OWN LANGUAGE

Yet there was something else that never ceased to amaze me—something that actually seemed more amazing as the days went by. Yes, writers are writing in all corners of the world. Yes, they are writing in countries rich and poor. Yes, they are writing despite threats to their freedom of speech or even to their very lives. Nonetheless, what intrigued me most as I continued to live with the IWP writers was that all of us, each and every one, were writing in our own language. Not only there in Iowa but everywhere on Earth, all kinds of writers were writing *in their own language*. It made no difference whether a writer's language had hundreds of millions of potential readers or a few hundred thousand; either way, they wrote in their own language, as if to do so were the most natural act imaginable—as if people had always done so, ever since the human race came into being. Of course, that is far from the truth. If one looks at human history, only in the modern era did the act of writing come to mean writing in one's own language. While the length of the history of writing varies from language to language, it is often a matter of a few hundred years or even a few decades. And yet, today, writers everywhere are writing in their own language as if people have always done so.

Moreover, at the IWP, for each writer, how deeply this notion of *one's own language* seemed to be connected to our feelings for our own country! When the gentle-faced Dashnyam talked in front of an audience, he projected an image of the expansive Mongolian steppe on the big screen from his laptop, played Mongolian music, and described Mongolia's natural beauty and the way people live in harmony with nature. (His computer skills were impressive.) He spoke less about his country's literature than about his country. His spirit of rebellion against the Soviet Union seemed alive and well, for he was writing about Genghis Khan, the Mongolian hero who was made the object of criticism in his own country at the height of Soviet influence. He also preferred using the Roman alphabet to the Cyrillic, not only because it was easier

to use on his computer, but because the latter symbolized his country's former oppressor. There was even a movement to resurrect traditional Mongolian script, he told me.

Or take Yevgeniya's Ukrainian, which is one of the languages that have
been tragically tampered with in modern times. In imperial Russia, publishing in Ukrainian was basically banned. The founding of the Soviet Union initially brought about a lift on the ban; to uproot pro-Russian antirevolution-
ary feelings, the Soviets welcomed the rise of Ukrainian ethnic consciousness
and promoted education and publication in the Ukrainian language. Stalin
reversed course in the 1930s. The Russian language was reimposed to uproot
any anti-Soviet feelings. Language control loosened under Khrushchev, but
the fate of the Ukrainian language since then depended on the whims of successive Soviet politicians, leading to a steady decrease in the number of users.
When the Soviet Union fell in 1991, Ukrainian users were already outnum-
bered by Russian-language users. But the new Ukraine government decreed
Ukrainian to be its *sole* official language. Today, even among citizens who use
Russian as their mother tongue, the majority consider Ukrainian their "real"
language. Russian is still often used in the media and in official documents,
and writers writing in Russian still outnumber those writing in Ukrainian,
but all this is likely to change in the future as more writers choose to write in
Ukrainian, like Yevgeniya. The recent turmoil can only strengthen national
identity among ethnic Ukrainians.

Or take Hebrew, the language of the vegetarian Shimon. People's passion
for their country resurrected this ancient language. It has a remarkably long
history as a written language; some even claim that it dates back more than
three thousand years. Jews, like so many others, were victims of the turmoil
of history, and the failed insurrection against the Roman Empire in the second century c.e. resulted in the Jewish diaspora. Written Hebrew was preserved in scripture, but the spoken language remained virtually unused for
nearly seventeen hundred years. The Zionist movement in the late nineteenth
century began its renaissance, secularizing the language. Then Hebrew even
became one of the official languages, along with Arabic and English, when
the British created Mandatory Palestine in 1920. When the state of Israel was
created in Palestine in 1948, Jews who gathered there from all over the world
began learning Hebrew, which the new generation now sees as its mother
tongue. And so a language that had mainly been used in religious rituals was
transformed into a modern language; a language that had virtually no speakers less than a hundred years ago now boasts over six million. Today Hebrew

and Arabic remain the official languages of Israel, but for the Jewish population, Hebrew is *their own language.*

Or take Norwegian, the language my friend the red-headed, freckled Brit was writing in. Starting in the late fourteenth century, Norway was under Danish rule for over four hundred years. During that time, Danish was the written language. After the country was liberated from Danish rule in 1814, a movement arose to come up with a national written language; much debate and experimentation followed for over a century until Norwegians eventually settled on two official languages. One is called Bokmål, or "book language," based on the Danish that was already familiar to Norwegians. When foreigners now study Norwegian, they learn Bokmål. The other is called Nynorsk, or "New Norwegian," a language with less Danish influence, single-handedly created in the mid-nineteenth century by a linguist named Ivar Aasen, who collected regional dialects from all over the country in his quest for a true national identity. As I understand it, Nynorsk can more vividly portray the traditional, rural life of the people who endure long battles with the severe climate, both by the ocean and in the mountains, away from the cities. It is also far richer in vocabulary.

Brit, who grew up in a fishing village, writes in Nynorsk even though she often uses the language in an urban context. That she chooses to do so means that she is deliberately limiting the number of her readers, for, though both Bokmål and Nynorsk are taught in school, Norwegians who actually read and write Nynorsk make up only about 12 percent of the population. The population of Norway is five million—12 percent of that is about six hundred thousand. This figure is not much different from the population of Suginami Ward—one of twenty-three wards in the city of Tokyo, where I live. For a Japanese writer like me, it would seem as if you were writing for your neighbors. According to Brit, though, many Norwegian writers choose to write in Nynorsk because the language is more colorful and they feel more deeply connected to it. It's a very poetic language, almost too poetic, she told me. People like Brit are writing in a language they feel is *their own language,* even if that language was artificially created only a century and a half ago and has only several hundred thousand readers.

All writers are writing in their own language, as if to do so was their mission in life. Walking down the hotel's empty hallway at night, I could sense the writers' presence on the other side of either wall as they sat facing their computer screens and writing, each in his or her own language. I could feel not only their presence but their passion and commitment. For every one of them, there were surely thousands of others similarly tapping on a keyboard or scribbling in a notebook, writing in their own language. Even as I acutely felt the dedication of those IWP writers on the other side of the wall, or rather, *because* I felt it so acutely, I could not help thinking about a major change that history is making us go through: English is becoming a universal language such as humans have never known before.

THERE IS A HIERARCHY AMONG LANGUAGES.

At the very bottom are the languages that have only a limited number of users and circulate only within a small tribe. Above those are the languages that circulate within an ethnic group, and farther above are languages that circulate within a nation. And on top are the languages that traverse a wide region of ethnic groups and nations.

Today the rapid increase in communication among different people is bringing about two extraordinary changes in the linguistic landscape. The first concerns the languages at the bottom of the hierarchy. These languages, most of whose names are not known to the rest of the world, are becoming extinct at an alarming rate. Of the approximately six thousand languages on Earth, it is often predicted that more than 80 percent may disappear by the end of this century. In the course of history, many languages have come into being and disappeared, but today languages are dying at an unprecedented rate, just like the plant and animal species affected by environmental change. The second change in the global linguistic landscape concerns, of course, the rise of the English language. There has never before been a universal language of this scale, a language that is not confined to any one geographical location, however vast, but sits atop all other languages and circulates throughout the entire world. This change could not leave other languages unaffected.

WHAT EXACTLY IS A UNIVERSAL LANGUAGE? SOME PREDICT THAT Mandarin Chinese will become the most powerful language of the twenty-first century because it has the largest number of native speakers. Indeed, learning Mandarin has become a worldwide fad. Such a prediction, however, is based on a fundamental misunderstanding. What makes a language "universal" has nothing to do with how many native speakers there are, and everything to do with how many people use it as their second language. It is high time we stop confusing the two figures. To be sure, changes in the world economy and population will likely make not only Chinese but also Spanish and Arabic more important than they already are today. Nonetheless, it is hard to imagine that any of those languages will ever dethrone English and be used among people of diverse nations. Certainly, Americans will not be using Chinese to trade with Russia or India—another country with a fast-growing economy and a mind-boggling population—anytime soon. (In fact, the rise of India, a former British colony, will only strengthen the dominance of English.) Spanish has the second largest number of native speakers, and the number is growing, but it's also unlikely to replace English. With the third largest number of native speakers, English is a big language in its own right; but that is not what matters. What matters is that English is already used and will continue to be used by the greatest number of *nonnative speakers* in the world.

The rise of English as the singular universal language resulted from an accumulation of historical coincidences. There is nothing intrinsic in the English language that made it attain such prominence. It is far from easy to learn. (A recent study found that it takes much longer for an infant to learn English than, for example, Spanish; the world would indeed have been better off if Spanish had become the universal language.) Unlike Latin or Classical Chinese, universal languages of the past, it did not develop primarily as a written language. With Old Norse and Norman French mixed into what was originally a West Germanic language, the grammar is messy, the vocabulary daunting, and the spelling cockeyed. And, for many nonnative speakers, English pronunciation is a nightmare.

Nonetheless, once a language comes to circulate widely, its circulation accelerates at a snowballing pace regardless of its intrinsic characteristics. The more people use it, the more new users it gains. Indeed, an analogy can be made between language and currency. A currency that many people use in transactions comes to be used by even more until the process reaches a critical point and that becomes the world currency. This principle of self-generating propagation—which, at some point, operates independently of how the initial process began—guarantees that the American dollar will continue to circulate as world currency for quite some time even after the relative decline of the American economy. The principle applies to a greater extent to language, a far more self-sustaining entity than currency.

And there is more. Today the added technology of the Internet is accelerating the spread of English. This universal language can now easily leap over the man-made walls of national borders as well as natural walls like the

Himalayas, the Sahara, and the Pacific. Apart from political, economic, or legal barriers, there is nothing the new technology cannot cross. Just how long human civilization as we know it may last is more uncertain than ever in today's world. Yet there is a strong likelihood that English will continue to grow as the universal language, with more and more nonnative speakers using it for at least a few centuries into the future—or even for as long as human civilization as we know it persists.

What will be the fate of written languages other than English one hundred or two hundred years on? Some populations will be cherishing *their own language* even more than before. Others will witness their language's fall—a fall that begins innocuously but all too soon becomes irrevocable.

Many linguists would dismiss such pronouncements as nothing but the idle talk of a layperson. The main current of linguistics today as I understand it is to grasp the structures of language based on phonetics. That means treating languages with and without writing as of equal value. Such a framework allows no room for the idea that written languages may fall. For linguists, languages cannot fall; they merely change. For them, a language dies only when its final speaker (or, more accurately, its final listener) disappears. When I talk of a language "falling" or "dying," I'm referring only to the possible fate of written languages, especially those that once achieved greatness by capturing and celebrating life—and at the same time celebrating themselves for performing such a wondrous task, each in its own way. What a loss it would be if such languages were reduced to mere shadows of their former glory. Just as civilizations fall, so can languages, too.

Perhaps because writers tend to be night owls, the minds of my fellow IWP writers seemed to become sharper at night. When I occasionally came across them in the hallway late in the evening, they didn't look as though they were going to unwind after a day's work; rather, they had the alertness of a soldier on the way to the battlefield—or the fierceness of a nocturnal animal on the hunt for prey. Their minds apparently occupied with their writing, they barely uttered a greeting before going in their rooms and shutting the door. Left alone in the hallway, I pictured them sitting in front of the computer screen and starting to move their fingers across the keyboard, already absorbed in the world they were creating with their words.

To a writer, the fall of one's own language means nothing less than the fall of one's national literature, of which every writer is a bearer. Did the others ever think about the future of their national literature? Did they ever consider the possibility that, having come into existence at a particular point in history, their national literature may have already peaked and be on its way to a fall? What would they say if I suggested that in a century or two, many national literatures may no longer be what they once were? What did they think of the significance of English becoming the universal language? Did they ever stop to ponder such things as I did?

Whenever there was some public event, ten or so of us showed up. Afterward, we walked back slowly under the broad Iowa sky, struggling to converse in English, not an easy task for many. The weather remained clear day after day. If you didn't notice that the leaves on the trees were turning yellow, it was as if time had stopped. Debating in any language is not my forte, so I did not bring this up while walking with the others, but I grew more and more haunted by the idea that we might be a group of people headed for a downfall. Every time we went on an excursion, we boarded the two minibuses, always more or less divided along the lines of whites and Asians. But in the sense that we might be headed for a downfall, we were all the same.

There was an exception. In addition to our two Anglophone writers— Gregory from England and Paddy from Ireland—Barolong, the poet from Botswana, wrote not in his mother tongue but in English instead. He was a manly man, big both in height and in weight, and I found his physical presence too intimidating to chat with him casually. He probably had no idea that a small Asian woman like me was interested in his being there. His participation seemed to me to symbolize one of the paths that more and more writers like him could take in the future.

Checking the map I had bought, I found that Botswana is just north of South Africa. It became independent from Britain and formed a republic in 1966. Barolong, born in 1957, must have been in elementary school at the time. His family could not have been poor, for he told me he had lived in England with his family for a while and attended secondary school in London. Yet—contrary to Virginia Woolf's assertion that writing requires "a room of one's own"—according to an anecdote he shared with us in his talk, his first published poem was written kneeling at the side of his bed, the only space that was all his own; so perhaps his family was not rich enough to let him continue his education in England.

For most people in Botswana, including Barolong, their mother tongue is something called Tswana. Under the British protectorate rule, English was the sole official language. It was only after Botswana's independence that Tswana became a legitimate medium of written communication and gained the status of official language, alongside English. Now some Botswanan writers write in English and others in Tswana, and between the two there is tension. When I asked Barolong why he chose to write in English, he answered that the secondary school years he had spent in England made him more adept at it—at least, that was his explanation. And, as if to atone for the sin of ethnolinguistic betrayal, he was working on English translations of Tswana proverbs. I found it fascinating that Africans with a command of Western languages are now taking over the task of those Western missionaries and anthropologists who once traveled to far-off Africa to collect regional folktales.

Already numerous writers from former British colonies write in Standard English, and some, like Barolong, are from sub-Saharan African countries that historically had no written language of their own. I used to wonder what it would feel like to write in a language not one's own. I also used to wonder if such writing could be considered part of "national" literature. Not anymore. Now these African writers seemed to me to be heralding a new era by embracing the English language and opening a new world with their writing. This may be a perverse thing to say, but they even seemed like a blessed group—not only because they could adopt the English language with such ease but also because they, at least, would not have to watch their literature and language irrevocably fall.

One French expression began coming back to me: *une littérature majeure* (a major literature). Someone used this expression in reference to Japanese literature when I was in Paris many years ago. I felt that these words, uttered casually at the time, were trying to tell me something important, but I could not pinpoint what that something was. One, two, then three years passed, the expression slowly fading from my memory, only to resurface on rare occasions. And then this invitation to participate in the IWP came to me—providentially, in retrospect.

As I lived under the blue Iowa sky while the leaves turned yellow, surrounded by writers all writing in their own language, and as I began to think that they and I might alike be on the road to a downfall, I began gradually to understand what it was that the expression *une littérature majeure* was trying to convey, assuredly far beyond the intent of the one who had uttered it. My thoughts turned to Japan's modernity. And I saw for the first time how extraordinary it was that my country had such an extensive body of modern

literature, dating back to the late nineteenth century. I even allowed myself
to call the phenomenon a "miracle." Yet this did not make me feel elated. On
the contrary, the more I marveled at the good fortune of Japanese literature in
the past, the more despondent I grew about where it was headed in the future.

THE MONTH I SPENT IN IOWA FELT LONG. THE TENSION OF LIVING
an unfamiliar life while enduring poor health made the time pass slowly. Still,
the laws of nature ruled as they always do, the sun kept rising and setting, and
finally my day of departure arrived. I was planning before returning to Japan
to visit New York to see some old friends. Since my heart never took root in
America the whole time I lived there, I had few friends worthy of the name.
The following scene took place with one friend I did have, a Japanese woman
roughly my age, known for her brilliant mind. We went to the same graduate school in the United States, and she was now a professor at a prestigious
American university. I had heard the rumor that while working on her M.A.
degree in Japan she had knocked other students out by reading Balzac's entire
oeuvre in the original. What knocked me out was her nonchalant remark, "I
was good in math, too." We nevertheless had one thing in common: our love
of the classics of modern Japanese literature.

We met one evening at a Chinese restaurant uptown. Neither of us is much
of a drinker, but we held our beer mugs like grown-up women should and
picked up the dumplings with the long plastic chopsticks that Chinese restaurants in America invariably provide. In our tipsiness, we fumed as we la-
mented the world and bemoaned Japan.

Her face now red from the bit of beer she had had, my friend said sauc-
ily, "You know, when I was little, I used to think that novelists were incred-
ibly smart people with really serious ideas—the most respected people in the
whole world. And look at the writers now in Japan. They've got no brains. I
just don't feel like reading the crap they write."

I have no idea what she thought of me. She has a vivacious mind with
plenty of room for mischief, so she may have been coolly including me in
the category of brainless writers of crap. But rather than feeling hurt, I nod-
ded my own reddened face and eagerly acquiesced: "True, so true!" All the
thoughts I had had during my month in Iowa came rushing back and circled
in my inebriated mind.

Perhaps both she and I belong to a generation so thoroughly imbued
with the classics of modern Japanese literature that we don't know how to

appreciate newer writing. Or perhaps most of the newer writing is in fact of lesser value. Long ago, while I was still living in the United States, whenever I thought of what it would be like to finally go back to Japan and start writing novels in Japanese, an image presented itself before my eyes of a deep forest where stately trees stood tall. I would write in their shadow, quietly and modestly, bits of trivial things befitting a woman. Though this was a sorry image for someone who was already getting a taste of gender equality, I had somehow assumed that my country would still be inhabited by men like the giants Fukuzawa Yukichi, Futabatei Shimei, Natsume Sōseki, Mori Ōgai, Kōda Rohan, Tanizaki Jun'ichirō—men of frightening intelligence, knowledge, and wit. It had never occurred to me that once I was back in my home country I might not be able to find any deep forest where stately trees stood tall. Yet that was what happened. I spotted a tree here and a tree there, but mostly the scenery was flat. Unsuited even for a poetic description like "bleak wasteland," it was more like a playground where everything was small and clamorous— just juvenile. I was left to wonder whether my compatriots had forgotten that those men I so admired had even existed.

Many people both in Japan and abroad would disagree with this description of the contemporary Japanese literary scene, and they may be right. But even if this description happens to be true, that in itself would be no cause for alarm. In the course of history, every art form rises and falls and rises again. There is no need to fear for the future of Japanese literature—not unless the Japanese language is falling, not unless Japanese people keep on letting it fall or, even worse, keep on doing everything in their power to accelerate its fall (which I'm afraid may be the case) now that we have already entered the age of English.

2. FROM *PAR AVION* TO VIA AIR MAIL

THE FALL OF FRENCH

T HE LANGUAGE THAT GAINED DOMINANCE IN THE MODERN ERA, FROM THE EIGHTEENTH CENTURY ONWARD, IS OF course English. However, during much of this time, English was not the world's most revered language. *Mais non!* It was French.

Let us begin by taking a look at *A Little Princess*, a children's story written by Frances Hodgson Burnett in 1905. Now a classic, it has continued to be read all over the world as well as adapted into films, television programs, musicals, and, naturally, anime. Its heroine, Sara Crewe, is an English girl born in India whose father is a very rich man, mining diamonds in the distant colony and contributing to the resplendence of the British Empire. The story starts when she is sent to live in a boarding school in London. Sara is not only a wealthy heiress but also someone with an exceptional mind, both intelligent and noble. Yet her unquestioned superiority over others becomes established on her first day of school, before anyone knows anything about her except that she is rich.

The title of the first chapter is "A French Lesson." Miss Minchin, the school's owner and headmistress, introduces Sara to the other pupils and, as if to demonstrate her authority, imperiously orders the new girl to begin studying the textbook before the French master Monsieur Dufarge appears. Mean, narrow-minded, and domineering, Miss Minchin epitomizes the nasty adult. She is convinced that Sara knows no French. Sara tries to explain to her that, though she "never really learned" the language, she knows it because she always used it at home, her deceased mother being French and her father loving the language. Miss Minchin has a secret: to her shame, she herself does not know the language. Not wishing to discuss the matter any further, she cuts the new pupil short: "If you have not learned, you must begin at once." Too polite to retort, Sara waits until Monsieur Dufarge enters the classroom, whereupon she rises from her seat and begins to explain to him in French how she came to know the language.

It is as if Sara has been enthroned that instant. Monsieur Dufarge exclaims to Miss Minchin, "Ah, Madame . . . She has not *learned* French; she *is* French." The rest of the class is in awe of her, or deathly jealous. Miss Minchin is mortified. The first French lesson has determined Sara's fate. Several years later, when the unexpected death of her father leaves Sara penniless, Miss Minchin, who despite her profound dislike of the girl had been treating her as the school's prize pupil, instantly turns against her. Sara, the "little princess," is quickly shoved up to a maid's room in the attic with only her doll and a dress that's already too short for her, and she becomes the target of repeated abuse.

Reading *A Little Princess* in translation while munching rice crackers in our Tokyo home was when I first vaguely understood the magical power of the French language. My own French lessons began in junior high school in the United States. Everyone was required to study a foreign language (though for me English was already foreign enough). We had three options: French, Spanish, or Russian. French was my natural choice, for I could not picture what it would be like to become a Japanese woman with a command of Spanish or Russian, never having read a novel with such a heroine. But I could easily imagine a Japanese woman speaking French. She would be elegant; she would have class. The lovely nobleman's daughter in Akutagawa Ryūnosuke's short story "The Ball" (Butōkai, 1920) waltzes with a handsome French officer while fluently conversing with him in his language, which seemed a bit fanciful even to a young girl but still quite wonderful. The French teacher in our junior high school had black, curly hair and was not exactly handsome; he was not even French but Belgian. But he was kind to me, the only Asian in the class, and soon, though I made no active effort to learn English, I would hole up in my room listening over and over to a record exclaim, "*Voilà Monsieur Thibault. Voilà Madame Thibault. Ils habitent à Paris, à la place d'Italie.*"

My ties with the French language lasted long beyond what I ever imagined at the time. After graduating from high school, I first entered art school but soon quit, and then, as I mentioned before, I ended up studying French literature not only in college but also in graduate school. I did not choose this path with a specific goal, aside from that of avoiding English. As a Japanese middle-class girl of the time, I took up French basically in the same spirit as one studied other things Western like piano and ballet. Circumstances led me to endlessly continue in this path almost by default—or that is how I understood the whole course of events until much later.

Only when I went back to Japan, was freed at last from having to deal with English, and even forgot most of the French I had learned did I finally begin to see another motive, a less innocent one. I had lived in the United States as an Asian girl without an adequate command of English. French was the perfect language with which a girl like me could gain an advantage over the monolingual Americans.

When people found out that I was a student, they would invariably ask, often out of courtesy, "What do you major in?"

I would proudly answer, "French literature!"

In the United States at the time, it was unusual for Asians to study French literature. Hearing my answer, Americans would often open their eyes wide with amazement and look at me with sudden new respect. I would return their gaze, cool as you please.

THE JOURNEY OF FRENCH TOWARD BECOMING THE MOST REVERED language in Europe perhaps started in the seventeenth century with the reign of the Sun King, Louis XIV, which lasted seventy-two years (1643–1715) and made France, with its cultural, political, and military eminence, the grandest nation in Europe. The refinement of the French court became the model for other monarchs. The venerable Académie française had already been established earlier under the Sun King's father, Louis XIII, with a mission to vigorously regulate the French language, to "render it pure, eloquent, and capable of treating arts and sciences" (founding document of 1637). French went on to become the lingua franca of the European ruling class. What later came to be known as the Age of Enlightenment followed in the eighteenth century with France and the French language at its center, thanks to *philosophes* like Montesquieu, Rousseau, Alembert, Voltaire, and Diderot, among others. In the nineteenth century, while the British ran the most powerful empire and Great Britain enjoyed military, political, and economic dominance, French continued to be revered as the language that embodied the essence of European civilization. Not only was French recognized as the official language of diplomatic affairs among European nations, but command of the language was considered integral to life as a cultivated person in Europe.

To most Europeans, having a command of English did not matter unless you aspired to be an intellectual, which required familiarity with more than one language. Yet all Europeans of a certain social class and above were expected to know French, just as European women of a certain class and above were expected to know how to do embroidery. This was true of the British as well, and it continued to be true even up to the early twentieth century, when the British Empire was at its zenith. Enough familiarity with French trickled down so that most people were on at least nodding terms with the language. Agatha Christie, writing in that period, created her famous detective Hercule Poirot, who is Belgian (and thus not at all dashy, as a Frenchman would be) and who—aside from throwing in French ejaculations such as "*Parbleu!*" and "*Au nom de dieu!*"—often speaks strange English that's a direct translation of French. Instead of "Do you understand?" he says, "You comprehend?" Instead of "Allow me to tell you," he says, "Permit me to say to you." Scattered throughout the novel, these peculiar English forms produce comedic effect, humorously highlighting the detective's foreignness. And it was because Christie knew her readers, representing a broad spectrum of ordinary people, would appreciate the humor that she invented a hero like Poirot in the first place.

With the spread of colonialism and European influence worldwide, French became a language revered even by non-Westerners. *La gloire* of the French language naturally reached all the way to Japan, which had, following the Meiji Restoration of 1868, finally opened its doors to the West. Until then, during more than 250 years of isolation, the Edo government allowed trade only with the Dutch, with the consequence that Dutch was the only Western language that any Japanese—and just a tiny segment of the population—knew. As the initial chaos brought on by the Restoration subsided, people turned their eyes to the outside world. While eagerly acquiring new knowledge, they also became sensitive to the relative cachet of different Western languages. And since those on the periphery embrace snobbery with greater earnestness than those closer to the center—a phenomenon well attested to by the fact that East Asia is now the biggest global market for European-brand products—the Japanese cultural elite espoused veneration for the French language with even greater enthusiasm than did Europeans themselves. Along with British military, political, and economic supremacy, British cultural prowess was already becoming evident. And yet, in Japan, the cultural elites regarded English as the language for practical affairs and French as the language that symbolized the soul of Western civilization. This was especially true of the new generation of writers who tried to embrace that soul by devouring Western arts and letters.

> I should like to go to France,
> But France is far too far.
> So I shall don a new suit
> And roam where fancy leads.[1]

These simple lines (the full impact of which is untranslatable [see chapter 7]) by poet Hagiwara Sakutarō eloquently express the longings of Japanese writers of the Taishō period (1912–1926), which came on the heels of the Meiji. Successful writers squandered their earnings to realize their dream of spending time in France just breathing the air of Paris. Yet for most, France was a country "far too far," which intensified their yearning all the more. Another poem by Hagiwara begins, "Like the scent of a French cigarette / One whiff and I'm transported." The yearning for France spread from writers to readers, and translations of poems by the nineteenth-century French poets Charles Baudelaire, Paul Verlaine, and Arthur Rimbaud came to be as familiar to the Japanese middle class as *waka* poems from more than a thousand years ago that girls were often required to learn by heart. And then there were the French films that reached the country during the first half of the Shōwa period (1926–1989): *Sous les toits de Paris, A nous la liberté, Quatorze Juillet, Le grand jeu, Pension Mimosas, Un carnet de bal, Pépé le Moko.* Rendered into Japanese, these titles became embedded in the Japanese psyche, reflecting the widespread infatuation with France around that time. Songs like "Quand refleuriront les lilas blancs" and "Mon Paris," routinely performed on the all-female stage of the Takarazuka Revue—whose audience was also nearly all female—became so popular that even men who usually had no interest in such trifles could hum the tunes. Moreover, after Japan's defeat in World War II, Shiga Naoya, a novelist often referred to—for reasons I personally cannot fathom—as *shōsetsu no kamisama* (patron saint of novels), made an astounding comment. After arguing that the Japanese people started the disastrous war in large part because they were using the Japanese language, he suggested that they abandon their language altogether and adopt French: "Perhaps Japan should take the leap and adopt the world's best, most beautiful language as its national language. I think French would best serve the purpose."[2] If only the French had known, he might have been awarded the Legion of Honor.

It was after the end of World War II that the decline of France finally became evident to everyone, including the Japanese. The end of the war marked the decline not just of France but of Europe as well. The United States, already the world's richest nation before the war, did not suffer from air raids; with its factories and infrastructures intact, its economic superiority became even more prominent. During the immediate postwar years, the country's GDP amounted to approximately half that of the world (today it is a little less than one-third). At the same time, war-weary people around the world hungrily consumed American culture through the media of music, film, and television, and the world's cultural center shifted from Europe to the United States. Japan, occupied by the United States, became virtually an American colony.

Still, French culture managed to bloom one more time. If American culture was for the masses, French culture still held sway over educated and semi-educated Japanese. In the 1950s, existentialism was the craze, and every college student was familiar with the names Jean-Paul Sartre and Simone de Beauvoir, along with that of the chanteuse Juliette Greco. Then in the 1970s, when structuralism and then poststructuralism became trendy, works by the next generation of French philosophers and writers were widely and reverently read by the Japanese, who joined in the critique of Western metaphysics quite as if forgetting that they themselves were not Westerners. French cultural influence remained strong until the mid-1980s, and at its core proudly stood, as it had always stood, *la gloire* of the French language.

When frequenting Paris as a student in the 1970s, I was struck by the difference between Japanese students who came to the United States and those who came to France. Those who came to America did so with the purpose of mastering a particular subject, be it journalism or nuclear science; English was merely a means to achieve that goal. Conversely, most of those who came to France did so with the sole purpose of learning French and just being there. Their highest goal in life seemed to be sitting in an outdoor café smoking Gauloises and speaking French like a native. In retrospect, that the French language no longer functioned as a means to learn something else portended its dark future.

Consider what has happened to the French language since then. Today a Japanese person who "should like to go to France" can board a direct flight from Tokyo and arrive the same day, for the kind of money a college student earns on the side. At the same time, the decline in the prestige of French as the language of high culture has become all too apparent. Books written in French will certainly continue to exert influence, but it is now difficult to imagine a whole intellectual movement originating in France that would gain the momentum it once did. (The decline of the humanities in general only adds to the decline of the power of the French language.) Woe to those around the world who have devoted years of their lives to learning French. Woe to the girl I used to be, holed up in her room listening to "*Voilà Monsieur Thibault*" while letting go to waste the privilege of growing up in the United States. But woe most of all to the French themselves.

The illustrious history of the French language is carved into the French mind since childhood; there is no way the French would stand back and allow their language to fall without a fight. Politicians travel to former French colonies around the world—Quebec, Haiti, Martinique, Vietnam, Morocco, Algeria, Tunisia, Mali, Nigeria, Senegal, Madagascar—to deliver speeches in beautiful incantatory French and mesmerize audiences in an effort to preserve these regions as Francophone. Yet that is no longer the real issue. Now the urgent priority is preventing the French language from falling in France itself.

France made the decision to protect its language and turned doing so into a national project. The Toubon Law, named after a minister of culture, was mandated in 1994 and enforces the use of French in government documents, public announcements, commercials, state-funded schools, workplaces, and so on. French television stations are under obligation to allocate at least 40 percent of airtime to programs produced in France. French films receive hefty state subsidies to counterbalance the onslaught of Hollywood films. The Académie française—whose honorable members are known as *les immortels* because they are to ensure the excellence of the language in perpetuity—is valiantly trying to stem the invasion of English loanwords by recommending French alternatives: *logiciel* for "software," *courriel* for "e-mail." But no amount of effort can stem the flood of English at this point. Today it is both a sign of distinction and a pastime among French intellectuals to lament the fall of the French language.

Yet I am certain of one thing. However much French intellectuals bemoan the fall of their language, it would never occur to them to compare French with a language like Japanese, much less to think of the two as being on a par. After all, French is French. How could anyone dare compare it with a language spoken in the Far East by people whose culture is marginal, a language that has no global resonance whatsoever, a language written with the strangest set of signs—in a word, a language that appears thoroughly incapable of embodying *l'esprit cartésien*. And yet, with the emergence of English as the most powerful lingua franca, French and Japanese are no different in one critical point: neither language is English.

WAS THIS ONE OF THOSE INSTANCES THAT FULFILLED THE PALM reader's prediction that I am fated to have ties with foreign countries? Several years before my stay in Iowa, I was given a chance to urge French intellectuals to face this rather humiliating reality when an invitation came to give a talk at a symposium in Paris. I had not been there in over a decade. Well pleased to be summoned back as a novelist to that magical city where I had previously stayed only as a student or a tourist, I snapped up the chance. I decided moreover to speak in French: for once in my life, I would actually put to use the language that I had spent precious time learning. I retrieved one French word after another from my rusted memory, checked my spelling in a dictionary, and had my draft reviewed by a French teacher at Berlitz before my departure. As always, I traveled economy class, which, as always, felt like being transported in a prison van or a cattle truck; but once I set foot in Paris, I was greeted with boulevards shimmering with new leaves and skies gloriously liberated from the dark of winter. It was in the month of May, just when the city so beautiful to begin with becomes more beautiful still.

"Time" being the theme of the symposium, I organized my discussion around the notion of time—temporality—and gave it a title: "La littérature moderne japonaise: Deux temps" (Modern Japanese literature: Dual temporalities). Here is what I said.[3]

THE TALK IN PARIS

I am not a courageous woman. But I have decided to be one just once in my life. So here I am, having decided to speak to you in French—in my rudimentary French. I will read slowly, trying to pronounce each word as clearly as I can. This is the first time that I have ever spoken French in front of an audience. This is the first time that I have ever spoken French in front of a *French* audience. To mark what is for me a very special occasion, I would like to begin by recalling my first encounter with the French language.

What was the first French expression that I learned?

It was *Par Avion*, which I wrote on a postcard to my father who was on a business trip to the United States. I was still a child. I still lived in Tokyo.

"Why do I have to write in French?" I asked. "There is an agreement between countries to use French in international mail" was the response I got. Maybe it was my mother, or maybe it was the clerk at the post office; I no longer remember. At the time, even English was an unfamiliar language for me, let alone French. From then on, every time I wrote the words *Par Avion* my heart fluttered with excitement. A few years later, just after I entered secondary school, my father was transferred to New York, and I moved there with my family. Too proud and too cowardly to restart life as an Asian girl in America—for we were not immigrants—I stubbornly resisted getting along either with the United States or with the English language. I kept writing *Par Avion* on the envelopes that I now was sending to Japan. And every time I did so, I felt as if I were battling against the English language, which surrounded me and invaded me from every corner. The battle lasted for a long time—for a very long time. Even after I finally returned to Japan, I kept writing *Par Avion*.

But one day it all came to an end. I was no longer writing *Par Avion*. I was writing "Air Mail." This transition must have occurred sometime in the mid-1980s, without my being quite aware of it. I stopped writing *Par Avion* one day. I simply stopped, just like that. Perhaps French was still the official language of international mail, but such a fine point seemed superfluous. No use resisting English. Needless to say, this transition from *Par Avion* to "Air Mail" corresponded with a larger transition that was taking place in the world. I would venture so far as to claim that it was a radical transition that would not leave any writers unaffected, regardless of the language they wrote in, be it French, Japanese, or even English.

Let me try to explain myself by going back a little in time.

In 1868, the isolationist Edo shogunate, which reigned over Japan for more than 250 years, finally came to an end. The Meiji Emperor took over power in what is called the Meiji Restoration, and Japan officially opened its doors to the West. Innumerable changes proceeded to take place in the country. One of them was the change in Japanese awareness of time—of temporality—which is directly related to the subject of this symposium. This awareness also concerns modern Japanese literature.

For Japanese people before 1868, Europeans were little more than curious beasts, strange and incomprehensible. Then, after the Meiji Restoration, everything changed. Along with European science and technology, European art flooded into Japan, all forms of it representing themselves as the universal—and most advanced—model. The same was true of novels. The Japanese, with characteristic diligence, began to read masterpieces of European literature, first in the original and then in translation. And such is the power of literature that through the act of reading, little by little the Japanese came to live the lives of Europeans as if they were their own. They began to live the ambitions of Julien Sorel, the happiness of Jane Eyre, the sufferings of young Werther, and the despair of Anna Karenina as if they were their own. They thus began living a new temporality—that which flows in the West, dictated by the Gregorian calendar, marked by major historical events in the West. And by so doing, they eventually joined what the Europeans called "humanity."

Bravo to my ancestors!

And yet, as you all know, joining humanity is never a simple matter. By beginning to live the same temporality as Westerners, the Japanese now had to live two temporalities simultaneously. On the one hand, there was Time with a capital "T," which flows in the West. On the other hand, there was time with a small "t," which flows in Japan. Moreover, from that point on, the latter could exist only in relation to the former. It could no longer exist independently, yet it could not be the same as the other, either. If I, as a Japanese, find this new historical situation a bit tragic, it's not because Japanese people now had to live in two temporalities. It's rather because as a result of having to do so, they had no choice but to enter the asymmetrical relationship that had marked and continues to mark the modern world—the asymmetrical relationship between the West and the non-West, which is tantamount, however abstractly, to the asymmetrical relationship between what is universal and all the rest that is merely particular.

Whereas the Japanese who joined humanity began also to live in universal, Western temporality, people in the West did not live in Japanese temporality. Japanese temporality was merely particular. In fact, since modernity, all educated people in the world have come to live in Western temporality in one way or another. Yet only the Japanese lived in Japanese temporality (with the exception of those colonized by the former Japanese Empire who had no choice but to live in even more complicated temporalities). Japan's entry into humanity meant living in this asymmetrical relationship.

Let's take my mother as an example.

Everyone is young once. Even my mother, who now walks with a cane, was a young woman before World War II. Like other modern city girls of the day, she passionately loved everything Western—music, fashion, food. It didn't matter what it was, she just loved it all. And this was because she loved reading foreign novels (in translation) and watching foreign films. Gérard Philippe and Gary Cooper were her Prince Charmings. My mother no doubt identified with the heroines on the silver screen and whispered softly to herself: "I am just as beautiful, just as elegant, just as passionate as them. Someday someone will fall head over heels in love with me, too; I will be loved, just like them." Yes, my mother was a bit vain when it came to her looks (and she still is).

Yet how different her life was from the lives of those heroines! She lived in a small row house made of wood and paper. She slept on the floor, on a thin futon, and not on the bed that she kept pleading for. But above all, her daily humiliation and frustration revolved around the presence of her mother—my grandmother—who was old, shamelessly shabby looking, and virtually illiterate. A former geisha, my grandmother could play the *shamisen*, a traditional three-stringed musical instrument; she could also perform traditional Japanese dance. But, alas! She couldn't even make an omelette! Naturally, she'd never read a single European novel. When she had to accompany my mother to movie theaters playing foreign films—girls' schools often required an adult chaperone—she wouldn't understand a thing and would immediately fall asleep. She would even snore. My mother's eyes would fill with tears. But this was the life my mother had to live. What a wretched life! The novels and films that gave her so much joy also inflicted on her no small amount of pain.

You will tell me that there always exists a chasm between the world depicted in novels and films and the world that people actually live in. It is the chasm between the world mediated by art and the world unmediated by art, formless and drab. You are absolutely right. The gap that my mother felt was not necessarily any deeper than the gap felt by a European girl who loved books and films. Yet there is one critical difference. For in my mother's case, the chasm between the world of art and real life also symbolized something more: the asymmetrical relationship I mentioned earlier—the asymmetrical relationship between those who live in only a universal temporality and those who live in both a universal and a particular one.

To make this discussion a little more concrete, let me introduce a character named Françoise. Françoise is a young Parisienne living before World War II. Like my mother, she loves reading books and watching films. Also like my mother, she lives in a small apartment with her mother, who is old, shabby looking, and illiterate. One day Françoise, full of artistic aspirations, writes an autobiographical novel. It is the tale of her life torn between the world of art and the world of reality. (Not an original tale, I must say.) The novel is well received in France. Several hundred Japanese living in Japan read this novel in French, and one of them decides to translate it into Japanese. My mother reads the novel. She identifies with the heroine and says to herself, "This girl is just like me!" Moved, my mother, also full of artistic aspirations, writes her own autobiography. That novel is well received in Japan but is not translated into French—or any other European language, for that matter. The number of Europeans who read Japanese is just too small. Therefore, only Japanese readers can share the plight of my mother's life. For other readers in the world, it's as if her novel never existed. It's as if she herself never existed. Even if my mother had written her novel first, Françoise would never have read it and been moved by it.

The difference between Françoise and my mother demonstrates the fundamental difference created by the asymmetrical relationship. Those who live only in the universal temporality can make their voices heard by the world. Those who simultaneously live in the universal and particular temporalities may hear voices from the other side, but they cannot make their own voices heard. They can only participate passively in the universal temporality, however much they may wish otherwise. This asymmetry can ultimately be reduced to the asymmetry between the two languages. French, and not Japanese, was the common language between the two. And this linguistic asymmetry itself can ultimately be reduced to a numerical asymmetry. In my mother's lifetime, for every French person who read Japanese there were hundreds of thousands of Japanese people who read French and could translate it. The fact that far more Japanese read both languages formed the very condition and base of the asymmetrical relationship between the universal and the particular.

Did all this asymmetry discourage Japanese writers from writing in Japanese, in a language so devoid of universality? The answer is no. On the contrary, Europe inspired them with a concept they had not known before: that of national literature. Europe, needless to say, is far from being a monolithic entity. Through the course of history, European people gradually came to live in the common temporality, but Europe itself has long been a region characterized by cultural and, more important, linguistic diversity. Naturally, that diversity was not lost on the Japanese when they joined humanity. Writers read a variety of European languages; translators translated from an even greater variety. This linguistic diversity in Europe reinforced in the minds of the Japanese the newly imported concept of *national language*, a language inseparably linked to a nation-state, founded—supposedly—on common ethnic blood and history. This concept of *national language*, in turn, reinforced

in the Japanese mind the newly imported concept of *national literature*, particular to each nation-state. Japanese writers—who had no choice but to live
in the two temporalities, to live in the asymmetrical relationship, and to remain silent in universal temporality—could at least identify with European
writers, for like them they too were writing for their national literature. They
wrote with great passion, leading to the flowering of Japanese literature, and a
handful of those works became known in the West through translation.

Then everything changed, as the rise of English gradually called into question the significance of writing for a national literature.

When did the change start?

Back when Columbus discovered America in 1492, Portugal and Spain
controlled the seas. Even when England defeated the Spanish Armada in 1588,
nothing was yet determined. When Puritans from England arrived on the
American shore in the *Mayflower* in 1620, Spanish, French, and Dutch colo-
nists were also settling on the shores of the same continent, and the Dutch, by
then the dominant sea power, were engaged in the world's first global commerce through the Dutch East India Company. England became the dominant sea power only in the eighteenth century; but the eventual triumph of
the English language was still by no means assured. Ironically for you French
ladies and gentlemen, the fate of your language may have been sealed by your
having been ahead of your time and leading the rest of Europe with your
revolution of 1789. The French Revolution gave rise to the formation of coali-
tions among European monarchs to attack the newly created republic, leading to the Napoleonic Wars. And it might well have been the consequences of
these Napoleonic Wars, themselves the consequences of the French Revolution, that destined the English language to replace French eventually as the
most powerful universal language.

For what happened because of the wars Napoleon waged and lost? First,
Britain, with its strong rival France finally out of the way, emerged as the
world's leading power for the next hundred-odd years—years that coincided
with the age of imperialism. At its height, the British Empire covered nearly
one-quarter of the planet, whereas the French Empire, the second largest,
covered only one-tenth. English naturally became the lingua franca of the
British Empire. Second, the United States as we know it emerged through
the Louisiana Purchase of 1803, when Napoleon sold off the vast French territories in the heart of North America to secure funds to wage war against
Britain. The sale was made at the astonishingly low price of three cents per
acre (under fifty cents per acre in today's currency). The Louisiana Purchase

meant that the United States, which until then had been clustered on the Atlantic shore, at once doubled in size and could then sweep farther on, acquiring fertile territories westward all the way to the Pacific Ocean without having to fight the mighty French army. When Britain's supremacy finally declined in the twentieth century after World War II, who should inherit the title of the world's leading power but the United States, another English-speaking country, ultimately making the English language circulate beyond the boundaries of former British colonies.

Today, a Japanese person speaking to a French person would use English as a matter of course. And the French have no choice but to answer in kind. In the history of humanity, there have been many languages, including French, that served as universal languages: Latin, Chinese, Arabic, and more. Yet none of them ever ruled the world the way English does today. No language has ever been as completely and absolutely dominant. Moreover, once the spread of a language gains momentum, it follows its own logic of propagation, independent of the economic, political, or military power that first propelled it onto the stage. Regardless of the future that awaits the United States, the hegemony of the English language can only expand in the years to come. The number of bilinguals—those who communicate with the outside world by using English—can only expand as well.

Now, where do novelists come into all this? A strong tie binds novelists to their mother tongue. Though novelists can and do write in languages other than their own, there is a common belief that a novel has a special, almost mystical affinity with the novelist's mother tongue. A novel not written in the novelist's mother tongue tends to be taken less seriously as a work of literature. This inevitably puts novelists today, even those writing in major languages, in a sorry position—except for those whose mother tongue is English. A great chasm divides the two. The asymmetry is stark.

To be sure, novelists writing in English have their own lament. They will argue that most of the English language now circulating globally—in academia, journalism, commerce, Hollywood, the Internet—is impoverished, degenerate, and uprooted. They have to wage war from day to day against facile English. Yes, I will reply, but you see, waging war against inane language that circulates almost automatically is a writer's eternal mission, and the day will never come when those battles are unnecessary. As a novelist who writes in Japanese, I have no sympathy for their complaints; they would certainly not dream of trading places with me.

Just think. Just think of all the readers who could go ahead and read your work in the original if you wrote in English. Aside from all those whose mother tongue is English, there are even more potential readers throughout Asia, Africa, Latin America, and Europe, those who truly make the English language circulate as the universal language. For literature, they are the readers that truly count, being almost invariably the best-educated and best-read members of society. As bilinguals, they also translate what they read into their other language. Both in the original and in translation, whether recent works or classics, novels written in English are increasingly dominating the world and can only continue to do so.

The act of writing is not mere masturbation. It is the writer's delivery of words somewhere far beyond the world right before her, beyond the world that surrounds her—beyond the immediate world of here and now. By delivering our words to an unknown future and space, we writers share them with our true readers—our spiritual comrades—people that we never have met and never will. The written word can overcome barriers in ways no spoken words can, and English written words are doing precisely that on a scale heretofore unimaginable. Take the case of Jane Austen, my favorite writer in English. If she found out how many spiritual comrades she has in the world today, she'd be embarrassed, even shocked. For while she was an ironist with a sharp tongue, she was also a perfect lady with a strong sense of modesty.

And that is not all. English no longer belongs to this or that group of people but to everyone who wishes to use it. At a certain point in history, the language became disconnected from its past. When those in the former British colonies first began to write in English, English must have felt like someone else's language. When the descendants of slaves, refugees, or immigrants first began to write in English, the same must have been true. Yet as those people swelled in number, English evolved into a language that everyone could claim as their own. English is no longer a national language, and texts written in English are no longer national literature. Today novelists using English, whether they be Canadian, Indian, or Nigerian, are novelists in a universal language. Inevitably, little by little, more will defy the notion of there being a special tie binding novels and one's mother tongue and choose to start writing novels in English *if*, by chance or effort, they acquire sufficient mastery of the language.

Which brings me to make this pronouncement.

My heart goes out to novelists who are writing in French today. No, I ought to be more honest. My heart is filled with discreet joy when I think about their new predicament. For I now have the pleasure of having such fine people join my company. I will cry out to them with my arms wide open:

Welcome! Welcome to my side of the asymmetrical relationship! You used to be on the other side, on the dominant side. No, you used to be more than that. Because of your past splendor, you were often the very symbol of that dominant side. Yet, alas, you are now sadly in the same sorry camp as me. You too are now made to live in two temporalities: the universal temporality that flows in texts written in English, and the particular temporality that flows in texts written in your own language. Like much of the world's population, you too can easily hear the voices of those who speak in the universal temporality, but you can no longer easily make your own voices heard. Moreover, this asymmetry does not end there. It even robs you of your past splendor. That's right. Until just a while ago, Racine was a figure on a par with Shakespeare. But look where he is now. Most high school students in the world—which has now come to include the whole non-West as well—are probably familiar with the name of Shakespeare. But what about Racine? Who *is* he? Probably only a very few high school students anywhere have heard his name. I am afraid their number may eventually dwindle to the number of those who have heard the name of Lady Murasaki Shikibu, the author of *The Tale of Genji*. What a shocking demise!

Yes, this is the pronouncement I would humbly make to novelists who write in French today. The asymmetrical relationship between the West and the non-West will continue to exist. That is inevitable. However, now, on top of it is added a new and in some ways equally fundamental layer of asymmetrical relationship: the asymmetrical relationship between the world of English and the world of non-English.

Now, please forgive my impudence and allow me to use the word "we" when talking about French novelists and myself. What could *we* do? What on earth could *we* do as novelists? The answer is, clearly, nothing. Even if we know that our voices will not reach the wider world, that doesn't stop any of us from writing in our own language. There's the desire—the psychological necessity—to do so. There's also the pleasure. Desire and pleasure combined are more than enough reason for any undertaking. And yet I would like to ask if there may not be some special gift endowed only to those of us who do *not* write in English. I dare say that there is.

If we were to compare ourselves with novelists who write in English, we might find our minds infused with countless unsavory sentiments such as jealousy, ill-will, anger, despair, and apathy, as if we had opened Pandora's box. Yet, just as "hope" was left inside the box, there is one thing left for us. On this one point, we have absolute superiority over novelists who write in English. For those of us who know we are living in this asymmetry are the only ones condemned to perpetually reflect upon language, the only ones forced to know that the English language cannot dictate "truths" and that there are other "truths" in this world that cannot be perceived through the English language. Of course, I am sure that many novelists writing in English also reflect upon language just like we do. Yet they are not *condemned* to do so in the way that we are.

They are not condemned to know, for instance, that the works that are usually translated into English are those that are both thematically and linguistically the easiest to translate, that often only reinforce the worldview constructed by the English language, and preferably that entertain readers with just the right kind of exoticism. They are not condemned to know that there is thus a perpetual hermeneutic circle—that in interpreting the world, only "truths" that can be perceived in English exist as "truths." They are not condemned to know that this hermeneutic circle is further consolidated by the honorable Nobel Prize in Literature, which inevitably suppresses all the problems inherent in the act of translation. Only we are condemned. Only we are forced to constantly reflect that when Proust's *maman* is replaced by "mom" or "mother," the very "time" that Proust retrieved is not the same. Similarly, replace my mother's *kaasan* with "mom" or "mother," and her story is not the same. Fortunately, I am not here today to represent contemporary Japanese writers. I do not know what they think about the things I have been talking about. I don't even know if they ever think about them. Yet everything I write is in one way or another haunted by the thought that I *am* writing in Japanese, that I *am* living in the asymmetrical relationship I have described. And this has much to do with my own personal history.

To use my remaining time effectively, let me briefly talk about my novel *Shishōsetsu from left to right* (An I-novel from left to right), published in 1995. In both its content and its form, this novel most directly addresses the question: What does it mean to write in Japanese in this day and age? The Japanese word *shishōsetsu* refers to a fictionalized autobiographical work, and my novel is just that. It's a story about a Japanese woman who left her native country as a girl and moved to the United States with her family. Instead of making the United States her new home, she turns her back on it, shuts herself up in her room, and spends every day reading Japanese novels. After twenty years of living in the United States—twenty years during which she absurdly rejects her new country while hesitating to return home—she finally decides one day to go back to Japan and become a writer.

Ever since Marcel Proust's *In Search of Lost Time*, what can be called "how-I-became-a-writer" stories have flourished in the world. *Shishōsetsu from left to right* is no doubt a variant. You may even detect in my novel that self-complacent, self-congratulatory tone that is characteristic of such stories. Yet my novel is also something else. For it is not just a how-I-became-a-writer story; it is also a how-I-became-a-Japanese-writer story. And this story is inseparably connected to another story that runs parallel to it and yet is a far more sober tale, full of regret: a how-I-failed-to-become-a-writer-in-the-English-language story. The female protagonist of *Shishōsetsu from left to right* went to the United States at a privileged age, a time when she was still young enough to adopt a new language and make it her own. Why was she so fixated on the Japanese language—a language that does not even belong to a major linguistic family, one that's used only in an island country in the Far East, one that's singularly isolated? In other words, why didn't she choose to adopt English? Why didn't she choose "correctly," like many others who moved to the United States at an age similar to hers—those who are now writing how-I-became-an-English-writer stories? How did she end up making such a terribly wrong choice? Why did it never even occur to her that she had such a choice until the choice was forever lost?

Why? It is true that as an Asian living in the United States, she felt she was an outsider. It is perhaps also true that she was too proud or too cowardly, afraid of the humiliation that necessarily accompanies the experience of learning a new language. Yet these sociological or psychological reasons are not sufficient to explain what in the last analysis represents a profoundly literary phenomenon. For what made the protagonist persevere in her resistance to English was the act of reading Japanese. The more she immersed herself in Japanese novels, the more irrevocably she turned her back on English. It was in reading that she encountered the irreducible material difference of the Japanese language from English, making it acutely uncomfortable for her to live in two worlds, to live with two subjectivities.

Hence the peculiar form of *Shishōsetsu from left to right*. As the awkward bilingual title indicates, the novel has some English phrases and sentences scattered here and there; to a limited extent, it is a bilingual novel. To realize the coexistence of the two languages—to allow the novel to be read without having to turn the book around—the novel is written horizontally, from left to right, unlike a typical Japanese novel that is written vertically, from top to bottom. It even begins with an overdramatic sentence in English: "Alas! Twenty years since the Exodus!"

I hoped, through this bilingual form, to attest to the linguistic asymmetry that I have been talking about. Any writer writing in English, even if she herself knew some Japanese, could not possibly expect her readers to understand Japanese phrases and sentences scattered in her novel. In contrast, any writer writing in a language other than English can reasonably expect her readers to understand some, if not most, of the English words she might happen to throw in. It would therefore be possible to replicate the bilingual form of *Shishōsetsu from left to right* in any language in the world—be it Korean, Bengali, or French—by translating the Japanese and leaving the English parts as they are. The only language in which this wouldn't work would be English. If we leave the English sentences as they are, how are we to replicate the bilingual form in the translation? Yet into what language are we to translate the English words and sentences? Indeed, the very impossibility of maintaining the bilingual form while translating the work into English, and the singularity of that impossibility, are clear testimony to the linguistic asymmetry we now face in this world.

That said, I would like to move on a little further, because throwing light on this asymmetry was not the only objective of the novel. Inextricably linked to that objective was another objective, an even more critical one. By juxtaposing the two languages, what I hoped to convey above all was the irreducible materiality of the Japanese language. What a bizarre and amusing language Japanese is, mixing Chinese characters with two sets of phonetic signs that look like the very opposite of each other: angular and masculine katakana and curvilinear and feminine hiragana! What a rough and yet refined language! Fast and loose in its logic, courtly in its honorifics. Through this bilingual form, I wanted to directly appeal to Japanese readers, to impress upon them that their language is different from English, different from any Western language, different indeed from any other language in the world. Not that I tried to make a case for the uniqueness of the Japanese language. I tried rather, through the bilingual form, to make a case for the irreducible materiality of all languages, the reason for which writing even in the most local of all of local languages becomes a worthwhile activity in itself.

Just imagine. Imagine a world one hundred, two hundred, three hundred years from now, a world in which not only the best-educated people but also the brightest minds and the deepest souls express themselves only in English. Imagine a world in which all other languages have been reduced to silliness.

Imagine the world subjected to the tyranny of a singular "Logos." What a narrow, pitiful, and horrid world that would be! To live in such a world would be infinitely sadder, I am sure, than to be confined to the asymmetry we have now.

You must all be aware that novelists are rather megalomaniacal people. I must admit that I am no exception. Even as I write in Japanese, in a language that has never played a major role in the history of humankind, I am doing so in hope of saving humanity from succumbing to that awful fate we, as humans, do not deserve.

MODERN JAPANESE LITERATURE: A "MAJOR LITERATURE"

When I finished this talk in Paris, a circle of people quickly gathered to say gracious things about it and shake hands with the novelist from afar. Since at that point *Merci!* was about the only French I could spontaneously come up with, I put on a big smile and repeated, "*Merci! Merci!*" Just as that circle began to wane, a middle-aged woman who had been standing at some distance approached me. I recognized her. She, too, had given a presentation a couple of days before; amid all the other presentations that were comically very French, bewilderingly philosophical with sentences lasting more than a minute each, hers was a notably clear talk in plain language. Framed by light brown hair mixed with some gray, her face revealed a well-cultivated mind, one nurtured by life and polished by education. French seemed to be her mother tongue, though she was teaching at a university in Israel.

Looking straight at me, she began telling me about her own parents, who were both novelists in Yiddish, a language used by ten million Jewish people in central and eastern Europe before the Holocaust. Then, apologizing for what she considered her impudence in comparing her parents to me, she mentioned how writing in languages like Japanese and Yiddish offers a kind of intimacy that is impossible when writing in more dominant languages. What struck me was the expression she used to describe Japanese literature: "I know I can't compare my parents with someone like you who's a writer in a major literature [*une littérature majeure*] like Japanese literature, but . . ." Even after she left my side, the words "major literature" rang in my ears. Even during the appropriately French posttalk reception with abundant offerings of wine and cheese arranged elegantly on tables, they stayed in my ears. Even when I left the crowd to go up to the rooftop to feel the May wind and stared blankly down at the Paris rooftops, even on my return flight, and even for a while after I arrived home, the expression stayed in my ears. In time, I came to recall it only intermittently. I never imagined that it would come back to me one day with such persistency and with far greater meaning than the speaker had intended.

AWARENESS OFTEN COMES TO US TERRIBLY LATE. IT FINALLY knocks on our mind's door months, years, sometimes decades after the scene, incident, or conversation that prompted it. Preconceptions we have unknowingly acquired keep us from seeing things for what they are. Blocked by preconceptions, we cease to think. Nonetheless, as time matures, we are sometimes graced with an occasion when truth reveals its simple, unforced, and also brutal self. At that point, we realize that we had somehow known the truth all along.

My generation was raised and educated by those who felt ashamed of the way the Japanese Empire once looked down on all other non-Western countries as backward and underdeveloped. If it never occurred to me to compare Japanese literature with other non-Western literatures, it was because the whole country, awash in a sea of guilt about its imperial past, never dared to make any such comparison. It also never occurred to me to consider whether other non-Western nations had as many works of modern literature written in their own language as Japan did.

The novels I immersed myself in as soon as I started living in a colonial-style house in a New York suburb in the 1960s were from a collection of modern Japanese literature published by Kaizōsha in 1926. Sixty-three volumes in all, this collection had great significance in the history of modern Japan. At the remarkably affordable price of one yen per copy, the first volume to be released sold 250,000 copies immediately after the advertisement came out. The collection ignited a boom for similar literary collections to follow. Of course, as a twelve-year-old girl I was unaware of any of this. I simply read whatever I could and kept yearning for a Japan that no longer existed anywhere but in literature. That such a collection had been published long before I was born never struck me as in any way remarkable. I must have taken it for granted that if I were a Mongolian girl, I would be immersed in a collection of modern Mongolian literature. It was only in Iowa when the expression "major literature" came back to haunt me that I began to realize how impossible it would have been at the time for any Asian girl outside Japan to read a collection of the modern literature of her own country published in 1926.

Suppose there was a bookish English girl who was brought to the United States at age twelve around the same time and did not feel at home there. She may have spent her days immersed in the Penguin Classics. Suppose she was French. She may have spent her days immersed in la Bibliothèque de la Pléiade. Yet what girl outside of Japan, what girl other than a Western girl, could have spent her days immersed in a collection of modern literature written in her own language, especially one published in 1926? Even for a Western girl, this luxury was not available for just anybody. Yet it never occurred to me as a teenager to think in those terms.

My blindness persisted even as I went on to college. I encountered many Americans who had read not only *The Tale of Genji* (*Genji monogatari*), written more than a thousand years ago, but also the works of postwar writers like Abe Kōbō, Mishima Yukio, and Ōe Kenzaburō, and even, to my pleasure, the lengthy *Makioka Sisters* (*Sasameyuki*) by Tanizaki Jun'ichirō. An aspiring writer that I once met—universally praised for his talent yet forever unable to finish his novel—expressed shock and dismay over the way Tanizaki ended the saga of the beautiful sisters. Raising his fists as if to curse God, he cried out, "It ends with, of all things, Yukiko having an attack of diarrhea! I can't believe it!" Those were the good old days when educated Americans read foreign literature in translation, even works written in non-Western languages. Still, while they may have read medieval works like *One Thousand and One Nights* and *The Rubaiyat*, never did I come across anyone who had read works of modern literature written in a non-Western language aside from Japanese. I, of course, made nothing of this.

I remained in the dark as I returned to Japan and then was called back to the United States to teach modern Japanese literature at Princeton—the first fulfillment of the palm reader's prediction. Japanese women of my generation grew up assuming that a job like university teaching had nothing to do with them. And so as I went back to the United States, I found the turn of events quite surreal. Then when I started teaching, another surprise awaited me: my students were a mixed bag, with ethnic groups I hadn't really been expecting represented in large numbers—Korean, Chinese, Singaporean, Indian, African American. Students at that relatively conservative East Coast university were mostly white at the time, yet there in front of me was an impressive range of skin tones, from ivory to dark coffee. Students looking for their identity in the non-West wanted to find out what on earth modern literature written in a non-Western language might be like, and thus they enrolled in the only such course Princeton then offered: my course on modern Japanese literature. Reading some of the masterpieces of modern Japanese literature with the students, I felt a not unreasonable pride. But still, I remained in the dark.

Many more years passed until I heard the woman in Paris utter the expression "a major literature." Still more years passed until, finally, everything fit. As the leaves turned yellow while I lingered under the blue sky of Iowa with other writers possibly on their way to a downfall, I began to think historically. And as I began to think historically, I became aware of something I had not realized when I gave the talk in Paris: the fact that Japanese literature is considered a major literature was the very condition that had allowed me to give such a talk in front of a French audience. For how could I even begin to talk about the asymmetrical relationship between the universal and the particular unless Japanese literature was important enough to represent the particular?

Not every national literature is a major literature, just as not every nation's cuisine is a major cuisine. When one uses the term "Mongolian literature" or "Lithuanian literature," the word "Mongolian" or "Lithuanian" basically functions as a simple adjective modifying the word "literature." That is not the case with the term "Japanese literature." The term circulates in the world as a recognized national literature—at least among readers who read literature in translation, who may be quite limited in number but whose presence is indispensable when thinking about world literature. Moreover, Japanese literature came to be recognized as such thanks not only to *The Tale of Genji* but also, and more crucially, to the wealth of the country's modern literature.

There is only so much fairness in the world. Good people are not rewarded, and fine works of literature—entire bodies of literature, even—are buried in oblivion without attaining the recognition they are due. That modern Japanese literature attained some recognition relatively early on is not necessarily a sign that it is superior to other, less recognized bodies of literature. As a matter of fact, the attack on Pearl Harbor, of all things, is what gave modern Japanese literature an edge. After the attack, the United States rushed to recruit brilliant young minds from all over the country to train them to decipher the Japanese language. Those people later became scholars and translators of Japanese literature: Edward Seidensticker, Donald Keene, and Ivan Morris worked for the navy; Howard Hibbett was in the army; Edwin Mc-Clellan, a half-Japanese Scotsman who grew up in prewar Japan, worked for Allied intelligence in Washington.

It was first and foremost thanks to the English translations by these men that the world came to know that there was such a thing as modern Japanese literature, which eventually led to Kawabata Yasunari's winning the Nobel

Prize in Literature in 1968. Whatever reservations one may—I think should—have about the prize, the event marks a significant historical step in pushing the boundary of what Westerners consider the "world." The first non-Western Nobel Prize in Literature went to Rabindranath Tagore of India in 1913, yet it was through his own English translation of his Bengali poems that he was awarded the honor. More than a full half century had to pass before a novelist writing in a non-Western language first received the prize in 1966. The recipient, Shmuel Yosef Agnon, was an Israeli who wrote in Hebrew, but he grew up speaking Yiddish—a variant of High German—at home in what was then the Austro-Hungarian Empire. It might be difficult to categorize him as a non-Westerner. Two years later came Kawabata Yasunari, who was as far removed from the West as a modern writer could be. Moreover, given that no author writing in a non-Western language would receive the award for the next twenty years, it is likely that no other non-Western literature was being translated to the extent that Japanese literature was. In time, a new generation of translators emerged, and, in addition to the classics of modern Japanese literature, contemporary works by young Japanese writers began to appear in English and in other Western languages, ultimately leading to Ōe Kenzaburō becoming the second Japanese writer to receive the Nobel Prize, in 1994. The translation of Japanese literature into foreign languages continues to thrive.

As of November 8, 2013, the *Encyclopedia Britannica* has an entry on "Japanese Literature" that consists of almost 13,400 words. (By comparison, Mongolian and Lithuanian literatures have entries of some 2,300 words and 600 words, respectively.) The entry begins as follows:

> Both in quantity and quality, Japanese literature ranks as *one of the major literatures of the world*, comparable in age, richness, and volume to English literature, though its course of development has been quite dissimilar. The surviving works comprise a literary tradition extending from the 7th century AD to the present; during all this time there was never a "dark age" devoid of literary production. (Emphasis added)

The entry's author is Donald Keene, one of the American scholars and translators mentioned earlier, first recruited to study the enemy's language during World War II. (Keene became a Japanese citizen in 2012.) It is uncertain if Japanese literature would have come to be recognized as "one of the major literatures of the world" if it were not for the arbitrary forces of history. Yet what is clear is that those recruited to decipher the language became intrigued enough by what the Japanese people were writing that they eventually wanted to translate it. And there is something more certain—and even more important. *Even if Japanese literature remained totally unknown to the rest of the world*, those Japanese who were well versed in literary gems of the world through reading them in the original and in translation could know with confidence that their own literature was filled with works in no way inferior.

By the time I was about to leave Iowa and its strikingly blue sky, I was ready to call the phenomenon of modern Japanese literature a miracle. Admittedly, "miracle" is a strong word, yet the more I thought about Japanese literature, the more I was convinced of its appropriateness—and of the necessity for me and my compatriots to understand and appreciate our country's literature in that exalted sense. For only then could we find a way to stop our present folly of doing all in our power to bring on our language's fall.

3. PEOPLE AROUND THE WORLD WRITING IN EXTERNAL LANGUAGES

HOW PEOPLE UNDERSTAND THE HISTORY OF THEIR LANGUAGE VARIES GREATLY. SOME POPULATIONS ARE LESS NAÏVE than others. Whether through foreign domination or ethnic conflicts, their history has taught them to be less naïve. Others are relatively more naïve—including the Japanese, islanders whose language has never been threatened from either within or without. Ask them how they as a nation came to read and write, and they will most likely give a short and simple answer like this: "Since time immemorial, we Japanese have always spoken Japanese. One day, some people from the nearby Korean Peninsula brought over Chinese characters, which our ancestors adopted for their own use. They added some phonetic signs they themselves invented and so created their own system of writing. This is how Japanese people came to read and write Japanese."

Such an answer isn't entirely false. After all, an answer so vague can be interpreted in any number of ways. Yet it is built on one mistaken premise—a mistaken premise by no means unique to the historically naïve Japanese but prevalent today: *that written language is a mere representation of spoken language.* Such a premise not only misconstrues the essential nature of written language but also ignores human history. For during most of the six thousand–odd years since the human race discovered writing, people usually have not read and written the language they spoke. More often they read and wrote an "external language"—that is, the language of an older and greater neighboring civilization that exerted its influence in the region. Several such languages have thrived in various parts of the globe at various times in human history. These are what I call *universal languages.*

Beginning with this chapter, I will develop my argument around three main concepts: *universal language, local language*, and *national language*. The last concept, national language, needs some clarification. Though the term is not much used in English, it is a helpful one found in many languages, and the concept has been important in Japan since the Meiji Restoration. A national language is basically the same as the official language of a nation, but the expression underscores the emotional connection people have with their language as the language of their homeland. National language may hence be defined as the language that the citizens of a nation-state consider to be their own language.

Naturally, this definition is fraught with problems. First of all, the borders of a national language do not always correspond with the geographical borders of a nation-state. In many cases, the same national language is used in different regions of the world; in other cases, a single nation can have several "national languages," since there are states with multiple official languages. In yet other instances, some nations have officially mandated a national language that is not used much in real life. I will not delve into these specifics. The history of human language is terribly messy and confusing. These three concepts—universal language, local language, national language—are merely tools for thinking as clearly as possible about the broad history of human language.

Two other expressions that have already come up in this book may need some clarification as well. First, the notion of a "bilingual." The word, as generally used, has a strong connotation of someone with an ability to *speak* two languages. Here, since my discussion centers solely on the written language, "bilingual" is used to designate those people who can *read and write* a language other than their own, with a stronger emphasis on their ability to read. The second is the notion of the "non-West." While it is a notion that is critical in understanding modernity, much ambiguity plagues the binary between West and non-West. Anglophone countries such as Australia and New Zealand can be categorized as belonging to the West, as well as countries like Hungary and Finland, both European nations using non-European languages. But what about a country like Israel, a Westernized nation using non-European languages and inhabited by many Semites? Or Mexico, which uses Spanish while the majority of its population is of mixed race? Again, I will not dwell on these subtle points and will simply emphasize that the notion of the non-West is here used as a cultural and linguistic concept and not a geographic or an ethnic one.

Let us begin by trying to better understand what a universal language is, for that will necessarily lead to a better understanding of both local and national languages. A brilliant and fascinating book—one that has had great influence worldwide over the past thirty years—gives us a perfect platform to think about the concept. It's not that the book offers any insight into the nature of universal language itself. On the contrary, the book has surprisingly little to say about it. Yet the very absence of a true appreciation of universal language paradoxically reveals its primary function.

The book is Benedict Anderson's now-classic *Imagined Communities: Reflections on the Origin and Spread of Nationalism*.[1] An analysis of the formation of modern nation-states, it is particularly well known among students of literature for the beginning section, in which Anderson discusses what turns out to be an inevitable relationship among national language, national literature, and nationalism. The book was published in 1983, and revised editions came out in 1991 and again in 2006. My own book would certainly not have been possible without Anderson's work.

I will confine my discussion basically to the introduction and first three chapters of *Imagined Communities*, as I want to focus on Anderson's understanding of the formation of national languages, not nation-states or nationalism, while fully recognizing that by so doing I am deviating from the main thesis of his book. Such a reading necessarily results in repeating the same "error" that many others seem to have committed and that Anderson laments in his preface to the second edition: it ignores one of the book's critical points, expounded in chapter 4, which argues that nationalism had its origins in the New World. Yet to examine his erudite work in its entirety is beyond the scope of my book—not to mention my ability.

The essential thesis of the beginning section of *Imagined Communities* may be summarized as follows: a nation-state is not a natural entity. Today, much of humanity—except for those living in countries that have come into being only recently—tends to take the existence of nation-states for granted. Yet, Anderson argues, nation-states are merely "cultural artifacts" of modernity, created through intertwining forces of history. Once invented, however, they invoke deep attachments that often defy logic.

Let me start by applying this thesis to national language: a national language is not a natural entity. Aside from scholars of language, literature, or history, much of humanity is under the illusion that the language they now use is something their people have always used since ancient times. But just as with nation-states, national languages are nothing but "cultural artifacts" of modernity, created through intertwining historical forces. And yet once such languages come into existence, the historical process of their formation is forgotten, and people come to believe that their language is an expression of their deepest national—and ethnic—character. National languages give birth to national literatures; national literatures, in turn, help to build and solidify nation-states—the "imagined communities" for which millions of people in the past, present, and future sacrifice their lives.

What seems to me to be most innovative about Anderson's understanding of the formation of national language—though apparently not everyone agrees—is his incorporation of the notion of "print capitalism" into his historical analysis. The invention of Gutenberg's printing press in mid-fifteenth-century Europe made it possible to print mechanically what had previously been copied by hand; the enormous impact the invention had on the history of written language is now well established. Yet according to Anderson, this invention alone would not have led to a profound transformation in society unless printed books could be distributed as market commodities. (In fact, the printing press itself had been invented in China and Korea well before Gutenberg's time.) The printing press proved transformational precisely because, in Europe, capitalism had by then developed to a point where books could circulate as market commodities. As books became commodities, they necessarily followed the market mechanism of supply and demand, eventually leading to the publication of books in what Anderson calls the "vernaculars," which, in turn, led eventually to the formation of national languages.

Let us follow Anderson's analysis in a little more detail by thinking about Europe just before Gutenberg's invention of the printing press. Nearly all books were sacred or exegetic texts that scribes copied by pen, word by word, onto parchment. And they were virtually all written in what was then the only written language for Europeans, Latin. What exactly is Latin? Anderson says, "The determinative fact about Latin—aside from its sacrality—was that it was a language of bilinguals." Latin was hence the language of all those people who spoke in their mother tongue in the streets while reading and writing in this "external language" as they entered the world of books. The number of such bilinguals was naturally quite limited: "Their readers were, after all, tiny literate reefs on top of vast illiterate oceans." Yet manually copying Latin one word at a time could not produce a sufficient number of books even for such a small pool of bilinguals. Then came Gutenberg. With his invention, the first printed edition of the Latin Bible, the Gutenberg Bible, was published and circulated in the market as "the first modern-style mass-produced industrial commodity." Taking on the idea first put forward by Marshall McLuhan, to call the Gutenberg Bible a "mass-produced industrial commodity" is Anderson's rhetorical device to highlight the role capitalism played in the process. The book was actually an exquisitely designed volume, a work of art. It was initially less expensive to have books copied by scribes than to have them printed by this precious machine. Even then, the Bible's becoming a market commodity meant that there was already a sufficient number of people capable of buying such a luxury item—a sufficient number of consumers. In terms of laws of the market, there was sufficient demand to meet the supply.

According to Anderson, the "vernacular revolution"—which later enabled the emergence of national language—took place as the next inevitable stage, complying with the same laws of the market. The Gutenberg Bible was followed by the publication of various books in Latin. However, those who could read Latin were limited to "a wide but thin stratum" of society, and the market was soon saturated. To create a new market, the laws of the market dictated that books written in the language of the street must come into circulation: "The logic of capitalism thus meant that once the elite Latin market was saturated, the potentially huge markets represented by the monoglot masses would beckon." Thus came "the vernacular revolution." One by one, various spoken languages in Europe were transformed into written languages, printed, and published. In Anderson's terminology, various "vernaculars" became "print languages." First to appear in these new print languages were translations of Latin, soon followed by books written directly in the print languages. In its social status, a print language ranked below Latin but above the vernacular, which was basically a spoken language.

Countless vernaculars existed in Europe, unique to each locality and class, akin to countless dialects coexisting in a region. In contrast, there could be only so many print languages, for in order for a book to make a profit as a "mass-produced industrial commodity," it needed to be published on a certain scale, which necessarily limited the number of print languages. Thus, following the vernacular revolution, countless vernaculars all over Europe were eventually subsumed into several important print languages: English, French, German, Dutch, Italian, Spanish, Portuguese, Czech, Danish, Russian, Polish, and so forth. And these print languages came to be shared by millions of people in each region.

The development from the vernacular revolution to the creation of the languages of nation-states did not progress at a uniform pace in Europe: some

European languages emerged as the language of a nation-state as early as the sixteenth or seventeenth century; others, as late as the twentieth century. Nonetheless, with the combination of the invention of print technology, the development of capitalism, and what Anderson calls "the fatality of human linguistic diversity," this progression was perhaps inevitable, and the process, largely unself-conscious. And once these print languages began circulating as the languages of emerging nation-states, they gave birth to a strong conviction among their populations that those who shared the same language belonged to the same community—the "imagined community." Whence arose nationalism, which these emerging states soon deliberately exploited. Europe's path since then was one in which states consciously manipulated nationalism as they went through conflicts over colonial territories, wars of independence, and border disputes. Furthermore, the nation-states that emerged in Europe provided a "module" for other regions that spread all over the world, along with nationalism.

Anderson writes:

Finally, [the nation] is imagined as a *community*, because, regardless of the actual inequality and exploitation that may prevail in each, the nation is always conceived as a deep, horizontal comradeship. Ultimately it is this fraternity that makes it possible, over the past two centuries, for so many millions of people, not so much to kill, as willingly to die for such limited imaginings. (Emphasis in original)

Contributing to the growth of nationalism was the spread of print media such as newspapers and, yes, national literature. National literature made it possible for an individual living in a nation-state to imagine fellow subjects inhabiting the same space at the same moment and to feel a sense of camaraderie with them. National language, the medium of national literature, was embraced as the essential expression of national character shared by all countrymen.

A good illustration of this sentiment is quoted in *Imagined Communities* from the late-eighteenth-century German philosopher and literary critic Johann Gottfried von Herder. Anderson cites the original German: "Denn *jedes* Volk ist Volk; es hat *seine* National Bildung wie *seine* Sprache" (emphasis in original). In other words, for *every* people is a People; it has *its own* national character expressed through *its own* language.

Now that I look back with these words in mind, all of us IWP writers in Iowa who were writing in our own language, shutting ourselves up every night in our hotel rooms, had a great task weighing on our shoulders: representing the "Volk."

In the thirty years since the first publication of *Imagined Communities* in 1983, the world has changed considerably. For one thing, the fall of the Soviet Union rendered obsolete Anderson's critiques of Marxist internationalism while further demonstrating how right he was in emphasizing the importance of nationalism in modernity. *Imagined Communities* continues to be essential reading for scholars and students. And yet, as a nonnative speaker of English, I cannot help sensing a strange lacuna in the book—a lacuna that, as more time passes, begins to seem like a selective blindness: there is no discussion anywhere of English turning into a formidable universal language above and beyond all others. English is treated as merely one of many national languages; it may be the most powerful, but only *primus inter pares*, first among equals. Anderson completely ignores the reality that English is becoming a language that functions on a different level from all other languages. Why does he fail to mention this? Could it be because thirty years ago there was not yet widespread recognition of English dominance? Or is it perhaps because the new technology that further accelerates the circulation of English—the Internet—was not yet widely available? As it turns out, these factors apparently had very little to do with Anderson's omission.

Not that the growing dominance of the English language continued to escape his attention as the years went by. In 2005, more than a decade after the second, enlarged edition of *Imagined Communities* was published in 1991, Anderson delivered two lectures in English at Waseda University in Tokyo. The lectures were published in a book in Japanese the same year. With a gentle, self-deprecating tone that comes through in the translation, he reflects on issues that he should have included but did not, even in the second edition of his book. English as today's universal language is not among them. And yet his lecture concludes with a strongly worded message that English alone will not do—an indication that he is quite aware of the language's growing dominance. Here are his final comments to the Japanese audience:

Before I conclude, I just want to emphasize the following.

In those days of "early globalization," and I think it's still true, there was an enormous amount of energy going into people learning to speak other languages, read other languages, to pass on information, pass on use, pass on thinking, pass on feelings, from one language to another.

What is really impressive, if you look at, for example, the correspondence of Filipino nationalists at the end of the 19th century, is that they were writing in Spanish, writing in English to Japanese, writing in French to French comrades, writing in German to scholars who were supporting the cause. They were making every effort to reach out across the globe, and certainly this was true of Chinese, Japanese, and many other people. That is, they were not interested in simply acquiring some master language for business. They were interested in entering into the mental world—getting emotional affiliation with people of other linguistic groups. And this is still extraordinarily important. That is, people who think that there are only two languages in the world worth learning, Japanese and English, are fooling themselves. There are many important and beautiful languages. Real international understanding can only come from this kind of inter-linguistic communication. English can't do it. I promise you. Thank you very much.[2]

One can almost hear the Japanese audience breaking into spontaneous and enthusiastic applause upon Anderson's reassurance: "I promise you." Well, the audience may have been reassured by his words and applauded wildly at that moment, but how many among them, on coming home and resuming their everyday life, would follow his advice and start studying Spanish, French, German, or Indonesian, for that matter? How many would decide that their children need not learn English?

Anderson's awareness of the dominance of the English language becomes even more manifest in the third edition of *Imagined Communities*, published in 2006, which includes a new concluding chapter. The new chapter traces the unexpected trajectory of the book's reception in the world through translations, scheduled to number twenty-nine by the end of 2007. Anderson then goes on to call the English language "post-clerical Latin": "This spread has much less to do with [my book's] qualities than with its original publication in London, in the English language, which now serves as a kind of global-hegemonic, post-clerical Latin." How right he is in his claim that the spread of his book is directly related to its being written in English and published in London. I say this not to disparage the quality of a book that I greatly admire, but as a plain fact. (Only books written in Standard English and published in major cities in the West circulate worldwide at this stage.) How right he is, moreover, in finally equating English with Latin. And yet Anderson seemingly has no interest in making use of this equation to begin to understand the true nature of universal language. On the contrary, he uses the very spread of his book around the world in diverse languages through translation to assert the strength of national languages: "On the other hand, this proliferation of translations suggests that the force of vernacularization, which, in alliance with print capitalism, eventually destroyed the hegemony of Church Latin and was midwife to the birth of nationalism, remains strong half a millennium later."

The reader is left wondering whether the force of vernacularization—the force of national languages—will eventually destroy the hegemony of English as well.

Anderson's position never wavers from that of multilingualism, a typical position taken by European intellectuals; it is a position that still resonates strongly in Europe, where a rich civilization was created through tensions among many languages. The European Union actively advocates multilingualism as an ideal, and currently the union of twenty-eight member nations has twenty-four official languages; member nations strive to train their children to be polyglots. Yet it is an indisputable fact that English dominates as a de facto common language within the EU—as in most other international institutions. I myself am a supporter of multilingualism, but multilingualism without a true understanding of universal language will only make us blind and ultimately ineffectual in realizing that very ideal.

Why did Anderson fail to see that English, or any other universal language, plays a unique role? I understand the inherent unfairness in posing such a question to the author of *Imagined Communities*, which, after all, is a book about the formation of nation-states, nationalism, and national languages ("print languages"). One cannot ask a book that treats oranges why it fails to treat apples. Yet I'm unable to resist the temptation to ask the question because Anderson's blindness—which persists for nearly a quarter century, from the first edition of *Imagined Communities* to the revised—seems to typify the general blindness of those whose mother tongue is English. That Anderson was born in 1936 in Kunming, China, that he is multilingual, and that he is fluent in a relatively minor language like Indonesian does not change the fact that his mother tongue is English, that he was educated in English, and that he, quite naturally, writes in English. Those whose mother tongue is English often are unaware that when they are writing in their own language, they are in fact writing in a universal language. They are unaware of what they would be deprived of if they were writing in a nonuniversal language—

beyond the sheer number of readers. To apply the phrase I used in the talk I gave in Paris, they are not *condemned* to reflect on language in the way the rest of us are.

Moreover, the naïveté of Anderson—who is anything but naïve as a thinker—on this topic seems almost inevitable when one takes a closer look at who he is. He is not simply someone whose mother tongue is English. Born of an Irish father and an English mother, he has kept his Irish citizenship when he could have become British or even American. We all know that the Irish are a people with strong literary talent and tradition who have produced an amazing—given the small size of the population—number of writers, including Jonathan Swift, Oscar Wilde, George Bernard Shaw, William Butler Yeats, James Joyce, and Samuel Beckett, all of whom greatly enriched English literature. Yet not many of us are aware that Ireland's first official language today is not English but Irish Gaelic. Hence the Irish people, while taking full advantage of their mother tongue of English, proudly claim Gaelic as their own language—a language that only about 5 percent of Ireland's population actually use on a regular basis. In 2007, they even succeeded in registering Irish Gaelic as an official EU language. The Irish people's proud embrace of Gaelic has its roots in the country's centuries-long virtual colonization by Great Britain, resulting in not only the tyranny of English rule but also the forced use of the English language. Since 1949, when Ireland finally and completely won independence, the Gaelic revival has been an important part of state policy. Government documents are now routinely written in both languages, and compulsory education devotes a significant amount of time to teaching Gaelic, so the language is gaining ground. Nonetheless, Ireland's goal is to become a bilingual nation. It has no intention of abandoning English and turning Irish Gaelic into its citizens' mother tongue. Indeed, Ireland's policy of protecting its own language is among the most enviable in the world; it is akin to someone who lives in a sumptuous palace putting up a shack with a thatched roof on the grounds in order to enjoy a bit of rustic life.

On a theoretical level, we can trace Anderson's blindness to his (mis)understanding of what he calls "sacred languages." In his terminology, sacred languages are what we have been calling "external languages"—the languages of old, great civilizations that exerted influence on their neighbors. They are the universal languages of the past. In Anderson's words, long before the birth of nation-states, much of humanity belonged to "religiously imagined communities": Christianity, Islam, Buddhism, Confucianism (though Confucianism is not a religion). And it was sacred languages that made membership in such communities possible: Latin of the Christian Bible, Arabic of the Qur'an, Pali and Sanskrit of Buddhist scriptures, and Chinese of both Buddhist scriptures and texts like the *Analects* of Confucius. The Hellenistic Greek of the Greek philosophers, as well as other influential languages, may also be included among them.

What was the distinctive character of these sacred languages? For Anderson, a sacred language like Latin was not only "a language of bilinguals" but, more important, a language used by a minority: "Relatively few were born to speak [Latin] and even fewer, one imagines, dreamed in it." His understanding that a sacred language was used by bilinguals leads him directly and inescapably to the understanding that it was used by only a small number of people, a minority he refers to as the "elite" or "high intelligentsia."

In fact, "arcane" is Anderson's word of choice in describing Latin, the sacred language of Europe. He repeatedly uses the word to emphasize his understanding of a sacred language as one that is comprehensible to only a few. The word itself derives from the Latin *arcanus*, which means "closed" or "hidden"; *arcanus* in turn derives from *arca*, meaning "a chest." Thus if the sacred language is "arcane," texts written in it are, for the vast majority of people, hidden in "a chest"—or, to use the expression of the Internet age, something people cannot access. Because of this "arcane" nature, the sacred language inevitably came to be abused by the literate minority, who constituted "adepts, strategic strata in a cosmological hierarchy of which the apex was divine." To hold on to their power, these people kept the acts of reading and writing "arcane." Indeed, for a thousand years, translating the Latin Bible into other languages was forbidden. Anderson points out that even at the dawn of the Reformation, the Roman papacy, struggling to protect its Latin fortress, compiled the *Index Librorum Prohibitorum* (Index of prohibited books) to prevent the spread of vernacular publications. In *Imagined Communities*, sacred languages thus end up as a villainous tool through which past oppressors tried to entrap the masses in ignorance.

Here, I think, is where Anderson stops too short. Even if a sacred language such as Latin came to function as an instrument of oppression by the few, that is not where its essence lay. Anderson, blessed with having a universal language as his mother tongue, could afford *not* to see any further. In fact, a sacred language is open, quite the opposite of arcane, and this openness indeed is the defining trait of a *universal language*. For though comprehensible to only a limited number of bilinguals, sacred language made it possible for bilinguals speaking diverse languages and living in diverse places during the millennium of Latin's ascendancy to communicate with one another in writing. Sacred language was the sole common language, the sole means of understanding one another, in a world of countless vernaculars. Far from being "hidden in a chest," a sacred language was actually a language open to the world.

WHAT IS A UNIVERSAL LANGUAGE?

Let me depart from *Imagined Communities* here and return to my initial question: What is a universal language? I consider it to be the language that most clearly defines the difference between written language and spoken language. A spoken word disappears into thin air the moment it is uttered. In contrast, a written word remains and can be copied. Not only can it be copied, but it also can be spread. The Rosetta Stone, onto which three ancient writings are carved, weighs approximately 760 kilograms (1,675 pounds) and cannot be moved by the mightiest of men. If successive generations always had to travel across oceans and mountains to Egypt to read what was carved on it, the Rosetta Stone would have made hardly any impact on humanity. The advent of parchment and paper made the written word something that could be copied again and again and spread afar, reaching speakers of different languages in distant lands, some of whom would learn to read and then to write that "external language"—the universal language. It is thanks to these characteristics specific to written words that humans have had the means to accumulate a wealth of knowledge over the centuries.

Homo sapiens means "wise man." And we humans are wise not only because we are more intelligent than other animals, but also because we seek knowledge and can hand down the knowledge we attain to following generations, through words. The invention of written language did not make us any more intelligent, but it allowed us to accumulate knowledge exponentially—which brings us to this conclusion: if all people in the world read and wrote a single written language, regardless of their spoken language, our pool of knowledge would expand most efficiently. I'm not here referring to all sorts of knowledge, but to knowledge with more or less universal applicability. In fact, the more universally applicable knowledge is, the more efficient it would be to expand it in a single written language. Our pursuit of knowledge in mathematics, the purest of the sciences, is conducted in a single common written language, the language of mathematics. This written language is comprehensible everywhere in the world, no matter what language a person speaks. Mathematical language, which isn't anyone's mother tongue, is the purest form of universal language.

No one knows for certain the origin of written language. It may have been invented to record trade, or it may have its roots in magical rituals. Yet one thing is clear: the birth of a writing system is extremely rare. Most of the writing systems that exist today are derived from some script that became a template for future variations. For the overwhelming majority of humans, written language was not something that they invented on their own but rather something that came to them from their neighbors.

Every culture begins as an oral culture, and at some point, some of them have a transformative first encounter with a writing system. Yet the transformation from oral culture to written does not take place just because a writing system arrives one day from next door. People do not immediately say, "My, my, here we have this wonderful thing, now let's try using it to write our own language," and suddenly create a written culture. Possession of a spade and a hoe does not turn people into farmers overnight; becoming a farmer requires an understanding of the meaning of farming. The principle is even truer when it comes to something as complicated as writing. Besides, what initially arrives from a neighboring community is not writing as an abstract entity but concrete items such as scrolls with writing on them. And the transformation of a culture from oral to written requires that a small number of people learn to read those scrolls, written in the "external language." It requires the emergence of a cadre of bilinguals.

Those scrolls may come in different ways: from enemies in war, from partners in trade, or from refugees arriving in waves. They may be brought as gifts from an emperor, carried preciously above the messenger's head; or by monks as part of their missionary enterprise; or yet again as words of heresy hidden deep in the pockets of exiles. Yet scrolls, even if they are placed in a golden box, differ from other treasures in a critical way. They surely need to exist as physical objects, but without the act of reading, they are nothing more than sheets of parchment or paper decorated with dots and squiggles. The essence of the written word lies not in the written word itself but in the act of *reading*.

Something critical happens when the cadre of bilinguals learns to read imported scrolls: they gain entry into a *library*. I use the word "library" to refer not to a physical building but, more broadly, to the collectivity of accumulated writings. Despite the historical vicissitudes of wars, fires, floods, and even book burnings, humans possess an ever-increasing store of writings, the totality of which is what I call *the library*. The transformation of an oral culture into a written one means, first and foremost, the potential entry of bilinguals into a library.

The importance of access to a library cannot be overemphasized. For if, after being introduced to writing, *Homo sapiens* became "wise men" on a totally different level, this change certainly did not come about because people were able to memorize all they read. The memory of an elderly sage in an oral culture would surely trump that of any bilingual in a written culture. No, what transformed *Homo sapiens* into those with knowledge on a higher level was people's newfound ability to enter, through the act of reading, the library of accumulated human knowledge. And doing so usually meant reading a universal language, necessitating that the reader be bilingual.

Some may object to this statement, pointing out, for instance, that the ancient Romans read and wrote the same Latin that they spoke. Such an objection is founded on the familiar, false premise that written language is a mere representation of spoken language. It ignores the fact that before those Romans began to read and write in Latin, they read and wrote in Koine Greek—a language that combined different dialects with Attic Greek, the Athenian dialect—which was then the universal language of the area around the eastern Mediterranean Sea. If Cato the Elder (234–149 B.C.E.) had not begun writing Latin prose, the Romans might well have continued to write in Greek. Educated Romans naturally remained bilingual even in the golden age of Latin literature. Any description of the prose of Cicero (106–43 B.C.E.) or Seneca (ca. 4 B.C.E.–65 C.E.) as "literary" is also founded on the premise that written language is a direct representation of spoken language—a premise that until modern times no one entertained even with their own language.

Needless to say, there was not just one library but various libraries in different regions, according to the reigning universal language. And all these various libraries initially centered on the most important written words of each region, the sacred texts—records of words uttered or written by those believed to have attained the kind of knowledge impossible for ordinary human beings to attain: Buddha, Confucius, Socrates, Christ, and Mohammad among them. For those who sought higher knowledge, the sacred texts were the "texts to read."

Now a question emerges: What kind of people want to read a universal language, a language that is often quite dissimilar to the one they speak? To put it another way, what kind of people go to the considerable trouble of becoming bilingual to gain entry to the library of an "external language"? In fact, all human beings seek knowledge from the time of birth. In all corners of the world, children start school with eager eyes. Yet those for whom becoming bilingual is essential, the ones I call "seekers of knowledge," are a breed apart.

Seekers of knowledge do not necessarily have noble minds; they are not necessarily courageous or fair or kind. They are simply driven by a stronger desire than others to know more. Historically, becoming bilingual required a high level of education. Those who could afford such an education were men of the privileged class. Even in that limited strata, those for whom becoming bilingual was essential were extremely few. Nonetheless, those few have existed in every stage of history, in every region of the world. And the "texts to read" accumulate further as some of those bilinguals begin not only to *read* but also to *write*.

For bilinguals, in the beginning, sacred texts were not only the texts they *ought* to read—or, more probably, to chant or recite. They were also something to reverently copy by hand. Yet as the seekers of knowledge read and copied the sacred texts, they were bound to take up writing themselves. Some would inevitably be tempted to write down their interpretations as addenda. Others would then be tempted to add their own interpretations as further addenda. And as such notes grew in volume, they would be compiled as hermeneutic texts. Soon there would be many hermeneutic texts, and later seekers of knowledge would try to discern which among them were superior; they would eventually turn those into new sacred texts and objects of interpretation, and start creating new hermeneutic texts about them. Later seekers of knowledge would do the same ad infinitum, creating a longer and longer chain of texts to be read. The act of writing that led to this accumulation of sacred texts was derivative of the act of reading, but the process was inevitable.

Universal language was the perfect medium for such a process to unfold. Though universal language is often used in trade for the sake of convenience, or in diplomacy to follow the dictates of custom or international law, its essence comes to light when it is used in the pursuit of knowledge. The validity of the knowledge one has acquired becomes apparent only through attaining the assessment of as many fellow seekers of knowledge as possible, a purpose best served by universal language. Before modernity, much of learning was confined to exegesis of sacred texts—in a word, theology. And theology, as the pursuit of knowledge, was carried out in various universal languages in various regions of the world.

THE ROLE OF LATIN AND THE BIRTH
OF NATIONAL LANGUAGES IN EUROPE

When we examine western Europe and the role Latin played there as the language used in the pursuit of knowledge, a very different picture emerges from the one portrayed in *Imagined Communities*. The period that interests us starts just before the Renaissance, when Europeans were being reexposed—often through Holy Wars—via Arabic translation to Greek philosophy, which had lapsed into oblivion in Europe after the fall of the Roman Empire and was preserved only in Islamic territories. Arabic translations were then translated into Latin. Through the writings of great scholars like Thomas Aquinas (1225–1274), Latin became a highly speculative language, one that could easily step beyond the boundaries of theology. Then with the waning of the power of the Church came the Renaissance. No longer confined to the sphere of Christian theology, Latin began functioning as the language of learning in totally different dimensions, playing a crucial role in Europe's bid to become the world's dominant power.

One such dimension was the natural sciences. As is evident from the phrase "Copernican Revolution," Nicolaus Copernicus made one of the truly great discoveries in the history of the human race: he found the contradictions in Scholastic geocentrism and advocated heliocentrism. He was born in 1473 in what is now Poland. Later, in 1609, sixty-six years after Copernicus's death, Galileo Galilei proved the veracity of heliocentrism using the telescope. Galileo was born in what is now Italy, more than 1,000 kilometers (600 miles) from Copernicus's Polish home.[3] Then came Johannes Kepler, Galileo's contemporary who defended his theory. Kepler was born in what is now Germany. Finally, in 1687, Isaac Newton provided mathematical proofs for the findings of both Galileo and Kepler. Newton was born across the channel, in England. The most important route traveled by modern science—from Copernicus to Newton—was a long journey that crisscrossed Europe, starting in Poland, moving through Italy and Germany, and reaching England nearly two centuries later. And this journey was made possible solely thanks to Latin: all these men published their major works in that universal language.

The same was true of thinkers in what is now called the humanities. Erasmus (1466–1536), the author of *In Praise of Folly* and one of the greatest Humanists, played a major role in Europe's shift from a religious world to a secular one. He was born in the Netherlands but lived, studied, and taught all over Europe—Paris, Leuven, Cambridge, Venice, Turin, Freiburg, and Basel.

He exchanged an astonishing volume of correspondence in Latin with politicians and philosophers throughout Europe, becoming friends with Thomas More (1478–1535) while disagreeing with Martin Luther (1483–1546). Not only Erasmus—and More and Luther—but many others wrote their major works in Latin: Thomas Hobbes (1588–1679), who was born in England; Baruch Spinoza (1632–1677), a descendant of Sephardic Portuguese Jews who was born in the Netherlands; Gottfried Leibniz (1646–1716), who was born in what is now Germany.

These men were all great seekers of knowledge whose names are familiar throughout the world. Yet rarely do we note that they all wrote in Latin. Scholarly writings generally have value independent of the language in which they are written. Moreover, because these men wrote in Latin, we often have only a vague idea of what country they were from or what their mother tongue was.

All this leads us to a simple conclusion: pursuing knowledge in disparate languages is uneconomical; a universal language is more efficient by far. Nonetheless, as we are all too aware, human society comprises many disparate languages; to quote Benedict Anderson again, we live with "the fatality of human linguistic diversity." And uneconomical though it may be to pursue knowledge in disparate languages, we humans started doing just that at a certain point in our history—that is, since the birth of national languages and nation-states. Before we ask how it was possible for people to pursue knowledge in disparate languages, we must first have a better understanding of what a *national language* is. And before we do so, we must first have a better understanding of what a *local language* is. The roles of these three kinds of languages can be grasped only in relation to one another.

Both theoretically and historically, a local language is a concept that forms a binary with, and is juxtaposed against, a *universal language*. People may live in a society where a cadre of bilinguals read, write, and sometimes even speak a universal language, but even those bilinguals use their mother tongue at home and on the streets like everyone else. That is their local language. Whether the local language has a writing system is irrelevant. What is relevant is that when two languages, the universal and the local, circulate simultaneously in a given society, there inevitably emerges a division of labor between them. The universal, which society places above the local, is assigned the heavy responsibility of aspiring to the highest excellence, not only aesthetically but also intellectually and ethically. In contrast, even if it has a writing system, the lower-ranking local language is primarily intended for only uneducated men and women. Plays, which must be understood by the listening audience, are usually written in local language, as are poems, which are often sung, but serious prose written in local language is extremely rare. A local language may at times be given the task of aspiring to aesthetic or even ethical excellence, but seldom if ever to intellectual excellence.

What, then, is a national language? I would say that it is an elevated form of a local language. And what has elevated local languages, thereby providing the key to the birth of a national language? The perhaps surprising answer I would propose is the act of *translation*. The role of translation has been undervalued or, worse, ignored in our understanding of the history of human languages, especially in modernity, when emphasis is placed on the author as the original subject of meaning. Yet it was through the very act of translation that what had once merely been a local language came to function on the same level as a universal language; that is, it came to be burdened with the task of aspiring to the highest excellence not only aesthetically and ethically but also intellectually. Hence the birth of a national language. While the birth of nation-states was a historical prerequisite for the emergence of national languages, this rather formalistic understanding of how national languages are born helps to better explain their nature.

Because we are deeply immersed in what might be called the "ideology of national language"—because we have so deeply internalized the premise that writing is a representation of speech—we have come to assume that writing means writing *in one's own language*. And because of that assumption, we have come to forget the critical role that the act of translation originally played in the development of national language. Historically, translation was necessarily an asymmetrical endeavor (as it still is, in its essence). It assumed the existence of a clear hierarchy between two languages. It was not about translating English into French or German, say, but about translating Latin (the universal language) into various vernacular languages of Europe. For the essence of translation lies first and foremost in the transference of accumulated knowledge otherwise inaccessible—and by extension, ways of thinking otherwise impossible—from a universal language into a lower one, the local language. Through repeated transference, a local language gradually and eventually developed a written language capable of functioning on the same level as the universal language. And so, along with the nation-state, national languages were born.

A caveat. As a novelist, I myself find it unsettling to define the act of translation in such terms. Translating literature is an artistic task that cannot possibly be reduced to the mere transference of knowledge or ways of thinking;

indeed, translation can even result in a text of a higher level of excellence than the original. Yet if we take a step back and reflect on the history of human writing, it is difficult to deny that such was its principal function.

With this in mind, let us return to western Europe, where nation-states first emerged, and see how, at the same time, national languages emerged from Latin. Our picture looks quite different from the one Anderson depicts in *Imagined Communities*. Because Anderson tries to understand the process in terms of market mechanisms, he basically sees the relationship between Latin and the "vernacular" in terms of numbers: after the small Latin market came the large vernacular market for the "monoglot masses." This description, though certainly not untrue, ignores the critical role played by the act of translation. It makes it seem as if some members of the monoglot masses just went on to write books in their own language to fill the ever-expanding market, when it was translations from Latin that first appeared—a fact he glosses over. Soon books written in vernaculars began to appear, and they themselves were then translated into Latin so that they could be read by bilinguals with a different mother tongue. Through this vibrant two-way process, local languages transformed into national languages in the course of a few hundred years.

Just as the role of translators has been undervalued or ignored in the history of written language, so has the role of bilinguals. If the act of translation was key to the transformation of local languages into national languages, the work of these bilinguals was no less so. Bilinguals were not necessarily translators in a literal sense. Often they were writers who wrote in both universal and local languages. And if national language owed its birth to universal language, it is perhaps no wonder that so many of those who are considered the father of a national language were themselves true bilinguals (or trilinguals even, especially if we include classical Greek).

One seminal bilingual was Dante Alighieri (ca. 1265–1321), who wrote the *Divine Comedy* in the early fourteenth century. As is well known, the Tuscan dialect he used in the work later became the normative written language for Italian, making him the father of the Italian language. He did not write only in Italian, however. He had recourse to Latin when writing prose. In fact, his very defense of the vernacular language, *De Vulgari Eloquentia* (On eloquence in the vernacular), was written in Latin. Francesco Petrarch (1304–1374) and Giovanni Boccaccio (1313–1375), born half a century later, also are regarded as fathers of the Italian language, and they too wrote Latin prose. Geoffrey Chaucer (1343–1325), their contemporary across the channel, is often considered the father of English literature, yet even he was versed in Latin and translated the Latin philosopher Boethius. Consider also Luther: his early-sixteenth-century German translation of the Bible—the New Testament was from the original Greek—became the model for today's German language, while at the same time, having been trained as a monk, he naturally read and wrote Latin on a regular basis, leaving his will in Latin as a matter of course. The Frenchman Joachim du Bellay (ca. 1522–1560), born nearly half a century after Luther, fought for the French language; a member of a group of French Renaissance poets, the Pléiade, he wrote a famous manifesto entitled "The Defense and Illustration of the French Language" that advocated the elevation of the French language to the excellence of classical Greek and Latin. Well versed in Latin, du Bellay not only borrowed expressions from classical literature in his French poems but also wrote poems in Latin. Michel de Montaigne (1533–1592), who came a little later, grew up in a home where everyone, including well-chosen servants, spoke Latin just so that he would prattle in that august language from his infancy. And it was the Latin-prattling Montaigne who wrote the essays that laid the foundation for French prose. This bilingualism persisted into the next century. René Descartes's famous phrase, "I think, therefore I am," is equally well known in Latin (*Cogito ergo sum*) and in French (*Je pense, donc je suis*), precisely because Descartes (1596–1650) wrote in both languages. These and many more bilingual men were all translators in a broad sense, and it is from their writings that national languages grew into what they are today.

Let us examine this development using the concept of the library. Before the Renaissance, there was only the Latin, or universal, library. And then, with the Renaissance, came the rediscovered Greek library, another universal library. At the same time, the number of books in local languages grew, starting with books in translation, until there eventually came to be many libraries, each in a different European language. A clear hierarchical relationship initially existed between the two universal libraries and the many local libraries, not only because the former enjoyed a higher social status but also because they had accumulated vaster knowledge and hence more texts demanding to be read. Both in quantity and in quality, their collections were far superior. Local languages transformed into national languages as, through translations from the universal to local languages, the accumulated knowledge in the universal libraries was steadily transferred to local libraries. The latter gradually caught up in quantity and quality and eventually surpassed the former— at least insofar as the accumulation of universally applicable knowledge is concerned. Seekers of knowledge who previously haunted the universal libraries now turned increasingly to the libraries of national languages. Indeed, by the late twentieth century, five centuries on, classical education in Latin and Greek had largely disappeared from the school curriculum. The once glorious, flourishing libraries of those universal languages were reduced to cobwebby book deposits frequented only by specialists.

THE EUROPEAN EXCEPTION

Now we are ready to ask the questions: How was it possible to pursue knowledge in disparate languages? Wouldn't the attempt be self-defeating? What does it mean to pursue scholarship in various national languages?

These questions necessarily lead us to take a look at the Enlightenment, the first intellectual movement to sweep through Europe in different national languages. The movement began to blossom in the late seventeenth century. John Locke (1632–1704) first wrote in Latin but switched to English in midlife. David Hume (1711–1776) and Adam Smith (1723–1790) wrote in English from the beginning. Across the English Channel, Montesquieu (1689–1755), Voltaire (1694–1778), and Jean-Jacques Rousseau (1712–1778) all wrote in French. Across the Rhine, Immanuel Kant (1724–1804) wrote entirely in German except for the academic papers he needed to obtain his university position. The Age of Enlightenment was when many of the fundamental concepts that define the society we live in first came into being: "human rights," "natural law," "separation of powers." And the thinkers who gave birth to these concepts all wrote in their own language. This being the case, the answer to the question of whether it is really possible to pursue knowledge in various national languages would appear to be a resounding yes. Evidently, it is indeed possible to write exclusively in one's own language and still enrich all humanity in a critical way.

But our "yes" has an important qualification: the pursuit of knowledge was conducted in diverse languages during the Enlightenment, *but they were all European languages.* The countries of Europe do not simply share a history, culture, and religion. They also share a language in the sense that nearly all European languages derive from the same origin and then were heavily influenced by Greek and Latin as they matured, allowing them to share abstract concepts. As a result, European intellectuals were able to read more than one foreign language in addition to Latin and Greek as a matter of course. It was only because of this unique linguistic condition, confined geographically to

Europe, that they were able to pursue knowledge efficiently even when national languages replaced Latin as a tool for learning.

If we look at the Age of Enlightenment solely from the perspective of the marketplace, as Anderson might do, we see that while sales of books in Latin diminished, sales of books in national languages steadily increased. This might suggest that as European intellectuals turned away from Latin, they began to read only what was written in their own languages. If, however, we look at the same historical period through the concept of the library rather than the market, we see a very different picture. For even as European intellectuals entered the age of national languages and read less Latin, they did not frequent *only* the library of their own language. They slipped into and out of other libraries as well. The Enlightenment thinkers I mentioned earlier could read one another's work in the original and had personal interactions across the channel or the Rhine.

Moreover, three principal languages that became the de facto universal languages of Europe compensated for the lack of a universal language: French, English, and a newcomer, German. (Though widely used under the reign of the Hapsburgs, German became a national language only in the eighteenth century, when hundreds of small nations were consolidated into the Kingdom of Prussia.) Other key languages—Danish, for instance—also came to bear double duty as national and universal languages in their own regions, but eventually, to reduce the time and effort spent on language study, European intellectuals settled on a tripolar system with French, English, and German as the main means of exchange. Once translated into one of these three languages, books originally written in less major languages became available to a wide readership. (Naturally, when Europe expanded its colonies, intellectuals worldwide set out to learn the three languages—with heroic, heartbreaking effort.)

What comes to the fore as Europe enters the age of national languages is, first of all, a fundamental asymmetry between the act of reading and the act of writing. Reading several foreign languages was one thing, but writing in all of them would require either extraordinary virtuosity or staggering effort. Hence, in contrast to the millennium when Latin ruled, the Enlightenment was a time when intellectuals read and wrote in different languages. They became polyglot readers and monoglot writers who wrote in their mother tongue.

This development would have far-reaching consequences. Humans have made great discoveries in the course of history. I would not go so far as to suggest that the emergence of national languages is of equal importance to the discovery of fire or the invention of money or writing. Nevertheless, the spread of the notion that our writing system *ought* to represent the language we speak was a critical step in the evolution of human civilization.

First, this notion led to far higher rates of literacy among populations— a prerequisite for the emergence of democracy, itself a prerequisite for the formation of modern nation-states. (Even nations that are in fact totalitarian promote literacy in order to uphold the banner of "democracy.") The acts of reading and writing were now within the reach of every citizen who spoke the language. Literacy rates climbed even higher as spoken language came to resemble written language more closely.

Moreover, together with the emergence of nation-states and nationalism, the democratic nature of national language soon gave rise to the "ideology of national language." This ideology—best articulated, as we have seen, in Anderson's quotation of von Herder, "Denn *jedes* Volk ist Volk; es hat *seine* National Bildung wie *seine* Sprache" (For *every* people is a People; it has *its own* national character expressed through *its own* language)—led to the idea that it was an obligation of the educated to write in their own language. By so doing, they would not only enable their compatriots to read what they wrote but simultaneously enrich their national culture. Intellectuals whose mother tongue had not yet fully matured as a written language felt this obligation even more acutely.

What happened in Russia is a case in point. Though the Russian language had a large number of speakers, it was late in establishing itself as a national language, the country being relatively less developed. As is widely known, French was the court language of the Romanov dynasty (1613–1917); it was also the language aristocrats used in everyday conversation. (Tolstoy's *War and Peace* opens with a splash of aristocratic French.) Slightly down the scale, high society routinely used French and German and, more rarely, English. Educated Russians hence wrote in one of the three principal languages as a matter of course. First came Alexander Pushkin, the father of modern Russian literature. Born in 1799, he wrote in French when he was young. Yet as the "ideology of national language" spread to Russia, in the 1820s he began writing poetry in Russian, and by the 1830s he was writing prose fiction in Russian as well. Shortly thereafter, with breathtaking speed, came Nikolai Gogol (1809–1852), Ivan Turgenev (1818–1883), Fyodor Dostoevsky (1821–1881), Leo Tolstoy (1828–1910), and Anton Chekhov (1860–1904). Around the same time, thinkers such as Vissarion Belinski (1811–1848), Alexander Herzen

(1812–1870), and Mikhail Bakunin (1814–1876) also appeared. Thus Russian, which had only a few decades earlier been a mere local language, was transformed into a national language used for the pursuit of learning.

By the mid-nineteenth century, many Europeans came to believe, almost religiously, that they *ought* to write in their own language even when writing learned books—and even when to do so might pose obvious disadvantages. Søren Kierkegaard (1813–1855), the Danish philosopher who paved the way for existentialism in the twentieth century, offers such an example. An avid reader of German literature, Kierkegaard could doubtless have written in German, a language closely resembling his mother tongue. Yet he made a point of writing his critique of Hegelian philosophy in Danish, a major language to be sure but not in the same league as German. Because he wrote in his mother tongue, his works such as *Fear and Trembling* (*Frygt og Bæven*) bear a highly personal flavor. Yet confining himself to Danish also meant that he had no inkling during his lifetime that his writings would be grouped with the classics, the "texts to read." Only through posthumous German translations did the rest of Europe come to know that such an eccentric figure had lived and written in a Nordic kingdom, questioning God in a most devout way.

One point still needs to be emphasized: the relative ease of translation among European languages. Through translations into one of the three principal languages, the works of Kierkegaard did ultimately enter the chain of "texts to read," first in Europe and then in the world. Danish is, after all, a European language. Over the centuries, European languages have become mutually translatable with minimal loss of meaning. Compared with a language like Japanese, Danish is infinitely closer to German or English—or even French.

All this might sound too crude to those who are aware of what seems like insurmountable differences among European languages. I myself cannot imagine reading *Pride and Prejudice* in French with the same pleasure that I find when reading it in English, or reading *Le Rouge et le noir* in English with the same pleasure that I find when reading it in French. In his famous essay "The Task of the Translator" (1923), the German literary critic and philosopher Walter Benjamin discusses how German *Brot* and French *pain*, both of which may be glossed as "bread," do not mean the same thing. Nonetheless, the difference between *Brot* and *pain*, however critical, cannot compare with the difference between, say, English "rice" and Japanese *ine*—the latter having been lyricized and mythicized for well over a millennium in Japanese culture. Numerous poems with the word *ine*, including love poems, are compiled in

Ten Thousand Leaves (*Man'yōshū*), the first Japanese poetry collection, dating back to the eighth century, and Japanese emperors still go through the ceremony of planting rice and harvesting it, a tradition said to have begun in the sixth century. A language such as Japanese is thus a world apart from those of Europe, where all the societies are culturally and linguistically kindred. To put it in terms of colors, if the Japanese language were red, then all European languages would be some shade of blue.

Thanks to this kinship among European languages and cultures, by the turn of the century and on into the twentieth century, learned books written in various languages entered the chain of "texts to read": *The Revolt of the Masses*, written in Spanish in 1930 by José Ortega y Gasset; *Prison Notebooks*, written in Italian from 1929 to 1935 by Antonio Gramsci; *Homo Ludens*, written in Dutch in 1938 by Johan Huizinga, to name just a few. That all these Europeans wrote in their own languages does not contradict our basic assumption about how knowledge spreads. Looking at the long history of humanity, we see that what took place in Europe at this time was an anomaly, which helps us better understand the fundamental nature of a universal language.

Balance, once it begins to keel, swiftly collapses. Once England, and then the United States, began to possess superior national power, the world's balance of power began to visibly shift. Universal languages have a self-sustaining capacity, so the tripolar system of English, French, and German continued for some time; but as English began to gain the upper hand, the essential connection between the pursuit of knowledge and universal language became undeniably clear.

Naturally the rise of English was not unaccompanied by pain for most Europeans, those whose mother tongue was different. The fate that befell the Polish economist Michal Kalecki (1899–1970) offers a poignant example. The field of economics once flourished in various European regions, but the publication of Adam Smith's seminal work *The Wealth of Nations* (1776), written in English, combined with the economic power of England and later the United States, changed everything; by the early twentieth century, economics had become a field of social science predominantly conducted in English. Knowing exactly what sort of age one lives in, however, is not always easy. In 1933, already one-third of the way into the twentieth century, Kalecki published an article, and not just any article: this historic treatise first put forth the principle of effective demand later expounded in *The General Theory of Employment, Interest and Money* by British economist John Maynard Keynes. Yet sadly, but predictably, because Kalecki wrote in Polish, his discovery went unnoticed. Two years later, he translated the article himself, but sadly again, the language he chose was not English but French. A year later, in 1936, *General Theory* was published, dramatically altering the course of economics. Seeing this, Kalecki claimed his intellectual property in another article. Unbelievably, he wrote *that* article in Polish, too. Poor Kalecki became known as a scholar who did not write in English.

Why didn't a brilliant scholar like Kalecki know enough to write in English? His homeland of Poland formed the Polish-Lithuanian Commonwealth in the sixteenth century and was once one of the world's great powers. Yet it began to disintegrate in the seventeenth century and finally disappeared from the map in 1795. For over a hundred years thereafter, the country had a tragic history of being divided by Russia, Austria, and Prussia, until it was able to reunite as a nation after World War I in 1918. In 1933, when Kalecki wrote his original article, nationalist fervor must have made the Polish people feel compelled to write in *their own language*. Kalecki must have espoused that fervor—to his own detriment.

Even if the "world" as the West saw it had been limited to the West, the prowess of England and subsequently of the United States would have ultimately toppled the tripolar system of the principal national languages. Yet another factor was at work to reinforce this development at the start of the twentieth century: the era when the "world" was limited to the West came to an end. Through colonization and improved means of communication, people from the regions of non-Western languages began to enter that world. This marked the end of an era when "a Christian" meant "a person"; the pursuit of knowledge could no longer comfortably remain Eurocentric. Though most of what is taught in universities all over the world is today based on Western disciplines, the universal applicability of these disciplines is under closer scrutiny from the non-West. Entering this new historical phase was bound to throw a light on the inevitable inefficiency of pursuing knowledge in one's own language. If non-Western intellectuals wanted their writing to enter the larger chain of "texts to read," the rational choice would be to write in English, the language that circulates most widely, however difficult that might be. The more non-Western intellectuals wrote in English, the more texts would circulate in English, thereby inducing more Western intellectuals to write in English as well. The entry of non-Western intellectuals into the "world" has had the effect of revealing with blinding clarity the essential nature of universal language: *it is in the single universal language—the "external language"—that knowledge is best pursued.*

THE NOVEL: A CELEBRATION OF NATIONAL LANGUAGE

The days are now long gone when Europeans unwittingly enjoyed the privilege of pursuing knowledge in their own language—the *golden age of national language*. That golden age coincided historically (and quite logically) with another: the *golden age of the novel as a literary genre*. At the basis of the latter was a new status bestowed on literature as something distinct from and even transcending the usual pursuit of knowledge.

Prior to the late eighteenth century in Europe, no distinction existed between literature and the pursuit of knowledge—or between literature and scholarship, or literature and science (the term "science" is here used in its archaic meaning of "knowledge in general.") The word "literature" then referred, as is well known, to any kind of writing. When learned priests wrote Latin treatises on theology, what they wrote was "literature" on theology, which was also the only "science" of the time. Divinity schools were the only places of learning. But as Europe gradually secularized, those divinity schools were transformed into today's universities. The pursuit of knowledge, now conducted in one's own language, increasingly became segmented into different academic disciplines, and the language in which to do so also became increasingly specialized. It was around this time that literature and the pursuit of knowledge—academia—became manifestly distinct from each other. The word "literature" was by this time used almost exclusively to refer to poems, plays, and novels, as it is today.

Something wonderful then happened to literature. Now that the language used in academic disciplines was far removed from the language of everyday life, people no longer turned to academic writings for words of wisdom—the sort that could address perennial human questions such as "What does it mean to be a human being?" and "How should one live?" Where previously they had sought these answers in religious texts, now they were turning to literature for enlightenment—particularly the modern novel, written in prose. Literature became something that transcended science.

Moreover, a national language was precisely the right medium for the novel as the new literary genre befitting a new age. For while a national language could function in the same way as a universal language, bearing intellectual and ethical responsibility, it could also, unlike a universal language, thoroughly exploit every merit of the local language, the mother tongue. Metaphorically, it had not only a father but also a mother. The novel developed while taking full advantage of both parents. On the one hand, as a genre with strong ties to universal language, it could discuss grand and high-flown ideas such as the existence of God, war and peace, the fate of humanity. Yet at the same time, as a genre with equally strong ties to the mother tongue, it could also depict in exquisite detail the life of a common individual—the new center of attention in the new era. It could depict the chain of the most mundane events that constitute everyday human life. It could tap deep into everyone's most vivid childhood memories—or even earlier, to moments when "memories" would be too concrete a word for fragmentary recollections of touch, smell, and soft murmurs. The novel could take us deep into the human psyche, capturing, examining, and lending dignity to our every fleeting thought or dream. It was inevitable that the national language should come to be thought of as a language that expressed one's innermost soul, a language of self-expression. The novel developed as a genre that celebrates the superiority of individual interiority over society; and the superiority of individual interiority was in fact the product of writing in the national language.

Indeed, the mother tongue is uniquely privileged. All languages are essentially external to us. As we begin acquiring our mother tongue while we are still inside the womb, we are unaware of the process and the arbitrariness of the connection between sign and meaning, unaware that the word "mother" has no inherent link to the woman who gave us birth. Benedict Anderson said of Latin that "few were born to speak it and even fewer . . . dreamed in it." But actually, nobody is born to speak (or dream in) any language.

As with any art form, the novel as a literary genre took a long time—a good two centuries—to realize its full potential. At the dawn of the genre, in 1722, Daniel Defoe wrote *Moll Flanders*, the life story of a woman by the same name. Here is Defoe's summation of her life in his preface: "Twelve Years a Whore, five times a Wife (whereof once to her own Brother), Twelve Years a Thief, Eight Years a Transported Felon." Yet as one reads through the story of her "sinful" life, one finds that she feels precious little for all that she has gone through. She displays an astonishing, or rather alarming, absence of interiority. Almost exactly two hundred years later, during a period that might possibly have seen the culmination of the novel, in his semiautobiographical novel *In Search of Lost Time* (1913–1927), Marcel Proust has his protagonist, a fully grown man, reminisce page after page about the time when, as a boy, he would lie in bed waiting for his dear *maman* to come up to his room and give him a goodnight kiss—something that often and tragically wouldn't happen when there were guests in the house. The author/protagonist is revealing a supremely personal moment, in language at once analytical and poetic, bringing readers to share in his search of a lost time when such a small ritual meant everything. Readers are then reminded of their own memories of childhood moments—moments that may have been insignificant in and of themselves but that, in retrospect, bestow the grace of a heightened sense of being alive.

As the novel continued to evolve, works often became more difficult to translate, even into closely related languages. As the libraries of national languages expanded, writers began to quote from, allude to, and parody the "texts to read" within their own language, and so the canon of "texts to read" written in the same national language began to form a unique chain of its own. Novelists began to take on such texts and play them off against one another; they also exploited the peculiarities of their own language through dialects and wordplay. The untranslatability that had been more or less characteristic of poetry all along began to extend to novels as well, culminating in a revolutionary work like *Finnegans Wake* (1939) by James Joyce. Since language produces meaning within an enclosed system, there is always a built-in untranslatability, which national languages began to deliberately pursue. The process added to the creation of an untranslatable "reality" that can be expressed only in a particular language. It also added to the discovery of untranslatable "truths."

Moreover, what became clearer through the separation of literature from the usual pursuit of knowledge is that there are two kinds of truths in this world. This distinction, I am aware, is a crude one that often fails to apply in reality, but it helps us to grasp what is at stake in the relationship between language and knowledge. On the one hand, there is the kind of truth that can be attained by reading textbooks; on the other hand, there is the kind of truth that requires reading the text itself.

Let me explain what I mean by this.

In the pursuit of knowledge, we are dealing with truths that are attainable through the reading of textbooks because they lie in the realm of science (using the word again in its archaic sense), where the accumulation of previously discovered truths enables the discovery of the next. Copernicus's heliocentrism of the early sixteenth century led to an accumulation of later truths that eventually made it possible for Einstein to formulate his theory of relativity in the early twentieth century. In this process, the later scientist need not return to any original texts, for the discovered truths they contain do not depend on the language in which they were written. (In the case of natural sciences, discovered truths ultimately do not depend even on human existence: Earth revolves around the sun and the speed of light remains constant whether we exist or not.) Because they do not depend on language, the truths accumulated in science are ultimately attainable through textbooks, where language is used clearly and economically to elucidate how one truth led to the next. The best example of this kind of pursuit of knowledge would be a textbook filled with mathematical formulas.

In contrast, the truths found in *texts* are not replaceable by textbooks. They depend on the very language that expresses them, and to understand them each person can only go back to and read the text itself. Moreover, this kind of truth does not reside only in literature in the modern definition. Aristotle's geocentrism was later proved not to be "true," yet Aristotle continues to be read because his writings include passages that are not transferable to a textbook. The truths found in the text are in the final analysis inseparable from the author's style of writing. Those truths depend on the author's choice, out of an infinite range of possibilities, of a particular word order; a particular noun, adjective, or verb; a particular turn of phrase.

Written language comes in many shapes, ranging from some that are completely transferable into textbooks to others that compel one to return to the original text. That range continues to signify the aporia between the possibility and impossibility of translation—which brings us to the final but crucial characteristic of the novel. Though a *text*, the modern novel is in this critical aspect more attuned for translation among different cultures than earlier forms of prose, for even though—or rather, precisely because—it is written in a national language, it belongs to a genre that is highly *global*.

As the language of a nation-state, a national language is a product of modernity. Unlike the Greeks or Chinese of a bygone era, citizens of modern nation-states do not look on those living outside their country as barbarians who babble incomprehensibly and observe strange customs. Citizens of modern nation-states are aware that they are surrounded by many other nation-states where other people, different from yet similar to them, are living and using languages of their own.

Writing a modern novel in a national language hence means writing with the awareness that you inhabit the same world as others around the globe. You see the same world map and the same world history as your contemporaries elsewhere, though how each of you interprets and relates the same historical events may vary greatly. You follow the same major scientific discoveries; you have read the same kinds of world classics; and you share with your contemporaries similar concepts of what humanity ought to be. If you were to write a novel today, for example, you would need to know not only that Earth goes around the sun but also that Earth is getting warmer. No matter how oppressive the society you live in, you would need to know that most people around the world embrace the universality of concepts such as "basic human rights" and "individual freedom." You can choose to criticize your own country or your own people from the standpoint of that global consciousness.

The act of reading a modern novel also presumes a similar global consciousness. An American I once met believed that *The Tale of Genji* was written in the era before Christ, generously giving the classic an extra thousand or so years of history. If he were reading a modern Japanese novel, he would no doubt have roughly guessed the time in which it was set. Readers of modern novels necessarily share a historical awareness.

To repeat, the novel flourished during an age when literature was believed to transcend science as a source of wisdom. During that time, seekers of knowledge not only wrote texts in their own languages but also read them— sometimes with amused laughter, sometimes with raised eyebrows, but always with devotion, passion, and respect. It was a time of the celebration of national languages of every stripe, golden years for those languages as well as for the writers and readers of national literature.

4. THE BIRTH OF JAPANESE
AS A NATIONAL LANGUAGE

"'FOREIGNERS ARE BEAUTIFUL, AREN'T THEY?' HE SAID."
This line occurs toward the beginning of *Sanshirō* (1909),[1] a novel by Natsume Sōseki, modern Japan's greatest novelist. Sanshirō, a young man from the sleepy southern island of Kyushu, is riding a train to the capital where, to his great pride, he will become a student at Tokyo Imperial University. A bearded and rather unimpressively attired passenger is sitting diagonally across from him, and they start a conversation. As the train comes to a stop, they see a Western couple on the platform, whereupon the man makes the observation about foreigners:

> Sanshirō could think of nothing to say in reply. He nodded and smiled.
>
> "We Japanese are poor things next to them," the bearded man continued. "We can beat the Russians, become a first-class power, but it doesn't make any difference. We still look like this, we still don't amount to anything. Even the buildings we build, the parks we make, they're just what you'd expect from people with faces like ours. . . . This is your first trip to Tokyo, isn't it? Then you've never seen Mount Fuji. We go by it a little farther on. Take a look. It's the best thing in Japan, the only thing we can brag about. The trouble is, it's just part of nature, something that's always been sitting there. We certainly didn't create it." He was grinning again.
>
> Sanshirō had never expected to meet anyone like this after the Russo-Japanese War. The man scarcely seemed Japanese. He said defensively, "But from now on, Japan is sure to develop."
>
> "Japan's headed for a fall," the man said coolly.

In 1908, three years had passed since Japan unexpectedly won the Russo-Japanese War, a war rife with symbolic meaning: for the first time, a non-Western nation had defeated a Western power. The precariousness of Japan's victory notwithstanding, the achievement was indisputable. The West had to accept that the ability to build a modern nation-state was not its exclusive prerogative; any ethnic group or race could do so. All the unequal treaties that Japan had been forced to sign with the Western powers since 1858 were nullified. The colonial ambitions toward Japan that the powers still harbored after the Meiji Restoration finally subsided, and Japan emerged as their rival in the Far East.

The bearded passenger, Sanshirō later learns with surprise, teaches at an elite preparatory college affiliated with Tokyo Imperial University, the educational pinnacle of modern Japan. His line, "Japan's headed for a fall," could as well be an authorial comment, as Sōseki himself once taught at that very college. Sōseki must have been well aware that Japan, despite its historic victory, was still immature as a modern nation. Indeed, after the publication of *Sanshirō*, Japan transformed from Asia's star of hope into another aggressor and then "fell" in less than half a century. One fact nonetheless remains: already in the first decade of the twentieth century, a novel like *Sanshirō* could be serialized in a major national newspaper and widely read—a novel exemplifying *national literature* in which a character critiques his own country and people from a global perspective, and that furthermore is a truly fine piece of literature, always fresh no matter how many times one rereads it.

The modern novel emerged in the West in the mid-eighteenth century. Jane Austen's *Pride and Prejudice* was published more than half a century later, in 1812, and by the mid-nineteenth century classic representatives of the genre had blossomed in profusion. Stendhal's *The Red and the Black* came out in 1830. Honoré de Balzac's *The Human Comedy* started appearing around the same time and continued to his death in 1850. The Brontë sisters' *Jane Eyre* and *Wuthering Heights* were written in 1847; William Thackeray's *Vanity Fair*, in 1848; Charles Dickens's *David Copperfield*, in 1850. Gustave Flaubert's *Madame Bovary* came out in 1856. George Eliot's *Middlemarch* was published a little later, in 1872. In Russia, Tolstoy's *War and Peace* was published in 1869; Dostoyevsky's *The Brothers Karamazov*, in 1880.

The Meiji Restoration of 1868 thus occurred just when the novel was at its peak in the West. Japan's own first modern novel, Futabatei Shimei's *Floating Clouds* (*Ukigumo*), dates from 1889, barely twenty years after the Restoration. Although unfinished, it is one of the enduring monuments of Japanese modern literature. Moreover, it was followed in quick succession by a slew of brilliant works: Higuchi Ichiyō's "Child's Play" (Takekurabe) and "Troubled Waters" (Nigorie), both in 1895;[2] Natsume Sōseki's *Botchan* (1907), *Sanshirō* (1909), and *Light and Dark* (*Meian*, 1916); Izumi Kyōka's *Song and Lantern* (*Uta andon*, 1910); Mori Ōgai's *The Abe Clan* (*Abe ichizoku*, 1913) and *Shibue Chūsai* (1916); Arishima Takeo's *A Certain Woman* (*Aru onna*, 1919); Naka Kansuke's *The Silver Spoon* (*Gin no saji*, 1921); Nagai Kafū's *A Strange Tale from East of the River* (*Bokutō kidan*, 1937); and Tanizaki Jun'ichirō's *A Portrait of Shunkin* (*Shunkinshō*, 1933) and *The Makioka Sisters* (1948). Together these remarkable, distinctive works filled the Japanese mind—and language—with inestimable riches.

That there should have been such a profusion of modern novels in Japan following the Meiji Restoration may at first glance seem only to be expected. Japan encountered the overpowering West; its people began writing modern novels emulating the overpowering West. What could be more natural, you may say. Yet things didn't work out that way in most other non-Western countries.

The question then poses itself as to how this was possible in Japan. The answer is beguilingly simple: after the Restoration, the Japanese language quickly established itself as a national language both in name and in practice—precisely the kind of language that makes possible the writing of novels and that the novel celebrates. The real question is how *this* came about. The answers could be as multifarious as the phenomenon was complex; I will begin by pointing to two conditions that have hardly been explored by scholars of Japanese literature but that seem to me to have been key in enabling the Japanese language to transform into a national language when the Great Powers of the West started eyeing the Far East. First, Japan already had a written language that was quite mature and held in high regard. Second, it enjoyed what Benedict Anderson calls "print capitalism" during the preceding Edo period, which enabled the written language to circulate widely.

JAPANESE AS LOCAL LANGUAGE

One crucial historical fact (again, virtually unexplored by literary scholars) must be made clear before moving on to a discussion of how Japanese transformed itself into a national language. For over twelve hundred years, the country remained part of the Sinosphere—the cultural sphere that used the Chinese writing system as a universal language. And, it must be noted, during that whole time the Japanese language was a *local language*. Despite the high level of maturity the Japanese language attained prior to the Restoration, it had nonetheless been a mere *local language* ever since people began writing in their own language. This point cannot be stressed enough.

That premodern Japan belonged to the Sinosphere may seem obvious—to everyone but the Japanese. Of course, children are taught in school that Chinese characters were brought to Japan by settlers from the neighboring Korean Peninsula and that the Japanese writing system grew out of those characters. Yet this historical fact is rarely truly appreciated. The Japanese are left thinking that if Chinese characters had not reached Japan, their resourceful ancestors would have invented their own writing system anyway, which seems hardly likely. Until the dawn of the Western age of exploration in the fifteenth century, much of the globe had no writing. It was only because of Japan's proximity to the Korean Peninsula that a writing system was introduced by the fifth century (or even earlier) and, by pure geographic luck, an oral culture was able to transform itself into a written culture. Other, more isolated Pacific islands followed a different course.

Let us go back to ancient Japan, as it became part of the Sinosphere. What reached the archipelago were bundles of precious scrolls with writing on them, scrolls that the Japanese learned to read from Korean settlers. To be sure, there were only a handful of Japanese bilinguals in the beginning, but their presence enabled Japan to join the Sinosphere alongside Korea and Vietnam. The Japanese thus gained entry into the library of Chinese texts, the library of an "external language"—the universal language of the region. And by gaining entry into this library, they also entered a society in which there was a linguistic double structure of "universal/local language," just as in the pre-Gutenberg societies of Europe—or indeed as in many premodern societies.

Like the Bible in Latin or the Qur'an in Arabic, which spread far and wide as sacred texts, what first reached Japan were Buddhist scriptures in Chinese, which, significantly enough, were themselves translations from Sanskrit. Initially, facing these beautiful calligraphic scrolls, Japanese people probably never dared imagine that they were anything other than texts to be deciphered with veneration—"texts to be read." The idea that the same characters used in them might be used to represent their own language—the language they chattered in the streets—would have seemed preposterous, all the more so because Chinese characters are ideograms and not phonograms; that is, they represent meaning and not sound. (More precisely, most Chinese characters are phono-semantic compounds, having a dual function, but I will use the term "ideogram" to simplify my argument.) Nonetheless, the general rule that a local language acquires a written language by translation of a universal language applies to Japanese as well. For it was through translation that the Japanese people started to use these characters to express their own language.

The process was a tortuous one that took centuries, not only because Chinese characters are ideograms, but because the Chinese and Japanese languages are totally unrelated. In fact, it seems almost surreal that two languages could be so far apart, given the geographic proximity of the two countries. Word order is opposite. Chinese follows the same subject-verb-object order as English, but this is reversed in Japanese; "I love you" becomes "I you love." Moreover, Chinese, especially Classical Chinese, is what is called an "isolating language," while Japanese is an "agglutinative language": in Chinese, each semantic unit is directly followed by another; in Japanese each semantic unit must be followed by a particle or suffix—a little bit of "glue"—that connects it to the next. So, in the example, in Japanese two particles must be inserted to mark the subject and object: "I (wa) you (wo) love." What is most astonishing and instructive to us who are the products of modernity is that, even faced with such a seemingly insurmountable linguistic barrier, Japanese people never thought of just going ahead and inventing their own letters or their own writing system to better represent the language they spoke—that it was as a by-product of the act of translation that they eventually acquired their own method of writing.

The Japanese who first learned to read Chinese from Korean settlers in the fifth or sixth century must have read it in the original word order, though this is impossible to establish. What we do know is that sometime during the Nara period (710–784), people were already reading Chinese as if it were Japanese, inverting the word order and adding small inversion marks to the text to indicate where and how the inversions should take place—a method still used today to read the Chinese Classics. This practice, called "Chinese writing, Japanese reading" (kanbun kundoku), was a primordial form of translation. (The Korean language has word order similar to that of Japanese, and Koreans may have already been doing something similar.) The next step was to add, in small lettering alongside the inversion marks, the particles and suffixes necessary to read the text as Japanese. Of course, at this point, the Japanese still had no distinctive letters of their own to represent the sounds of their language. They compensated by taking the meanings away from certain Chinese ideograms and using them simply for their sound value, as phonograms.

Using this method of writing, they gradually succeeded in amassing a vast collection of indigenous poetry that is still read and loved today: *Ten Thousand Leaves*. Visually, the poems appear to be Chinese, but phonetically and semantically they are Japanese. Chinese characters used this way are called *man'yōgana* (letters of *Ten Thousand Leaves*).

The following Heian period, when Lady Murasaki Shikibu wrote the masterful *Tale of Genji*, represents the true birth of vernacular writing. Since the seventh century, the Japanese government had been sending missions regularly to China to learn from the higher culture, but the practice came to a halt at the beginning of the Heian period for various reasons, the collapse of the mighty Tang dynasty being one. (The final mission was canceled in 894.) Chinese influence remained strong, but without any direct and centralized contact with China, indigenous culture began to flourish. More self-confident, Japanese people turned their method of translation into something more elaborate.

Besides the little inversion marks, particles, and suffixes, people began to write full translations alongside the text, still using Chinese characters as phonograms. These additions—interlinear texts of a sort—first appeared in minuscule writing, as if they knew they didn't belong. Gradually, the characters used for this purpose were simplified, requiring fewer brush strokes and slowly evolving into distinctive letters in their own right. In the process, they split into two systems of phonograms or "syllabaries," as they are known, each letter representing a syllable of Japanese. Thus were born today's katakana and hiragana, the indigenous products of translation.

To give you an idea of what these syllabaries look like, here is the word "katakana"—which originally meant "partial characters"—written in katakana: カタカナ. It is composed of straight lines, exuding masculinity. And here is the word "hiragana"—which originally meant "easy characters"—written in hiragana: ひらがな. As you see, unlike katakana, hiragana is composed of curved lines, exuding femininity. The word "kana" is used when referring to both syllabaries. Chinese characters, meanwhile, were called *magana* or "real characters," written 眞仮名. The difference between kana and *magana* is visually obvious.

Why two sets of kana? True, the language could perhaps have done just as well with one. It ended up with two because of the split created by the very binary between the universal language and the local language. Katakana continued to be used when translating the universal language and long remained subordinate to it. As Japanese people became more comfortable writing in their own language, interlinear texts using the two syllabaries grew larger and bolder, but because of katakana's close relation to the universal, its process of enlargement took much longer than its counterpart.

Hiragana became distanced from Chinese early on as it was quickly relegated to the role of writing the local language. First it became the medium of choice for writing indigenous *waka* poetry—poetry in syllabic groupings of 5-7-5-7-7 that was a precursor to haiku. Then it was used in headnotes, prose descriptions of the situations in which those short poems were composed, like this one from the first imperial anthology of *waka* poetry, compiled in 905: "On hearing the call of a wild goose and thinking of a friend who had gone to Koshi."[3] These descriptions grew longer—often longer than the poems they introduced—and eventually evolved into short fictional narratives centering on poems. And who should be the greatest users of hiragana but well-educated ladies, for whom it was socially unacceptable to write in Chinese? (The exclusion of women from learning the universal language is the norm in any society where there is a binary between the universal and the local.) Ladies began writing prolifically in various prose genres—fiction, essays, literary diaries—using hiragana. The association with women's writing became so close that hiragana was often referred to as "women's hand" (*onnade*) in those early years. Such writing in hiragana also became known as *yamato kotoba*, literally "Japanese words," to distinguish it from writing in Chinese. *The Tale of Genji*, a work of astounding psychological subtlety, is the greatest exemplar of *yamato kotoba*.

However, it would be naïve to assume that *yamato kotoba* was something like a direct expression of the Japanese soul (*yamatodamashii*). *Waka*, literally "Japanese song," must have had its origin in oral incantation, but as a literary form it was created by readers familiar with Chinese poetry who gradually shaped their own poetry with Chinese models in mind. A nationalistic myth, both modernist and romantic, long had it that many of the poems in Japan's oldest collection, *Ten Thousand Leaves*, were composed by men and women from all walks of life, including soldiers garrisoned on the frontier, using *man'yōgana*, the precursor of *yamato kotoba*. Many scholars now believe, however, that these poems were most probably composed by aristocrats well versed in Chinese poetry. The first imperial *waka* anthology, which came out about a century and half later, includes not just allusions to but innovative adaptations of Chinese poems. If it is generally the rule that writing in a local language is created derivatively through the act of translation, Japanese follows this rule to a tee.

Some might ask how a language that produced the glorious *Tale of Genji* could be called a *local language*. Some might even consider the term an affront to Japanese literature. It is true that Heian court ladies turned their forced linguistic exclusion into an advantage by writing in *their own language*, in the process giving birth to *Genji* and other works of literature that continue to delight the world a thousand years later. They triumphed brilliantly by standing the patriarchal taboo on its head. And yet that triumph was recognized only in the modern era, when the "ideology of national language" was imported to Japan and scholars reconstructed the history of Japanese literature, playing down the importance of Chinese texts. During the Heian period, the hierarchy between the universal language and the local language was an absolute given that not even the brilliance of *The Tale of Genji* could alter. Male bilinguals not only read and wrote official documents and pursued knowledge in Chinese but also composed poetry in that language—a practice that persisted into the twentieth century. The ability to compose Chinese verse was the hallmark of a highly cultured man.

Katakana and hiragana long maintained their respective roles, but the distinction grew increasingly lax, and toward the end of the Heian period a new kind of writing emerged that would become the foundation for modern Japanese prose. Using kana as the base, the new writing mixed in Chinese characters with varying degrees of frequency. Some texts were densely Sinicized, while others were heavily vernacular with only scattered bits of Chinese. This flexibility allowed the Japanese people to read and write almost anything, and so they began reading and writing more and more in Japanese. Indeed, after Heian, through the Kamakura (1185–1333), Muromachi (1337–1573), and Edo (1603–1868) periods, prose writing in pure Chinese gradually became confined, aside from official documents, to the domain of Buddhist and Confucian texts.

Even so, during this time the hierarchy between writings in Chinese and Japanese never disappeared, not even during the Edo period, when the local culture thrived as Japan closed its doors to the outside world and the government allowed only limited access by Koreans, Chinese, and Dutch. Any attempt by native Japanese to leave the country was punishable by death. This period of hothouse seclusion led to striking literary achievements epitomized by the Genroku era (1688–1704), which is now remembered for three towering literary figures: a poet, a novelist, and a playwright, all of whom wrote not in Chinese but in Japanese. Matsuo Bashō (1644–1694) wrote a seventeen-

syllable haiku about the splashing sound made by a frog that led later generations to spend a million syllables speculating on its meaning: "The ancient
pond / a frog jumps in / the sound of the water." Ihara Saikaku (1642–1693)
wrote stories on a whirlwind of topics, everything from business cunning to
amorous adventures, both hetero- and homosexual in variety; and Chika-
matsu Monzaemon (1653–1725) is best known for his lyrical love-suicide
plays. Yet this perception of Genroku literary achievement is the product of
a particular narrative, a narrative of national literary history created after the
importation of the "ideology of national language." For despite this remarkable flowering of literary genius in the Japanese language, at the time Chinese
writings by Confucian scholars such as Itō Jinsai (1627–1705) and Ogyū Sorai
(1666–1728) possessed by far the greater prestige. *Kaitai shinsho* (New book
of anatomy), published more than half a century after the Genroku era in
1774, is usually described as the first Japanese translation of a Western book—
Ontleedkundige Tafelen (Anatomical tables, 1734), itself a translation into
Dutch from the original German work, *Anatomische Tabellen* (1722) by Johan
Adam Kulmus (1689–1745). Yet the translators actually rendered the text not
into Japanese but into Chinese, as was proper, since it was a book on human
anatomy—a book of knowledge. Japanese-language texts remained caught in
the "universal language/local language" hierarchy.

The first official document ever issued in Japanese—though heavily Sinicized—was the Five Charter Oath (1868) proclaimed by the Meiji Emperor.
The event marked the beginning of a new era, one in which Japan saw itself
as a modern nation-state no longer confined to the Sinosphere. A society
cannot throw away tradition overnight, however. Children of the educated
class continued to begin their studies by learning Classical Chinese. It took
a couple of decades before the emphasis shifted to learning to read and write
in their own language. It took nearly a century for people well versed in the
Chinese language to fade away.

The following anecdote shows something of the lingering prestige and influence of the Chinese idiom at this transitional period.

Uchimura Kanzō (1861–1930), the well-known founder of the Nonchurch
(Mukyōkai) movement in Meiji Japan, embraced monotheist Christianity at
a young age and enthusiastically engaged in evangelical work to spread the
faith. However, to his great dismay, his own father expressed no interest. As
Uchimura Kanzō wrote in his English-language autobiography, *How I Became a Christian*, "The arch-heretic was my father, who with his learning and

strong convictions of his own, was the hardest to approach with my faith. For three years I had been sending him books and pamphlets. . . . But nothing could move him."[4]

One day, Uchimura came up with a fine idea. At the time, the five-volume *Commentary on the Gospel of St. Mark* by Dr. Ernst Faber, a German missionary in China, was gaining acclaim. The commentary was written in literary Chinese without inversion marks, and Uchimura wrote, "I thought the difficulty of reading it, if not any thing else, might whet my father's intellectual appetite to peruse it." He thus spent his savings on the five volumes and presented them to his father. The elder Uchimura initially threw the books away, but his son persistently put them back on his desk, and in time he began to read them. Uchimura exulted, "Finally . . . I prevailed; he went through the first volume! He stopped to scoff at Christianity!" As the father read through the second, third, and fourth volumes, he began to change. "*He would not touch his wine any more*" (emphasis in original).[5]

Uchimura appears to have been greatly moved by the power of Christianity to make his father stop drinking. I, however, am more struck by the picture of an old-time samurai sitting erect, turning page after page of Western religious philosophy written in Chinese. I can't help thinking what a huge transformation in the literate life of the Japanese people was to come in the ensuing hundred-odd years.

THE ESCAPE FROM THE CHINESE IMPERIAL EXAMINATION SYSTEM

That the Japanese language remained for over a millennium merely a local language is perhaps typical. That its writing was created through the act of translating a universal language is indeed typical. What is surprising is the level of sophistication written Japanese attained. Usually, the nature of a local language is such that even if a learned man wrote in it, he would be writing not for his peers but rather for his wife or children. Yet Japanese developed into a language shared by male intellectuals.

To see how this turn of events came about, let us start by picturing the Japan archipelago lying in the sea by the Chinese mainland. If its proximity allowed it to become part of the Sinosphere and acquire a written culture, its distance benefited the development of indigenous writing. The Dover Strait, separating England and France, is only 34 kilometers (21 miles) wide. A fine swimmer can swim across it. In contrast, the shortest distance between Japan and the Korean Peninsula is five or six times greater, and between Japan and the Chinese mainland, twenty-five times greater. The current, moreover, is deadly. The missions the Japanese government sent regularly to China between the sixth and ninth centuries were life-risking endeavors often ending in shipwreck. Japan's distance from China gave it political and cultural freedom and made possible the flowering of its own writing.

Nowhere is the effect of Japan's distance from the continent more manifest than in the country's escape from the powerful pull of the imperial examination system invented by the Chinese. As is well known, the imperial examination was a means of soliciting the most brilliant minds from all over China to become high-ranking bureaucrats. The earliest example of democratic examinations in the world, the system demonstrates how advanced Chinese civilization once was. Begun in the sixth century, the examination system lasted for an amazing fourteen centuries and exerted control over Chinese politics and culture. The content of the examination changed little with the times, however, and once China entered modernity and fell prey to the imperialistic ambitions of the West, the system proved practically useless and was abolished in 1904. The imperial examination system became symbolic of the stagnation of Chinese civilization.

What concerns us is the relationship between such a system and the learned male population. Because the imperial examination was initially implemented to counter the power of the military, it was thoroughly literary in nature. The content was based on Confucian scholarship and required memorization of the Classics; the system produced not just officials but scholar-officials. On top of this, every conceivable mechanism encouraging fierce competition was built into the system: the examination was supposedly open to any male regardless of origin (though in reality only those of the learned class had the means to prepare for such an examination); once someone passed the exam, his entire clan would share in his power, glory, and wealth; and the top three successful candidates were assured particularly prestigious positions.

It is easy to see what would come out of such a system. Those in the learned class would select the brightest boy in the clan, and the whole clan would invest in his education. All across China, boys who particularly excelled in reading and writing would spend their entire childhood, youth, and even part of their adulthood studying single-mindedly for the examination. The average successful examinee was around thirty-five. That such a system lasted not only one or two hundred years but well over a millennium means that every bright male in the country was continually drawn deep into the changeless Chinese civilization—deep into the vast library of Classical Chinese writing.

Moreover, Classical Chinese was an "external language" even for Chinese themselves. For erudite Romans in the first century B.C.E., Seneca's prose, literary as it was, must have been comprehensible by ear. But Classical Chinese texts, so concise and dense, had little tie to the spoken language of ordinary people at any point in history. This is true quite aside from the fact that the Chinese spoken languages—Cantonese, Shanghainese, Fukienese, Mandarin—vary so greatly that they could be considered different languages altogether. Thus, while preparing for the imperial examination enabled educated Chinese to communicate in a highly sophisticated manner, it hindered them from creating vernacular writing. Vernacular fiction began appearing only in the sixteenth century and was never held in high regard.

What would happen when countries surrounding China adopted such a system is then apparent. Their bilinguals—seekers of knowledge—would be absorbed into the Chinese library in a similar way. Without the participation of those bilinguals, writings in those countries' local languages would inevitably fail to mature.

Both Korea and Vietnam, which are located on geographic extensions of the Chinese mainland, adopted the system, as did later the Ryūkyū Kingdom (present-day Okinawa), which is much closer to China than to Japan. The Japanese made an attempt to adopt the system once during the Heian period. Yet as the country stopped sending regular missions to China and centralized, direct ties with China gradually ended, there was no longer any incentive for Japanese to follow the Chinese model. This turn of events was a blessing for the Japanese language. Japanese bilinguals, because they were not forced to compete fiercely in order to excel in written Chinese, soon began to read and write in the local language as well. These men had no qualms about using hiragana, the "women's hand." On the contrary, they apparently used it whenever occasion permitted.

When the first imperial anthology of *waka* poetry was compiled, the poet Ki no Tsurayuki (872–945) wrote two prefaces, one in Chinese and the other in Japanese, mostly hiragana. He then went on to write the groundbreaking *Tosa Diary* (*Tosa nikki*, 935), which describes, in Japanese, a long journey to the capital. (Some scholars speculate that he kept a diary in Chinese during his travels and rewrote it after his return.) Moreover, to experiment once again in writing hiragana-based Japanese, he went so far as to adopt the persona of a woman. Writing a diary was something men did more often than women, but male diarists of his time invariably wrote in either Chinese or Sinicized Japanese—never in hiragana.

The opening passage of *Tosa Diary* is quite perverse: "Men write diaries, but I, a woman, will try my hand at it too." This one sentence, written mostly in hiragana, crystallizes the wonders of Japan's literary history. Men were not "supposed" to be writing in hiragana, except when composing *waka*, but they were reading it (and probably writing it, too). Even before *Tosa Diary*, there already existed a collection of anonymous short stories called *The Tales of Ise* (*Ise monogatari*, mid- to late ninth century). Because each story is a narrative revolving around *waka*, it is written in hiragana, but the collection, sometimes bawdy, was certainly not meant just for women. Nothing in *Tosa Diary* suggests that it was meant just for women either. And there is more. Even women authors, who always wrote in hiragana, were far from having a solely female readership in mind. The two lady rivals, Murasaki Shikibu, author of *The Tale of Genji*, and Sei Shōnagon, author of *The Pillow Book* (*Makura no sōshi*, 1002), were both well versed in Chinese Classics—though they made their erudition known only by slipping in allusions here and there—and they reveled in compliments from male readers. By writing brilliantly in their own language, they must have given men the desire to do the same. The binary of the universal and the local did not coincide with the binary of the educated and the uneducated in Japan.

As men began to write more freely in hiragana, hiragana writings began to incorporate Chinese characters more freely, increasingly blurring the difference between hiragana-based and katakana-based texts. Some Buddhist writers began using hiragana for their less scholarly works. Then, during the Edo period, with the emergence of protonationalism and a school of thought called *kokugaku* (national philology), there even appeared some scholarly texts that were hiragana-based. When *kokugaku* apologists criticized the dominance of "foreign" Chinese learning, they were in fact criticizing the dominance of universal language while using what circulated as merely a local language. In their writings, the local language had become a language that bore intellectual, ethical, and aesthetic burdens, just like the universal language; it had come to function almost like a national language.

Chinese people, proud of their advanced civilization, were highly Sinocentric. They little knew or cared that people across the sea had created their own strange system of writing by using and adapting Chinese characters for their own purposes. They little knew or cared that that system of writing was being used to compose poems about cherry blossoms, autumn leaves, and the transience of life. What they did know was how poor Japanese mastery of the Chinese language was compared with that of Koreans and Vietnamese. Japanese people's Chinese was generally looked down on inside the Sinosphere, doubtless with good reason.

Yet from a modern historical perspective, the Japanese achievement in developing a local language and literature early on was quite remarkable. The Western experience was different. In medieval Europe, learned bilinguals remained absorbed in the library of the universal language of Latin for a thousand years under the authority of the Church, very much like those absorbed in the Chinese library under the imperial examination system. European vernacular writing started appearing only in the twelfth century and began to flourish from the Renaissance period on: Dante's *Divine Comedy* in the early fourteenth century and Chaucer's *Canterbury Tales* later that century, followed by François Villon's poems in the mid-fifteenth century and Shakespeare's plays in the late sixteenth and early seventeenth centuries. Moreover, all these works—with the exception of some parts of *The Canterbury Tales*— were poetry or plays, not prose. Not until the seventeenth century did the first pinnacle of prose fiction in the West, Miguel de Cervantes's *Don Quixote*, appear—some six centuries after *The Tale of Genji*.

THE DEVELOPMENT OF CAPITALISM IN THE EDO PERIOD

Let us next briefly touch on the second condition that I believe enabled the Japanese language to quickly establish itself as a national language: the development of what Anderson calls "print capitalism" during the Edo period. However refined, Heian court literature alone, known only to a handful of aristocrats and their entourage, would not have led to the speedy establishment of a national language. What was needed was a thriving bourgeois literature, widely enjoyed by middle-class townsmen.

Under the more than 250 years of peace during the Edo period, Japan, though basically cut off from the rest of the world, enjoyed steady economic growth. Living in a mountainous island country with many rivers and inlets proved handy during the premodern age, when water was the principal means of conducting trade. Added to this topographical advantage was the system called *sankin kōtai* (alternate residence) by which the Edo shogunate required feudal lords, or daimyo, to reside in Edo and their domain in alternate years: this system created a strong need for cash for the daimyo, to make the costly annual journey and to reside in the capital with style. The Edo period saw increasingly heavy trade between the capital and the provinces as well as among the provinces themselves, and the country soon became the wealthiest in the non-West—though the Japanese had no idea of this. The development of capitalism is always accompanied by a rise in literacy; one must be able to count and read and write to join the marketplace. Thus by the end of the Edo period, the country was filled with schools, including public schools for members of the samurai class and temple schools for children of ordinary people. Japan boasted a literacy rate among the highest in the world. Print technology (mainly woodprint) had existed well before the Edo period, but now the active economy and high literacy rate combined to create Anderson's "print capitalism." To be sure, a unified written language did not yet exist. A bewildering variety of forms of written language coexisted. Moreover, none of them was anything close to the spoken language, and there was no such thing as a unified spoken language either. (The diversity of dialects at the time is unimaginable for Japanese today.) And yet Anderson's point that the development of print capitalism leads to the increased circulation of writings in the local language holds true in Japan, too. The growing market for books came to absorb more and more monolinguals. Indeed, by the time of the Meiji Restoration, Japanese writing was circulating on a scale scarcely seen in any premodern society.

It was against this background that, soon after the Restoration, two books appeared back to back and became Japan's first best sellers. *Self-Help* (1859) by Samuel Smiles, a Scottish reformer, was translated and published in 1871, only three years after the Restoration. It became an instant must-read and sold a million copies altogether. Then in the following year came *An Encouragement of Learning* (*Gakumon no susume*) by Fukuzawa Yukichi (1835–1901),[6] an influential educator who played a key role in the Westernization of Japan. (We will be touching on his fascinating autobiography later.) Written in a relatively simple style that Fukuzawa claimed "even a monkey could read," it was initially published in pamphlet form and sold so well—700,000 copies in all, plus pirated editions that led him to complain about the lack of enforcement of copyright law—that he decided to issue it in book form in 1880. The book went on to sell an astonishing three million copies.

TO REITERATE, JAPAN WAS FORTUNATE FIRST IN ITS GEOGRAPHIC position—close enough to China and Korea to receive an early introduction to writing, far enough away for its own indigenous writing to grow and flourish—and second in its economic development, which allowed that writing to spread among the population at large. These were the two conditions, virtually ignored by literary scholars, that made it possible for Japanese to establish itself as a bona fide national language shortly after the Meiji Restoration. However, while these two were prerequisites, they alone were insufficient. For the Japanese language to transform itself into a national language so swiftly, there was yet another, absolutely indispensable, historical condition, one that has been not just ignored but virtually suppressed: Japan had to escape from the Western powers.

THE ESCAPE FROM THE WESTERN POWERS

From the nineteenth century to the twentieth, Western powers spread through Asia and Africa, colonizing nearly all the non-West. Japan, however, managed to escape this fate (though it soon enough turned neighboring nations into colonies of its own). At the time of the Meiji Restoration, non-Western countries besides Japan that were not colonies or protectorates, and also not divided or leased, could be counted on the fingers of one hand. In Eurasia there were Korea, Thailand, Afghanistan, and part of the Ottoman Empire; in Africa—not counting Liberia, founded by freed American slaves with the aid of the U.S. government—there was only Ethiopia. Japan was thus one of the lucky few.

This came about thanks to a group of clear-sighted men who saw that Japan's only hope lay in dismantling its isolationist policy, engaging in international trade, and transforming as quickly as possible into a modern nation-state. Once again, geographic location helped. Situated at the extreme eastern end of the world (from the Western perspective), Japan was far removed from the West, including the United States, whose maritime route to Asia at the time went through the Indian Ocean.

The neighboring Qing dynasty (1644–1912) had resisted the West, only to end up fighting the disastrous Opium Wars, a fate that Japan observed with horror. In the years leading up to the wars, the British treated China in a way they would never have dared to treat any Western country, illegally exporting large amounts of opium they grew in India in an effort to acquire Chinese silver. The First Opium War started in 1839 when the Qing emperor, understandably alarmed at opium's rapid spread, banned the underground traffic. Britain countered with military force. Lacking a modern army, China was quickly defeated and subjected to humiliating conditions: concession of Hong Kong, large indemnities, unequal treaties. Then in 1856, Britain found a pretext to wage the Second Opium War. This time, the other European powers got in the act, and China was half colonized. Alert patriots in Japan saw all too clearly what the consequences would be if their country did not voluntarily open its doors to the West and modernize, but fast.

Along with geography, history worked in Japan's favor, or else the patriots' goal might have remained elusive. Japan was indeed a tempting country to colonize: it was conveniently located for maritime trade; it produced copper, silver, tea, silk, and porcelain that the Western importers coveted; and it had a large population and a developed capitalism that made it a good market for Western exporters. The Western powers could have tried to grab some of its land for lease or tried to divvy it up; even worse, one of them could have colonized it outright. The vastness of China limited their ambitions to obtaining concession territories along the coast and sharing prerogatives, but Japan was an easy target.

None of this happened, however. Commodore Matthew Perry's squadron entered the port of Uraga in 1853, surprising the Japanese with four huge navy vessels known forever after to the Japanese as "black ships" and demanding that the country open its doors. Perry came back the following year to Yokohama, this time with nine vessels, making the same demand. Faced with cannonballs for the first time in their history, the Japanese had no choice but to agree to supply American ships with fuel, water, and food; then the Europeans joined in, all demanding more concessions. Things looked dark for Japan, but history soon intervened as a series of wars broke out among the Western powers. The Crimean War, fought by Britain, France, and Turkey against Russia, took place between 1853 and 1856. The American Civil War began in 1861 and lasted until 1865. The Franco-Prussian War was fought in 1870 and 1871. These wars debilitated the Western powers for a while; in the meantime Japan began to turn itself into a modern nation-state, complete with a modern military.

What if Japan had become a Western colony? Today, nearly a century and a half after the Meiji Restoration, the possibility may appear all too distant and far-fetched. Yet for Japanese living at the time, the possibility was all too real. In his celebrated and wonderfully funny autobiography, published in 1899, Fukuzawa Yukichi, the aforementioned best-selling writer and one of the key figures in Japan's modernization, reflects back on the tumultuous years immediately following the Restoration from the perspective of an "old man" (he was sixty-four) and reveals how precarious Japan's independence actually was.

Through many an intrigue and skirmish between the Edo shogunate and the rebels who favored restoring imperial rule, the shogunate finally fell. Yet the situation was a complicated one. Often the very ones who worked to bring about the Restoration were incensed by the shogunate's weak-kneed dealings with the West and yearned to rid the country of Western influence once and for all. Those in favor of opening up the country were initially in the minority. Fukuzawa writes that he was unsure if the new Meiji government was willing to embrace change, which he knew was the only way that the country could maintain its independence: "In truth I could see that the officials of the government knew nothing better than the dregs of the Confucian philosophy with which to guide their actions. They were simply lording it over the people with arrogance and pretense."[7] He further writes that Western diplomats who initially favored Japan's self-governance turned skeptical on arriving in the country and seeing its people firsthand, citing the example of Lincoln's secretary of state, William H. Seward, who asserted that "after seeing the condition of things, he could not say much more in commendation of Japan. He was sorry, he said, but Japan with her inflexible nature could hardly be expected to keep her independence." Fukuzawa knew that unless the country opened in the true sense of the word, there was a good chance that it would be colonized even after the Restoration.

Fukuzawa reflects:

> I have never told anyone of the dire, helpless state of my mind at that time. But I am going to confess it now. Watching the unfortunate condition of the country, I feared in reality that we might not be able to hold our own against foreign aggressiveness. . . . If in the future there should come signs of foreign aggression and we were to be subjected to insult from foreigners, I would probably find some way to extricate myself. But when I thought of my children who had longer lives to live, again I was afraid. They must never be made slaves of foreigners; I would save them with my own life first. At one time I thought even of having my sons enter the Christian priesthood.[8]

This last was an outlandish idea, since Fukuzawa himself was a nonbeliever—a thorough rationalist. Whether having his sons "enter the Christian priesthood" would have spared them humiliation at the hands of foreigners remains an open question. For Fukuzawa's fears did not materialize: fortunately the new government, once in power, quickly grasped the course it had to take and began implementing drastic reforms. Fukuzawa concludes, "As I look back today—over thirty years later—it all seems a dream. How advanced and secure the country is now! I can do nothing but bless with a full heart this glorious enlightenment of Japan today."[9]

Let us here consider the "what ifs" that Fukuzawa feared.

To start with, what if the American Civil War had not broken out so soon after Perry's squadron entered the port of Uraga? Japan could have become a United States colony. Preposterous, one might scoff, but not if one exercises an imagination informed by modern history. At the time, every non-Western country was up for grabs. Itself a former British colony, the United States was divided over whether to join European countries in colonization—but that did not stop it from taking the Philippines from Spain.

What if Japan had become a United States colony like the Philippines—what would have happened to the Japanese language? Like all other colonized countries, Japan would surely have become a bilingual society where the languages of the colonizer and the colonized were used side by side. Unlike that previous bilingual era when Japan belonged to the Sinosphere and people's access to the Chinese language was more or less limited to written texts, a colonial power would have exercised far more direct and extensive influence. Americans would have arrived in person and trod all over Japan, whether in muddy military boots or shiny civilian shoes, controlling everything from foreign relations to internal governance, including the three branches of government as well as businesses and, of course, higher education. Naturally, English would have become the official language. Under such conditions, as is always the case with colonized countries, the best upward path for locals would have been to excel in English and serve as liaisons, relaying orders from above and claims from below. If the system for selecting such liaisons were fair, it would have attracted the brightest minds from all over the country, encouraging more and more people to become bilinguals and receive higher education in English. The best Japanese minds would have been absorbed into the library of English.

To be sure, the Japanese written language, already mature and widely used, would have remained in circulation. People would have continued to use the traditional epistolary form to write letters. They would have continued to compose *waka* and haiku in their leisure. They would even have continued to compose Chinese poetry for a while. New works of the popular traditional fiction called *gesaku* (playful writing) would have continued to be written, depicting the new society. The general population would most probably have been taught reading and writing in Japanese.

Yet colonization would have had drastic effects on how the Japanese language developed. First of all, it is likely that the use of Japanese in critical thinking would gradually have been abandoned. What is known as the *gen-bun itchi* (unification of spoken and written word) movement, a movement to create a standard form of prose closer to the spoken language, probably would not have come about, or, if it did, would not have attained much sophistication. Moreover, it is even possible that the ruling Americans would have enforced the use of the Roman alphabet. (As I will discuss later, after Japan's surrender in World War II, the United States Occupation forces proposed this very change.) All this on top of the fact that Japanese society itself would have become polarized, as is typical of colonized societies, with a deep gap between a small number of bilinguals and a large number of monolinguals.

In short, if Japan had become a colony, the Japanese language would in all likelihood have been reduced to a typical local language. Of course, the age of colonization would eventually have come to an end. Nationalism would demand that, with independence, the Japanese language would transform into a national language. Nonetheless, to what extent could it have become a national language in a true sense?

Thanks to the expanse of the British Empire, by the time Perry's "black ships" appeared off Japanese shores, the English language was already the world's most dominant language. At the same time, the United States was well on its way to becoming the world's richest and most powerful nation, so if Japan had indeed been a U.S. colony, by the time it regained its independence, English dominance would have been even more entrenched. Unlike the people in Japan's former colonies of Taiwan and Korea, who did not hesitate to abandon the Japanese language once they were liberated, the Japanese people might easily have chosen to stick with English. Even if they had decided to relegate it to the status of "second official language," which language would the government actually have used? The universities? Which language would novelists have elected to write their novels in?

THE BIRTH OF JAPANESE AS A NATIONAL LANGUAGE

The Japanese language escaped threats from the outside. Yet the path to becoming a national language is fraught with difficulty, as is shown by what happened next. After the Meiji Restoration—however incongruous this may seem—the Japanese language was faced with threats from inside, from the Japanese themselves. Many Japanese intellectuals at the time doubted whether their language could be turned into the language of a modern nation-state. One such doubter was Mori Arinori (1847–1889), a contempo-

rary of Fukuzawa's who became the first minister of education. Mori implemented important educational reforms, but he remains a controversial figure,
mainly because he initially advocated that Japan abandon the use of its language and adopt English instead.[10] In 1873, he wrote a short article in English
for American readers entitled "Education in Japan." Here is an excerpt:

> The absolute necessity of mastering the English language is thus forced
> upon us. It is a requisite of the maintenance of our independence in the
> community of nations. Under the circumstances, our meager language,
> which can never be of any use outside of our islands, is doomed to yield
> to the domination of the English tongue, especially when the power of
> steam and electricity shall have pervaded the land. Our intelligent race,
> eager in the pursuit of knowledge, cannot depend upon a weak and un-
> certain medium of communication in its endeavor to grasp the principal
> truths from the precious treasury of Western science and art and religion.
> The laws of state can never be preserved in the language of Japan. All
> reasons suggest its disuse.[11]

Notice Mori's descriptions of the Japanese language: a "meager language,
which can never be of any use outside of our islands . . . doomed to yield to
the domination of the English tongue"; "a weak and uncertain medium of
communication"; a language in which the "laws of state can never be preserved." The Japanese who today criticize Mori for his seemingly unpatriotic
assessment of his own language lack historical imagination. They fail to see
that Japan was in such precarious circumstances that someone like Mori, who
was fluent in English and could look at the world from a global perspective,
felt compelled to consider the radical option of abandoning Japanese altogether. To remain independent, Japan needed a language that would allow
it to function as a modern nation and gain parity with the Western powers.
Many intellectuals, even those who opposed Mori's proposal, were genuinely
skeptical as to whether their language was equal to the task.

Mori's proposal for the adoption of English was rejected before he became
minister of education. It was not compatible with the ideology of national
language, which was gradually penetrating Japan from the West. The new
ministry made no attempt to adopt English but tried instead to come up with
various ways of reshaping the language into one befitting a modern nation.
The heated discussion dragged on for years. Nonetheless, those involved in
the task were nearly unanimous on one point: they all wanted to do away with

Chinese characters. Not only did Chinese characters symbolize an "external language," which went counter to the ideology of national language—worse, they were ideograms, then thought to be a symbol of underdevelopment.

At the time of the Meiji Restoration, alongside the ideology of national language, social Darwinism was also in full force in the West. In Japan, the works of its advocate Herbert Spencer (1820–1903) began appearing in translation around 1880. Social Darwinism, which saw Western civilization as the pinnacle of human evolution, was applied to writing systems as well, suggesting that human writing evolved from ideograms to phonograms. Among the varieties of phonograms, syllabaries like hiragana and katakana that combine a consonant and a vowel in one letter were considered less evolved. Those that separate consonants and vowels and thus are closer to phonetic signs were considered more developed, and somehow the Roman alphabet was given a privileged status. (It is perhaps no accident that powerful Western nations happened to use the Roman alphabet and not Cyrillic.) In other words, social Darwinism was inextricably connected to phoneticism or, more precisely, what would a century later be criticized as "phonocentrism"—an understanding of language that gives primacy to spoken language as a spontaneous expression of the human mind, thus reducing written language to the status of mere representation of spoken sounds.

Chinese characters, by exemplifying ideograms, went blatantly against such phoneticism. Though regarded as more evolved than Egyptian hieroglyphs, they came to symbolize the backwardness of East Asia, crystallized in China's defeat in the Opium Wars. Such a view was bound to influence how people in the former Sinosphere regarded their own writing systems. In fact, as we shall see in the final chapter, the fall of the Qing dynasty presaged the fall of Chinese characters in the former Sinosphere, as country after country came to espouse the ideology of phoneticism.

In Japan as early as 1866, six years after the Second Opium War and two years before the Meiji Restoration, a pro-Western intellectual named Maejima Hisoka submitted a proposal to the fifteenth and final shogun to abolish the use of Chinese characters. The new Japanese government, which had assigned the Ministry of Education the task of "improving" the Japanese language, in 1890 sent linguist Ueda Kazutoshi to study in Germany, where the ideology of national language reigned and a linguistic group called Young Grammarians (Junggrammatiker), focusing its attention on languages' sound, was attracting brilliant minds. Ueda returned to Japan in 1894 even more passionate a proponent of phoneticism than before, and later the Ministry of Education appointed him to head the newly founded National Language Research Council.

The council kept soliciting illuminati who upheld phoneticism in various forms. Some advocated using only katakana or hiragana; others—among them Mori, who had previously called for abandoning Japanese in favor of English—advocated using the Roman alphabet; still others advocated creating a totally new system. However different their solutions were, their goal was the same: to gradually reduce the use of Chinese characters until they were entirely gone.

Their goal never materialized. While the illuminati in the National Language Research Council under the Ministry of Education were debating how to get rid of the accursed Chinese characters, a practical kind of written Japanese was already taking shape, one that continued the tradition of mixing kana and Chinese characters and that depended on those very characters as never before. This development, which involved orders from higher levels of the government, arose from the urgent need to translate Western languages. And it arose precisely because Japan had so far managed to escape colonization. Not only Fukuzawa but those who were running the country knew all too well that in the eyes of the Western powers, the Restoration meant little more than a regime change in a small, vulnerable nation off in the Far East. The only way to avoid the indignity of further unequal treaties, or division or even an outright takeover, was for Japan to seize on knowledge accumulated in the West and get it speedily translated. Orders to translate as many Western books as possible, as soon as possible, were issued by the Great Council of State (Daijō-kan) and the Chamber of Elders (Genrō-in), followed by the Ministry of Finance, the Ministry of Justice, the Ministry of Education, and more. To accomplish such a formidable task, Chinese characters, being ideograms, could not have been better suited for the task.

Chinese characters have the ability to succinctly express abstract concepts and, when combined, to create new words without end. Those people chosen as translators, being from the educated class, were well versed in Chinese and knew how to take full advantage of the conciseness and versatility of the ideogram. Writing in a style of Japanese with a generous admixture of Chinese characters, working day and night, these translators played a critical role in helping Japan to preserve its independence.

It is telling that one of the very first books to be translated from a Western language—via an original Chinese translation—was a guide to international law, *Elements of International Law* (1836) by Henry Wheaton (1785–1848), an

American legal scholar. To rectify the unequal treaties, Japan first needed to learn the rules of the diplomatic game. Of course, that alone would not make the West willingly give up its gains. Japan also needed to build a modern military and manufacture its own guns and battleships. It had to build railroads and plumbing; it had to produce printing presses and monies; it had to provide modern education for its people. In short, Japan had to make each and every bit of Western knowledge and technology its own. And in the process, the act of translation, this time from a set of different universal languages, provided a new birth for the Japanese language. Now the Japanese language took its first tentative steps toward becoming a language capable of functioning on the same level as Western languages.

Furthermore, though the act of translation may have been prompted by the goal of sustaining Japan as an independent nation, it was not this alone that drove the translators of the time. The ultimate driving force behind any act of translation is the human desire to seek knowledge—a desire independent even of concern for one's nation's viability. This desire is what makes humans *Homo sapiens*. Translating Western languages as a national project in the early years after the Meiji Restoration resulted in an amazing quantity of translated materials. Even more amazing was the diversity of their subject matter. The government ordered translations on topics with no direct relevance to the nation's survival, including even aesthetics—perhaps the most useless of topics as far as nation building is concerned.

The impetus to seek knowledge did not come just from the top. Many of those who became translators were primarily seekers of knowledge who truly wished to know the world better. Even before the Restoration, as these people glimpsed the libraries of Western languages, they immediately understood that here was an immense trove of knowledge, universal in its application. Overwhelmed by the richness of this trove, they tried mightily to gain access to it on their own. No book illustrates this process better than the autobiography of Fukuzawa Yukichi, written thirty years after the Meiji Restoration.

FUKUZAWA YUKICHI: FROM DUTCH TO ENGLISH

Fukuzawa tried to learn Western languages against all odds simply because he wanted to know more than he did. Or better, he wanted to know everything that humanity knew. Knowing more than his fellow samurai was also a way for him to challenge those in power; he was angry with the shogunate for maintaining a rigid social and political hierarchy and with the Confucian scholars who gave the shogunate legitimacy. Yet what drove him most profoundly was his sheer passion to learn. Concern over Japan's fate came only later, when he realized that his country was headed for cataclysmic change.

Fukuzawa's autobiography gives a vivid picture of his hungry search for knowledge in the years leading up to the Restoration. The image of Fukuzawa with cropped hair—a sign of modernity—is familiar to present-day Japanese through his image on the ten-thousand-yen bill, but he was born in 1835, when the great woodblock print master Hokusai was still active. He thus belonged to a generation of men used to wearing a topknot, and he experienced the Restoration as an adult in his thirties. His father, Momosuke, a low-ranking samurai in the conservative Okudaira domain located on the southern island of Kyushu, was stationed in Osaka to carry out market transactions for his domain, and it was there that Fukuzawa was born, though he grew up in Kyushu. In his youth, he excelled in the study of Confucian texts, like his father, a bibliophile and a Confucian scholar in his own right. But Momosuke was never able to rise above his inherited rank, which led to Fukuzawa's well-known declaration, "Feudalism is my father's mortal enemy."[12] Knowing firsthand the humiliations suffered by low-ranking samurai in the Okudaira domain, Fukuzawa was already thinking of somehow getting out when the news came that black ships had arrived off Japanese shores, threatening the country with cannons. Told by his older brother that the country needed people to study gunnery and that to study gunnery one needed first to study Dutch, he gleefully sought and gained permission from domain authorities to move to Nagasaki to learn the language: "I would have been glad to study a foreign language or the military art or anything else if it only gave me a chance to go away" (22). This was in 1854, when he was nineteen years old.

Just off the western tip of Nagasaki was a small, artificial island whose ports had provided the only window on the West ever since the Edo government imposed an isolationist policy in 1636. The policy was the outcome of a major peasant uprising organized by Japanese Christians who had converted to Catholicism through missionaries sent by the Portuguese. The shogunate feared the spread of Christianity but was not willing to put a total stop to trade. The Netherlands, a great sea power in the seventeenth century, promised not to engage in any missionary activities, and so the Dutch East India Company was allowed to establish a trading post on that little island. From then on, the meager information Japan managed to glean of the Western world came via the Dutch language. The few Japanese intellectuals who chanced to come into contact with Western knowledge were impressed, and so, despite the dire shortage of books and teachers, not to mention the near nonexistence of dictionaries, they established schools all over Japan to teach the Dutch language along with Western science, especially medicine. Some progressive domains encouraged such "Dutch learning" (later called "Western learning"), but the Okudaira domain, where the Fukuzawa family had served for generations, was not among them. The best way for Fukuzawa to absorb Dutch learning was thus to go to Nagasaki.

On arriving, he saw the Roman alphabet for the first time in his life and was shocked: "I could hardly believe these ABC's to be signs of a language" (37). He quickly set about learning the language, but his one-year stay was not as fruitful as it could have been. The Okudaira domain saw no point in anyone seriously learning Dutch. Fukuzawa was assigned to stay as a nonpaying boarder, half-secretary and half-servant to a family that owned precious copies of Dutch books and drawings on gunnery and rented them out to inquirers from all over Japan. Put in charge of the family rental business, he soon acquired a good deal of knowledge about gunnery—without ever laying eyes on an actual gun—but was never allowed to officially learn the Dutch language. He had to pick up what he could by seeking out doctors who practiced Western medicine or interpreters who conducted trade negotiations. On uncovering a silly intrigue by a jealous rival who wanted him out of the way, he left Nagasaki, intending to go to Edo, present-day Tokyo, to start learning Dutch in earnest. An arduous journey without money took him only as far as Osaka, the place of his birth, where his older brother was temporarily stationed, their father having by then passed on. The brother urged him to take up the language then and there. It turned out to be good advice.

Osaka was home to Ogata Academy, run by Ogata Kōan (1810–1863), a doctor trained in Western medicine. It so happened that this was one of the best places to acquire Dutch learning in all Japan. Fukuzawa's stay at the academy lasted for three years, and he made the most of it. At one point, the death of his brother required him to return to the Okudaira domain, but though he was now the head of the family he refused to stay and, unmoved by recriminations from his relations, headed back to the academy after raising money for travel expenses by selling off valuable family possessions. Only his aged mother, who would be left at home alone, gave him her blessing.

Fukuzawa's vivid descriptions of academy life capture the rowdy mischief, anarchic behavior, abject poverty, and in-your-face filthiness typical of such Edo-period students—all of them frantically learning Dutch as if their lives depended on it.

One day, taken sick, Fukuzawa noticed that he had no pillow. He then realized that for the past year he had never actually had a decent night's sleep:

> I realized suddenly that I had not used [a pillow] for the whole year that I had been there. I had been studying without regard to day or night. I would be reading all day and when night came I did not think of going to bed. When tired, I would lean over on my little desk, or stretch out on the floor resting my head on the raised alcove (*tokonoma*) of the room. I had gone through the year without ever spreading my pallet and covers and sleeping on the pillow. So obviously the servant could not find *my* pillow, for it did not exist anywhere in the apartment. This incident may illustrate our intense manner of studying. In this I was not unusual; all my friends lived in this way. We could not have studied harder. (79)

Moreover, since the academy had only ten books in Dutch, in order to study students had to copy out the original, taking turns. They each had to soak rice paper in alum so the ink would not smear, and make their own quill pens. Furthermore, as for the essential Dutch–Japanese dictionary, three thousand pages in all, there was only one precious copy. Students gathered around it to look up words. Before exams there was always a line.

One day, Ogata Kōan brought an expensive Dutch book on loan from a daimyo, Lord Kuroda. Kōan first called in Fukuzawa, who was the student representative, and handed him the book. "It was a new text on physical science recently translated from English," Fukuzawa wrote. "The contents seemed to hold much that was new to us, especially the chapter on electricity." The book described the structures of a battery, and his "heart was carried away with it at first sight." His ability to perceive at a glance that this book represented the latest developments in science is testimony not only to his own ability but to the high scholarly level at the academy. When he took this "text on physical science" to show the other students, they "rose up as one and crowded around" (88) in awe.

The book was theirs for only two nights, while Lord Kuroda was visiting Osaka. Just to stare at it was meaningless, and to copy a thousand-page book in two nights was impossible. But Fukuzawa wanted to copy at least the part about electricity, and he mobilized everyone for the task:

> If we could have broken the book up and divided the copying among the thirty or fifty "ready-quill men," the entire contents might have been kept.

But of course injuring the nobleman's possession was out of the question. However, we worked at full speed, and the Ogata students could work expertly. One read aloud; another took the dictation; when one grew tired and slowed down, another was waiting with his quill, and the exhausted one would go to sleep regardless of time, morning, noon, or night.

Thus, working day and night, through meal hours and all, we finished the whole chapter in the time allotted, and thus the section on electricity, about three hundred pages including its diagrams, remained with us in manuscript. (88–89)

The students wanted to copy more, but there was just not enough time: "[W]hen the evening of Lord Kuroda's departure came, we all handled the book affectionately in turn and gave it a sad leave-taking as if we were parting with a parent" (89). The image of young men affectionately caressing the book that was a repository of human knowledge and bidding it a sad farewell is striking.

Looking back, Fukuzawa himself seems puzzled over why they sought knowledge at such cost, and in the end he suggests that intellectual snobbery or pride may have been at work:

[H]owever much we studied, our work and knowledge had practically no connection with the actual means of gaining a livelihood or making a name for ourselves. Not only that, but the students of Dutch were looked upon with contempt by most men. Then why did we work so hard to learn Dutch? It would seem that we were simply laboring at difficult foreign texts for no clear purpose.

However, if anyone had looked into our inner hearts, he would have found there an untold pleasure which was our consolation. In short, we students were conscious of the fact that we were the sole possessors of the key to knowledge of the great European civilization. However much we suffered from poverty, whatever poor clothes we wore, the extent of our knowledge and the resources of our minds were beyond the reach of any prince or nobleman of the whole nation. If our work was hard, we were proud of it, knowing that no one knew what we endured. "In hardship we found pleasure, and the hardship was pleasure." To illustrate, our position was like that of someone taking bitter medicine without knowing exactly what it was good for. We simply took it because nobody else could take it—the more bitter it was, the more gladly we took it. (90–91)

What a brutal shock it must have been when, having made this super-human effort to study Dutch, Fukuzawa realized that the language was nearly useless. With the Dutch golden age a thing of the past, the Dutch language was of minor importance in the world. Some in Japan already suspected this, but Fukuzawa did not face the fact until later, when he visited Yokohama.

In 1858, the Okudaira domain belatedly accepted the need to learn Dutch and summoned Fukuzawa to its Edo compound to teach the language. That was the year when the Ansei Five-Power Treaties were signed and Western-ers first began living in Yokohama. One day, Fukuzawa decided to try out his Dutch and walked all the way from the Edo compound to Yokohama, a distance of about 30 kilometers (19 miles). "There was nothing of the town of Yokohama then—a few temporary dwellings had been erected here and there by the foreigners, and in these the pioneer merchants were living and showing their wares" (97). Yet to his astonishment, those foreigners did not understand Dutch:

To my chagrin, when I tried to speak with them, no one seemed to un-derstand me at all. Nor was I able to understand anything spoken by a single one of all the foreigners I met. Neither could I read anything of the signboards over the shops, nor the labels on the bottles which they had for sale. There was not a single recognizable word in any of the inscrip-tions or in any speech. It might have been English or French for aught I knew. (97)

Faced with this unexpected reality, Fukuzawa turned on his heel and walked back to Edo in shock: "I had to leave home just before the closing hour and return before the same hour of the next day. This meant that I had been walk-ing for twenty-four hours" (98).

Far greater than his physical exhaustion was the mental blow he had re-ceived—yet what is astounding is his quick recovery:

[T]he fatigue of my legs was nothing compared with the bitter disap-pointment in my heart.

I had been striving with all my powers for many years to learn the Dutch language. And now when I had reason to believe myself one of the best in the country, I found that I could not even read the signs of merchants who had come to trade with us from foreign lands. It was a bitter disappointment but I knew it was no time to be downhearted." (98)

He was back on his feet the very next day:

Those signs must have been either in English or in French—probably English, for I had had inklings that English was the most widely used language. A treaty with the two English-speaking countries had just been concluded. As certain as day, English was to be the most useful language of the future. I realized that a man would have to be able to read and converse in English to be recognized as a scholar in Western subjects in the coming time. In my disappointment my spirit was low, but I knew that it was not the time to be sitting still.

On the very next day after returning from Yokohama, I took up a new aim in life and determined to begin the study of English. (98)

So began his study of English. The only person rumored to know some English in the whole of Edo was too busy to teach him. And even that person did not know very much. English–Japanese and English–Chinese dictionaries were nonexistent, and even an English–Dutch dictionary was hard to come by. When he invited his former classmates from the academy to join him in studying English, they took off, groaning that they could not bear to go through such an ordeal all over again. He finally met someone willing to study with him, and the two of them did whatever they could to learn English, latching on to children who lived near foreigners and had picked up scraps of the language or former shipwreck victims who had been stranded abroad. In the course of time, they realized that English was not too different from Dutch after all, and their former efforts were by no means a total waste.

The following year, in 1860, Fukuzawa pulled strings and managed to wangle a ride to the United States aboard the *Kanrin-maru*, the first Japanese navy vessel—built by the Dutch. He stayed for a few months and brought back one of the first two copies of Webster's dictionary to enter Japan. After that, he continued his study of English while teaching the language at the school he had founded originally to teach Dutch. Soon he was sought out as a translator by the shogunate's Gaikoku-kata, corresponding to today's Ministry of Foreign Affairs, and in 1862 they dispatched him to Europe with other government officials. As a sign of his untiring pursuit of knowledge, he alone used his entire stipend, a substantial amount, to purchase English books to bring back. He kept climbing the social ladder as he rode the wave of Japan's opening to the world.

Fukuzawa Yukichi is remembered today as the founder of Keio, one of Japan's top universities, but he made an even more fundamental contribution through his translation work. Words that he coined using Chinese ideograms include *enzetsu* (public speaking), *sansei* (agreement), *tōrōn* (discussion), and *hanken* (copyright).[13] Today, nobody in Japan thinks of Fukuzawa when using these common, everyday words. But translations by him and other knowledge-hungry men of Meiji—Nishi Amane, Mitsukuri Rinshō, Nakae Chōmin, Tsubouchi Shōyō, and others—helped the Japanese language to evolve so that writers could address the same issues as the rest of the world, with global consciousness and synchronicity. Japanese began transforming into a national language. And by doing so, it turned into a language in which Japanese writers could write modern literature—especially the novel, a celebration of national language.

5. THE MIRACLE OF MODERN

JAPANESE LITERATURE

UNIVERSITIES AND CREATIVE GENIUSES MAY SEEM STRANGE BEDFELLOWS WHEN IT COMES TO ART, INCLUDING LITERATURE. Of course, plenty of universities nowadays offer courses on creative writing that are taught by acclaimed writers. Yet the romantic in us wants to believe in geniuses who dwarf the annoyingly erudite in their ivory towers. That romantic belief harks back to the golden age of national literature, an age when literature was separated from academic disciplines and transcended them as a source of knowledge. But in non-Western countries, universities had to play a crucial role in creating a national literature—however unromantic the fact may be. Genius was not enough.

The previous chapter was devoted to the discussion of three conditions that enabled the rapid establishment of the national language in Japan after the Meiji Restoration: a mature written language when the country was still part of the Sinosphere, a robust print capitalism during the preceding Edo period, and freedom from Western colonization at a time when nearly all the non-West was colonized. We will begin this chapter by first directing our attention to something that was made possible only by the last of the three: Japan's founding of its own universities.

First, let us revisit the question of what might have happened to the Japanese language if Japan had become a colony of the United States. Quite assuredly, the Japanese universities we now know, where classes are taught in Japanese as a matter of course, would never have existed. The children of the wealthy would have crossed the Pacific to study in American universities, and other bright youths would have been selected in large numbers to do the same. Sooner or later, universities would surely have sprung up on Japanese soil, but the courses would have been taught in English. (When Japan founded universities in its colonies, Taiwan and Korea, the courses were taught in Japanese.) Only the escape from colonization allowed Japan to build its own universities, which, in turn, made it possible for Japanese people to pursue knowledge in their own language.

Nothing better illuminates the truth of this statement than the fact that, at the outset, most university courses in Japan were *not* taught in Japanese by Japanese professors. Universities erected brick buildings modeled on Western architecture and purchased mounds of leather-bound books from the West, but no Japanese could teach the necessary subject matter of "Western learning"—the Western academic disciplines. Universities therefore hired foreign teachers, turning not just to qualified Westerners already residing in Japan but also to scholars from afar. These teachers were considered so invaluable that many are said to have earned more than cabinet members. Only gradually were they laid off and replaced by Japanese back from studying in the West. And it was when such returnees began teaching in their own language what they had learned abroad that the Japanese language began transforming into a language in which the pursuit of knowledge was legitimately possible— that is, into a *national language* not only in name but also in practice.

This was a good start, yet such is the nature of asymmetry between West and non-West that this auspicious turn of events did not make Japanese universities centers of learning in quite the same sense as Western universities. Rather, they came to function above all as major institutions for translation. Early in the Meiji period, there naturally were no Japanese books in which to study the Western subjects that students were supposed to learn; acquiring knowledge necessarily went hand in hand with acquiring proficiency in Western languages. The main role of Japan's higher education was therefore to teach Western languages. Entry to national universities, which resembled today's graduate schools, was preceded by preparatory classes at national colleges where students were required to learn two of the three major European languages, one as a major, the other as a minor. Learning these languages played such a fundamental pedagogical role that students were grouped according to the language of their concentration and, after intensive training, often formed a lifelong bond with their classmates, like troops in a hard-won battle. Students earned pocket money through translation.

After graduating from universities, some of them went on to become educators-cum-translators, making what they had learned accessible to the general public by writing straightforward translations or introductory, explanatory, or interpretive books in Japanese. They were called "scholars" in Japan and certainly considered themselves as such, but from a larger perspective (and I say this without any intention of disparaging their endeavors), they were basically translators—transmitters, not creators, of knowledge. Generation after generation of these dedicated men—and later women—ultimately made it possible for nearly all important Western knowledge to be available in Japanese, so that today's university students no longer have to read a single book in the original to know what the world expects them to know. Other bilingual or polyglot university graduates who did not become educators or translators per se read widely in European languages and then wrote in Japanese, contributing en masse to transforming Japanese into a language that presumed a global consciousness. The ideology of national language would later have it that a humble peasant who tilled the soil and did not know what "democracy" meant even in Japanese was held up as the true sage, possessing a kind of wisdom that the educated could not possibly attain. This jaundiced view of higher education was possible only for those Japanese who could take for granted the existence of the Japanese language as it is today, who came late enough to be blissfully ignorant of how their language and literature developed.

The Englishman Daniel Defoe was, as we have seen, one of the pioneers of the novel. Writing in English in the eighteenth century already meant writing in one of the universal languages, and Defoe had no need for an Oxford or a Cambridge education to achieve what he did. The same was not true for Japanese writers. Of all the male Japanese writers born in the nineteenth century, each one a pioneer in his way, the number who attended Tokyo Imperial University or its college (both of which were closed to women) and thus were bilinguals, if not polyglots, is astonishing. In fact, it is mind-boggling, bizarre even. Beginning with Natsume Sōseki, the list is virtually endless: Tsubouchi Shōyō, Mori Ōgai, Masaoka Shiki, Yamada Bimyō, Ozaki Kōyō, Ueda Bin, Osanai Kaoru, Suzuki Miekichi, Saitō Mokichi, Shiga Naoya, Mushakōji Saneatsu, Naka Kansuke, Kinoshita Mokutarō, Tanizaki Jun'ichirō, Yamamoto Yūzō, Uchida Hyakken, Kishida Kunio, Kume Masao, Akutagawa Ryūnosuke, Osaragi Jirō, and Kawabata Yasunari, among many others. As if that weren't enough, well-known private universities such as Keio and Waseda simultaneously produced their own schools of literature and their own set of leading writers. Going to university meant being at least bilingual, and, however counterintuitive it may seem now, bilingualism was a sine qua non of becoming a standard-bearer of Japanese national literature—for male writers, anyway.

That said, remaining in academia and pursuing a career there in nineteenth-century Japan was not an attractive choice to young men of aspiration, especially those with literary inclinations. Virtually all the university curriculum consisted of Western disciplines that seemed to have no direct bearing on the country at the dawn of its modernity. The two societies, Western and Japanese, were too far apart. Natural sciences, of course, had universal relevance to any society. Yet it was not so with other disciplines, especially those falling under the rubric of "liberal arts." Aside from traditional fields of learning—Buddhist studies, the classics of China and Japan—all other disciplines in the liberal arts were basically Western: philosophy, sociology, psychology, linguistics, history, anthropology, aesthetics, musicology, literature, and so forth. Their study was inseparable from the study of Western languages. There was an underlying Eurocentrism in all of them, a tendency to perceive the world from the Western perspective and find human universality in Western modes of being.

The pursuit of that kind of knowledge in academia was bound to prove frustrating and alienating for Japanese men of talent and ambition. First, no matter how brilliant such a man might be, his work could not really enter the global chain of "texts to read" as long as he wrote in Japanese, which he almost inevitably did. He had to remain in the role of a translator, introducing Western learning to Japanese readers. Second, no matter how much he wrote in Japanese, as long as he remained within the confines of academia, his prose had to read like a translation of some Western treatise and so be cut off from Japan's rich literary tradition. No allusions to poetry could be allowed, either Japanese or Chinese, nor any of the rhetorical devices specific to Japanese prose that make fine writing so much more than a mere message. Third, the Western academic disciplines gave a writer no way to capture vividly the excitement of what was happening right in front of him—the messy reality of a Japan rapidly transforming after the arrival of Commodore Matthew Perry's black ships. From trams and gaslights to hats and shoes, the everyday look of Japan was mutating at dizzying speed, and how was one to write about that? Writing as an academic must have felt to many men of talent and ambition like being forced to write with both hands tied.

And yet these challenges were a blessing for modern Japanese literature. Remember, this was the era that celebrated national language, the era when the language of literature was regarded as transcendent over the language of scholarship. And precisely because of the challenges that Japanese intellectuals faced, there was a far greater urgency in Japan than in the West for the language of literature to transcend. The language of literature carried the heavier intellectual, ethical, and aesthetic burden of making sense of the maelstrom of change. Writing fiction was a somewhat disreputable profession at the time, but these men overcame the opposition of teachers, parents, and wives and chose that path, forsaking the chance for a more stable and respectable career.

It often happens when a national language is formed that there emerges, almost magically, a national figure who single-handedly comes to embody that historical process. In Japan, Natsume Sōseki, the author of *Sanshirō*, was such a figure. After having spent two and a half years in London, Sōseki returned to Japan in 1903 and became the first Japanese to teach English literature at Tokyo Imperial University, replacing Lafcadio Hearn, an English-language writer best known for introducing Japanese ghost stories to the West. Sōseki naturally conducted his classes in Japanese, thus heralding the conversion of university instruction to the vernacular and elevating the language in the process. Moreover, because he went on to leave the university after only a few years to become a novelist, he also came to embody the dilemma faced by Japanese intellectuals then and now.

THOSE IN *SANSHIRŌ* WHO READ EXTERNAL LANGUAGES

Let us take a closer look now at Sōseki's novel *Sanshirō*, which was cited earlier.[1] It is a sort of bildungsroman about a naïve young man who leaves his family—probably landowners—in the rustic southern island of Kyushu to attend Tokyo Imperial University. As the novel progresses, he meets urbanized, sophisticated people for the first time in his life; develops an unspoken infatuation with a woman who breaks his heart by abruptly marrying someone else; and, amid confusion and turmoil, achieves a measure of growth.

A fine novel captures the hearts of readers across time, and I am sure that many Japanese identify with Sanshirō even today, especially those who, like him, have left the countryside to study in a big city. It is natural that even today, many readers should identify with the innocent young protagonist so full of the future, so full of dreams.

Nonetheless, a very different *Sanshirō* emerges when we take a step back and see the novel as a kind of metanovel. Set in and around the university campus, it could first be read as an analysis of how a university functions in Japan. But it could also be read as a work that allows the reader to see, more lucidly than any work of scholarship, why so many Meiji intellectuals turned to writing novels and why novels were destined to flourish in Japan. To push our interpretation further, *Sanshirō* highlights the historical necessity for national literature to thrive during this time of rapid modernization.

Let us go back to the scene on the train bound for Tokyo. The night before, Sanshirō has had a rather humiliating experience. When he got off the train in Nagoya for the night, the woman sitting across from him got off as well and asked him to help her find an inn. He did not have the nerve to say no. He found a seedy-looking inn befitting the third-class passengers that they were; the innkeeper instantly mistook them for a couple, and before Sanshirō knew it, he was forced not only to stay in the same room with the woman but also to share the same futon with her. Hastily making up some nonsensical excuse, he rolled up a towel to create a barrier between them and spent the entire night lying beside her wide awake, rigid with tension. When they parted in the morning, she broke her silence, saying suddenly with a mocking smile, "Quite a coward, aren't you?" Now, on the train from Nagoya, Sanshirō ruminates on her words: "Not even his mother could have hit home so accurately." He recalls the woman's mocking smile. He cannot help but feel depressed. Then, to lift his spirits, he imagines the bright future awaiting him: "He was going to Tokyo. He would enter the university, associate with famous scholars, befriend students of taste and character. Do research in the library. Write books, win acclaim. Make his mother happy." He goes on self-indulgently in this vein.

While all this is going on his mind, spread on Sanshirō's lap is a book that he took from his bag a little while ago and has been pretending to read: Francis Bacon's *Essays*. Now, here is a question few Japanese readers may have bothered to ask: Is the book a translation or the English original? The novel does not tell us. The present-day reader, long accustomed to the idea that every important book from the West has been rendered into Japanese, is likely to assume that it's a translation. But if one stopped to consider that the novel was written over a hundred years ago, one might conjecture that the book was in the original—which I think would be the case. At the time, translations of Western books were rare. Once we can picture Sanshirō perusing a book in English, we have already taken an important step. We can expect this novel to be about bilingual intellectuals of the Meiji period in whose lives reading Western languages, particularly English, played a central role.

We soon find out that Sanshirō is enrolled in the Department of English Literature at Tokyo Imperial University. We see him reading English—or trying to. The bearded man he met on the train in the scene quoted in the previous chapter, Professor Hirota, is not just a teacher at the university's affiliated preparatory college but a teacher of English. We see Hirota reading English all the time. Another important character, a research physicist named Nonomiya who comes from Sanshirō's hometown and is a few years his senior, also reads English as a matter of course. Even the beautiful Mineko, with whom Sanshirō eventually falls in love in his timid and inarticulate way, reads English, though she is "merely" a woman. Her pronunciation, Sanshirō thinks, is excellent.

The university library is quite naturally filled with books from the West: "Some of the books were piled so high you needed a ladder to reach them. Books darkened by handling and greasy fingerprints, books with titles of shining gold. Sheepskin, cowhide, two-century-old paper and, piled on top of it all, dust. Precious dust that took two or three decades to accumulate." These books piled with "precious dust" are books that the university has been working hard to acquire, volume by volume, language by language, since the Meiji Restoration.

Sanshirō is stunned to realize the diligent use people have made of the library: "He was amazed to discover that every book he handled, no matter what it was, had been read at least once. There were pencil marks scattered throughout. Once, just out of curiosity, he picked up a novel by an author named Aphra Behn. Nobody will have read this, he told himself before opening it. But again, there they were, the neat pencil marks. This was really too much."

And who should be one of those people who have read Aphra Behn but Professor Hirota! Of the main characters, Hirota reads English the most and hence uses the library the most. He informs Sanshirō that Aphra Behn was England's first female writer to become a professional novelist. He even tells him that a man by the name of "Southerne" subsequently wrote a play based on her work. Professor Hirota also has a substantial private collection of books in English, which he seems to lend out generously. Indeed, although he has never traveled abroad, he knows more about the West than anyone else, having read more books in Western languages than anyone else. He tells Sanshirō the curious story of Leonardo da Vinci injecting arsenic into the trunk of a peach tree experimentally, to see if the poison would circulate to the fruit. He also informs him about the construction of a Greek theater and explains the meaning of certain Greek and Latin words: *theatron, orchêstra, skêne, proskênion.* Sanshirō learns from him that, according to some German or other, the theater in Athens could seat seventeen thousand, which was on the small side, as the largest one could seat fifty thousand. The professor even knows that there were two kinds of tickets, ivory and lead, and that a day's performance cost the equivalent of twelve sen; a full three-day program, thirty-five sen. Professor Hirota, who seems to know everything, is a seeker of knowledge par excellence.

Professor Hirota represents not only the most knowledgeable but also the wisest character in the novel, universally respected. This comes out in the scene at the very beginning of the novel where Sanshirō looks at him and sees only a shabbily dressed, middle-aged man with a mustache who, at his age, is still riding third class; Sanshirō inwardly looks down on him, comfortably contrasting the man with himself and the bright future he has in store. Yet the man says things that Sanshirō has never heard before: Japan's victory in the Russo-Japanese War hardly made the country a first-class power; it's actually a sorry place with just one thing to be proud of—Mount Fuji, a product of nature. The professor's unmincing words astonish Sanshirō, who is fresh out of Kyushu. He feels compelled to offer a counterargument:

> . . . He said defensively, "But from now on, Japan is sure to develop."
> "Japan's headed for a fall," the man said coolly.
> Say a thing like that in Kumamoto and you'd get a punch in the nose, or be called a traitor. The atmosphere Sanshirō grew up in left no room in his head for such an idea. Just because he was young, was the man having some fun at his expense? The man kept on grinning. Yet his way of talking was perfectly composed. Not knowing what to think, Sanshirō held his tongue.
> His companion went on, "Tokyo is bigger than Kumamoto. Japan is bigger than Tokyo. And what's bigger than Japan is . . ." He paused and looked at Sanshirō, who was listening intently. ". . . the inside of your head. That's bigger than Japan. Don't let yourself get bogged down. You may believe your way of thinking is for the good of the nation, but you could actually be bringing it down."
> When he heard this, Sanshirō felt he had indeed left Kumamoto. And he realized, too, what a small person his Kumamoto self had been.

What makes the inside of one's head "bigger" than a nation? It is thinking in a national language that came into being through translations of *universal languages*. On his way from Kumamoto to Tokyo, Sanshirō encounters for the first time his own language used as a national language—a language that can transcend and critique one's own nation-state, a language that presumes a global consciousness. A naïve young man, Sanshirō does not fully appreciate the invaluableness of someone like Professor Hirota. The first chapter ends: "The bearded man never told Sanshirō his name. There were bound to be men like this everywhere in Tokyo, Sanshirō thought, and never bothered to ask."

Needless to say, this portends that even in Tokyo, the likes of Professor Hirota are hard to find.

Professor Hirota appears as someone who can use Japanese in such a way precisely because he is constantly reading books in Western languages and thinking, while mentally translating what he has read into Japanese. Indeed, scenes abound in which the subject of translation comes up. Meeting Sanshirō again in Tokyo, Professor Hirota recognizes him and asks out of the blue: "Did you ever try to translate Mount Fuji?" When some young people, including Sanshirō, help the professor move into a new rental house with all his foreign books, he asks them how to translate the English proverb, "Pity is akin to love." And a discussion on how to translate ensues. Easily influenced, even Sanshirō, as he thinks of Mineko, starts having thoughts like this: "Beautiful women could be translated any number of ways." Mineko herself puzzles Sanshirō with a question: "Do you know the English translation for 'lost child'?"

And it is through the character of Professor Hirota that the novel stealthily asks the critical questions: What does it mean to pursue scholarship in Japanese? Is it truly possible to do so? Such questions underlie the fact that Professor Hirota, with all his knowledge and wisdom, can be seen as little more than a walking encyclopedia, someone who makes no good use of the vast store of knowledge and wisdom he has acquired. Though he reads more Western books than anyone else, he never writes anything himself. He absorbs all the glories of the world's knowledge and never emits any light of his own. This is why he is referred to as "the Great Darkness" by Sanshirō's classmate Yojirō, the clown in the novel, who lives with Professor Hirota as his disciple-cum-houseboy. Professor Hirota is always smoking a cigarette and, in Yojirō's words, "emitting his customary puffs of philosophy." He does not have a single published book to his name. He occasionally writes essays of sorts, but nobody pays any attention. And he is content with teaching English at the preparatory college.

Feeling sorry for Professor Hirota and frustrated at the same time, Yojirō works behind the scenes to try to get him a position on the English literature faculty at Tokyo Imperial University. He first publishes a long magazine essay entitled "The Great Darkness" in which he sings the professor's praises in extravagant terms. The essay is "particularly severe on foreigners teaching foreign literature in the university" and argues that the university should hire Japanese professors: "Of course, the situation cannot be helped if there is no one suitable, but here is Professor Hirota." Yojirō then goes on to organize a student gathering where he delivers a ringing speech: "We've got to get hold of someone who can satisfy the youth of the new age. A foreigner won't do. They don't have what it takes."

Yojirō's efforts are in vain. The position goes to someone "who had until recently been studying abroad under government orders"—in other words, to a man like Sōseki himself, who in real life obtained the very position in question after studying abroad under government orders. Sōseki's mischievous humor has Yojirō say he heard a rumor that "the other fellow was pulling strings." This subplot is a light sideline in which Yojirō ends up causing trouble for all concerned. But the historical background of the subplot is anything but light. The incident symbolizes the incremental replacement of foreign faculty by Japanese that had to take place for the Japanese language to be elevated into a language used in academia.

Professor Hirota himself does not seem the least bit disappointed at the failure of Yojirō's scheme. He scoffs at Yojirō's long essay and goes on teaching at his college, unruffled. The reader is led to believe that this is because he is a man who transcends the worldly. Yet I would argue that there is a deeper significance. Professor Hirota attaches no great importance to becoming a professor of English literature at Tokyo Imperial University. Indeed, how on earth could he or any Japanese become a true scholar of English literature? Even if the Japanese were able to pursue scholarship in their own language, so long as they all *wrote* in their own language, how could anybody's writing enter the world's chain of "texts to read"?

Though he has no publications to speak of, Professor Hirota seems to be idly working on a magnum opus that, Yojirō fears, will amount only to "a heap of scrap paper" when he dies. He is a lazy scholar not *despite* having read more books from the West than anyone else, but precisely *because* he has. He understands all too well how ultimately futile it is for a liberal-arts scholar like himself to write and publish in Japanese, how impossible it is for him to make a contribution in the field that way. And yet the West is too far, psychologically as well as geographically, for him to try writing in English—or in any other European language for that matter. Furthermore, even if, against all odds, he did write his book in English, what Western scholar of the time would read it? What Western scholar in his right mind would trouble to read a book on English literature written by a Japanese?

True, some Japanese people around the same period did write in English, notably the Christian reformer and writer Uchimura Kanzō, as we have seen, and the government official and artist Okakura Tenshin (1862–1913). Westerners welcomed the former's *How I Became a Christian* as gratifying proof of their religion's universal validity, and the latter's *The Book of Tea* (1906) as a source of wisdom embodied in the exotic tea ceremony. But a treatise on English literature by a Far Eastern man would have been unlikely to find a publisher. Even if Professor Hirota were promoted and thus given more time to write his magnum opus, his role from a global perspective would remain that of a translator introducing Western scholarship to Japan.

A character in *Sanshirō* who is Professor Hirota's polar opposite is Nonomiya, the young physicist. In many ways, the two are similar. Nonomiya, too, is a man who transcends worldly matters. He, too, is content with low pay and goes about doing the same thing for ten long years, secluding himself in a cellar-like laboratory, staring into a telescope, and conducting research on the pressure exerted by light, a subject that seems remote from everyday life. He, too, is unknown to the general public. And yet there is a crucial difference between him and Professor Hirota: he is known to those around the world who are engaged in research similar to his. "Everyone in that field, even Westerners, knows the name of Nonomiya," we are assured. "Nonomiya is celebrated in foreign countries." As a scientist, Nonomiya not only reads but writes and publishes in English, for the language of science is close to the language of mathematics, the universal language par excellence. His writings can thus enter the chain of "texts to read." This is why, even though he is a man with little worldly interest, he is highly sensitive to trends in his field. "Research nowadays moves fast; if you don't stay alert, you're quickly left behind," he tells Sanshirō.

Sanshirō astutely grasps the difference between the two men:

Around Professor Hirota he felt easy and relaxed. Competition just didn't seem to matter anymore. Nonomiya had an otherworldly air too, like the professor, but in his case lofty ambitions seemed to distance him from conventional desires. So when Sanshirō talked with Nonomiya one on one, he would start to feel that he too must hurry and do his share, make his contribution to the world of scholarship. He grew anxious. By contrast, Professor Hirota was tranquility itself. He was just a college language teacher and that was it—not a very nice thing to say, granted, but he hadn't published any research. And yet he seemed totally unconcerned. That must be what put Sanshirō so much at ease.

That Professor Hirota should remain "the Great Darkness"—a master of mere trivia—is structurally imposed by the futility of pursuing Western scholarship in Japanese, and that futility itself is imposed by the historical dynamics of modernity, manifesting itself in the linguistic asymmetry.

Not everyone is blessed with the kind of mind that allows him to spend his days in peace when entrapped in such a situation. Sōseki must have admired men who possessed such tranquility of mind, must have aspired to be like them. Yet he was no Hirota. He accepted the position on the faculty of English literature at Tokyo Imperial University, replacing Lafcadio Hearn—and thus becoming what he later sarcastically called a "captain of Western learning."

Sōseki's next step, however, was extraordinary. He tried to explore the only path that seemed meaningful and valid to him, the only path in which he would be more than a "captain of Western learning," more than a transmitter of knowledge. The result was the notoriously hard to read book *Theory of Literature* (*Bungaku ron*, 1907), a compilation of his lectures at the university from 1903 to 1905. The book begins with a rather startling declaration:

One can perhaps approach the form of literary substance with the expression (F + f). F here indicates impressions or ideas at the focal point of consciousness, while f signifies the emotions that attend them. In this case, the formula stated above signifies impressions and ideas in two aspects, that is to say, as a compound of [the] cognitive factor F ("large F"), and the emotional factor f ("small f").[2]

In other words, the impressions a reader receives from literature derive from the combination of F, which stands for cognitive function, and f, which stands for emotive function—a contention so basic that it is difficult either to agree or to disagree. It is less what he says than the way he says it that concerns us here. Sōseki had a highly analytical and scientific mind. In trying to teach

English literature in the Japanese language to Japanese students, he tried to step outside not only English literature but also the literary language commonly used in discussing literature, and to address, in a most formalistic way, the fundamental question of what literature is.

What Sōseki avoided was repeating the ideas of Western teachers in Japanese and thus acting as a mere conduit. A good example of what he presumably did *not* want to do as a teacher can be found in *Sanshirō*. On Sanshirō's first day of classes at the university, he waits for the professor to enter the classroom, his heart filled with awe. Then a "distinguished-looking old man, a foreigner" walks in and begins "to lecture in fluent English." What does Sanshirō learn from this guru? He learns that the word "answer" derived from the Anglo-Saxon word "andswaru." He learns the name of the village where Sir Walter Scott went to grammar school. In short, he learns things that are hardly relevant to Japanese people. It would not be worth Sōseki's while to teach in Japanese if he only replicated this sort of class. It was the mission of him or someone like him— a person who could look at English literature from the outside—to relativize works in English as variants of literature's universal formula.

Modern history forced Sōseki to become a formalist, more than a decade before the Russian formalists came on the scene. And yet he was unsatisfied with *Theory of Literature*, which he later called a "deformed corpse": Why did he feel so bitter about it that he felt compelled to doubly degrade it, calling it not just a "corpse" but a "deformed corpse"? "Circumstances compelled me to give up my contemplated task long before it was completed. My *Theory of Literature* is thus not so much a memorial to my projected 'lifework' as its corpse—and a deformed corpse at that. It lies like the ruins of a city street that has been destroyed by an earthquake in the midst of its construction."[3] Was Sōseki frustrated by the limitation of pursuing academic learning in the Japanese language? We do not know. All we know is that he quit his teaching post after only four years. By that time, he had already earned a considerable reputation as a writer through works he wrote in his spare time, such as the satirical comic novel *I Am a Cat* (*Wagahai wa neko de aru*, 1905–1906). The *Asahi Shimbun* offered him a full-time position as an in-house novelist who would write serially for the paper. His decision to walk away from what was then one of the most exalted positions in Japan, that of faculty member at Tokyo Imperial University, to become a full-time novelist created a sensation. Yet in fact, it symbolized a typical predicament of intellectuals in modern Japan: there was a structural necessity for bright minds to leave the university behind to write.

Let us go back to the beginning of *Sanshirō* when, during his train ride to Tokyo, Sanshirō tries to cheer himself with self-indulgent dreams. He would "do research in the library. Write books, win acclaim. Make his mother happy." The novel ends a year later, when his first year of the university life has come to an end. What will become of Sanshirō now? Is he going to write books in academia, as he first dreamed of doing? Or, like Sōseki, is he going to leave the university behind to write books as a standard-bearer of national literature? I cannot read *Sanshirō* without wondering what the future holds for him.

Writing outside academia, someone like Sanshirō could write books that would enter the chain of "texts to read," at least in Japanese. His language would not need to be cut off from Japanese literary tradition. He would be free to pose urgent questions for which academia had no room: What does the West mean for Japan? Does the Western construct of "Asia" really exist? What is modernity? Indeed, many men besides Sōseki left universities in order to pose these questions, and in the process some became writers, critics, and preeminent public intellectuals.

To be sure, fine Japanese scholars did exist back then, and not just in the natural sciences. Yet they were in the minority. Most Japanese scholars stuck to absorbing Western scholarship, translating it, and introducing it to Japanese readers. A barrage of new ideas arrived almost daily from across the ocean. They had to scramble just to keep up, without the luxury of clarifying how a new idea related to the one before. Those writing outside academia, meanwhile, tried to capture the reality of Japan, a country suddenly confronted by what is often referred to as the "shock of the West," leaving behind the fine writing that still captivates readers today.

THE DISJUNCTION OR "SUDDEN TWIST"

The birth of modern Japanese literature did not come without a price: the "shock of the West" created a deep disjunction in the Japanese literary tradition. Today's Japanese readers cannot browse literature from before 1887, the year Futabatei Shimei began writing *Floating Clouds*. A man only three years Sōseki's senior, Futabatei was thoroughly schooled in Russian, loved its literature, and is considered Japan's first modern novelist and translator of Western literature.

Floating Clouds, which appeared two decades after the Meiji Restoration, was the first work of fiction written in the new prose style of *genbun itchi*, which was closer to spoken language. Born out of translations of Western writings, the *genbun itchi* style emphasizes the referential function of language—how words refer to reality rather than to literary traditions—and thus places importance on representing facts, things, and human thoughts as they "actually" are. Hence the importance of realism. Inevitably, this new prose style entailed change in content as well. *Floating Clouds* has as its protagonist an ordinary clerk, albeit one of the samurai class; it also gives unheard-of prominence to the internal monologue as the feckless protagonist agonizes over his one-sided love. Though *Floating Clouds* still stirs readers, probably more people in the Meiji period read traditional *gesaku* works such as *Agura nabe* (Sitting around the beefpot, 1871), written only sixteen years earlier by Kanagaki Robun (1829–1894). *Agura nabe*, however, is linguistically and thematically a mere curiosity for present-day readers. Anything earlier, no matter how popular or culturally important it may have been, is even more inaccessible now. The disjunction in the Japanese literary tradition is all but unbridgeable.

As a result of this disjunction, the word "modern" (*kindai*) has taken on a peculiar usage in Japanese, one that separates the Western literary tradition from that of Japan (and probably other non-Western countries). In the Western literary tradition, "classical literature" usually designates literature written in Greek and Latin, while "modern literature" remains a vague notion, its meaning shifting depending on the context. Vernacular literature before the advent of print is often called "early modern," but after that, literature is more often divided by century: the eighteenth-century novel, twentieth-century poetry, and so on. Since the establishment of the vernacular as "print language," Western literature has followed more or less a smooth trajectory until the present. There is no clear break that marks the beginning of "modern literature." English-speaking teenagers can pleasurably read Jane Austen's *Pride and Prejudice* (1813) or even Samuel Richardson's *Clarissa* (1748). French people today have no trouble reading a classic like *The Dangerous Liaisons* by Pierre Choderlos de Laclos, first published in 1782, or even *The Princess of Cleves*, going back to 1678, probably written by Madame de Lafayette. German youth can easily dip into Heinrich von Kleist's *Collected Short Stories* (1810–1811) or Johann Wolfgang von Goethe's *The Sorrows of Young Werther* (1774). This is not the case with Japanese literature. "Modern literature" in Japanese designates literature written after the "shock of the West"; the term implies the disjunction created in the Meiji period.

Nowhere is this disjunction more manifest than in the loss of ties with the Chinese literary tradition. To translate the Western languages that were new universal languages, Japanese writers retained the use of Chinese characters but distanced themselves from Chinese literature, which had long been the pillar of their literary tradition. Over time, the number of Chinese-literate Japanese dwindled to a few specialists, and thus Chinese writing in Japan eventually died. Japanese literature was severed from a major part of its past.

Again, no writer better exemplifies the path of literature in Japan's modern era than Sōseki. As we have seen, he became the first to teach English literature in Japanese in a Japanese university. He then left the confines of the university to become a full-time writer, and by so doing he came to symbolize the inevitability of the language of literature surpassing the language of scholarship in conveying an understanding of the world in which the Japanese lived. But Sōseki as a writer symbolizes yet another path that modern Japan had to follow. Because of his lifelong love of the Chinese Classics and his outstanding knowledge of them, he perhaps more than anyone else experienced the disjunction brought on by the "shock of the West" as a personal loss.

In the well-known preface to *Theory of Literature*, Sōseki ruminates on his different emotional connections to Classical Chinese and English literature. Fond of studying the Chinese Classics from a tender age, he eventually yielded to the tenor of the times and devoted himself to studying English literature. But he did so on the assumption that English literature would be similarly rewarding, only to feel "cheated." He writes, "[W]hen I graduated, I was bothered by a notion that lingered at the back of my mind—that somehow I had been cheated by English literature."[4] How was it possible for his "sense of like and dislike between the two to be so widely divergent despite [his] having roughly equal scholarly abilities"[5] in Classical Chinese and English? Why was he so attached to Classical Chinese and so disenchanted with English literature?

In *Grass Pillow* (*Kusamakura*, 1906), which he wrote in roughly the same period, Sōseki compares the poems of Percy Bysshe Shelley with those of the Chinese poetic geniuses Tao Yuanming (365–427) and Wang Wei (655–759), coming to this damning conclusion: "Western poetry . . . however poetic it waxes, scurries over the ground, never forgetting to count its small change." In contrast, he writes, quite predictably, that Eastern poetry is "emancipated from the worldly." Sōseki repeatedly professes his aversion to English literature—and the English language—around the same time, perhaps because that literature symbolized certain personal disappointments: the unpleasant-ness of his stay in London, the proprietary airs of foreigners in Japan, his need to teach English to make a living. In a letter he wrote after quitting the university, he declares, "If I cannot make a living, I will become anything, even a dog. Teaching English is about the same as barking like a dog, so I'll do it if I have to. It was through a misfortune that I began to study English."[6]

And yet, despite his avowed distaste for the world of English letters, Sōseki's own novels swiftly departed from Chinese tradition, coming more to resemble Western novels. *The Poppy* (*Gubijinsō*, 1907), which he wrote shortly after leaving the university, was written with constant reference to an ancient anthology of Chinese poetry. Heavily Sinicized, classical, and ornate, it is also the work of Sōseki's that was most popular during his lifetime. In contrast, his final, unfinished novel *Light and Dark*, written some ten years on, shows the greatest influence of the West both in its plot and in its use of language, one example of the latter being the repetitive use of personal pronouns equivalent to "he" and "she"—which, amazing as it may seem to Westerners, did not ex-ist in premodern Japanese. The main character is a man about twenty years younger than Sōseki, someone who "could not read books dense with noth-ing but square, multistroke characters"—in other words, a man no longer ca-pable of appreciating Chinese literature. While Sōseki's own life was imbued with a deep familiarity with the Chinese Classics, he was well aware that a generation of Japanese quite different from him was emerging. And he is still read today precisely because, seeing the inevitability of that historical change, he wrote novel after novel for readers who, like his own protagonist, were los-ing touch forever with the Chinese literary tradition, with "books dense with nothing but square, multistroke characters."

Indeed, Japanese readers today, including Sōseki scholars, mostly read Sōseki's later novels. Those novels offer no clue about how closely entwined Sōseki's life was to the Classical Chinese literary tradition, quite unlike the lives of today's readers. While Sōseki was writing *Light and Dark*, after work-ing in the morning he would spend his afternoons composing Chinese poetry to escape what he saw as the all-too-mundane world of the novel. During his lifetime, he not only wrote a considerable number of Chinese poems but, following the Chinese literati tradition, practiced calligraphy and painting as well (though his painting was not very good). Any Japanese museum-goer who encounters Sōseki's Chinese calligraphy and poetry in the original is bound to be brought up short. Despite his beloved place in our hearts, despite his towering stature in Japanese literature, a portion of Sōseki's oeuvre close to *his* heart is illegible to Japanese people today.

When I contemplate the distance between the literary culture that Sōseki lived in and our own, I am struck by the loneliness he must have felt. It is the loneliness of the writer who knows that his readers will never share the same world that he lives in, never share the same culture that he is part of. It is the very loneliness experienced to some degree by all Japanese people of Sōseki's time.

In a public talk, "Gendai Nihon no kaika" (The development of contemporary Japan), Sōseki describes the cultural transformation Japan had to go through as a "sudden twist [*kyokusetsu*]." According to him, the development within the West was "internally driven," that in Japan "externally driven." He argues that although in the past Japan certainly developed under the influence of Korea and China, that influence was of a nature that prompted gradual, internally driven development. In contrast, the "shock of the West" experienced by modern Japan was of unprecedented magnitude, forcing on Japan a "sudden twist":

> *From that moment on, Japan's development took a sudden twist. It experienced a shock so great that it could not help but do so.* To use the phrase that I used earlier, Japan until then had been internally driven but suddenly lost the power of self-determination and, pushed by external forces, had no choice but to do as it was told. . . . Since Japan probably cannot exist as Japan without forever being pushed in the way it is today, there is no other way to put this than being externally driven.[7] (Emphasis added)

Sōseki concludes in a slightly comical tone: "Call us unfortunate, call us wretched or what you will—we Japanese have fallen into one hell of a predicament." But in fact, it was not only Japan that was forced to go through this type of "externally driven" development.

It was a drama that continued in all the non-Western regions throughout the twentieth century and that continues to this day. Since the fifteenth century, with the advancement of maritime technology, and on through the age of colonialism, externally driven development spread through the non-Western world and is now omnipresent under the name of "globalization." Beginning over one hundred years ago, modern Japanese literature told this narrative from the non-Western standpoint—a narrative that will likely continue to be told in various parts of the world.

THE MIRACLE OF MODERN JAPANESE LITERATURE

What a fascinating body of literature emerged in Japan, though, precisely as a result of what Sōseki calls the "sudden twist"! The first prerequisite for fine literature is that the writer must see the language not as a transparent medium for self-expression or the representation of reality, but as a medium one must struggle with to make it do one's bidding. Japan's historical "twist" forced—condemned—Japanese writers to struggle with their language in ways they had never imagined. Using the tragedy of the twist as a launching pad to come up with a new language that could capture the new Japan, they traced their language back over a thousand years, examining each and every word as in a treasure hunt and exploring all the possibilities that the language possessed.

In the early years of modern Japanese literature, all writers—including those not endowed with a particularly great gift—were forced to address the issue of language. And in so doing, they produced a body of literature that often seems to transcend the individual writer—one in which layers of tradition sing in mesmerizing polyphony.

The new *genbun itchi* prose flourished in many variations. At one end of the spectrum, there initially was even a surge of heavily Sinicized writing, exuding manliness, which befitted the newly found ground for political discussion, heroically exhorting freedom and civil rights. At the other end of the spectrum were the writings based on hiragana—the "women's hand"—where the use of ideograms was sparse; stylistically these ran the gamut, by turns feminine, innocent, elegant, colloquial, or vulgar, often treating the imported concept of romantic love. Whether it took the form of a novel or an essay, all prose could draw from the various tones in between these disparate styles. There was also a brief reaction against the *genbun itchi* movement, reviving the language of the literary height of the Edo period—the seventeenth-century Genroku era—and reconnecting readers to that bygone era in a new way.

Poetry thrived, too. Stimulated by the *genbun itchi* prose, which aspired to realism, both *waka* and haiku poetry also tried to depict the "real," rather than engage in intertextual play with tradition, and in doing so experienced a golden renaissance. Free verse joined the parade. Katakana, which had been closely associated with Chinese characters, came almost overnight to represent the sounds of Western loanwords, transforming itself into a chic set of letters that reeked of the West. The more one sprinkled Western loanwords using katakana in one's writing, the more modern one sounded. Meanwhile, translations of Western works ended up with a marked style, often quite distinct from that of works written originally in Japanese; even today when Japanese read translations, they tend to shift modes of reading, like a driver shifting gears at the wheel of a car. I know of no Western literature that has mixed such a diverse array of writing systems and literary traditions and, moreover, so clearly retained the historical marks of each of them, so that layers of different heritages are visible on almost every page.

To be sure, of the astonishing quantity of literature published since *Floating Clouds*, not all is of fine quality. Full-length novels that deserve to be called masterpieces are rare; unlike their Western counterparts, Japanese writers generally do not excel in constructing a fictional universe that stands on its own. Yet the corpus of modern Japanese literature is filled with such diverse linguistic and literary wonderment that it is a true embarrassment of riches. It is also filled with "truths" visible only through the Japanese language—in passages often highly resistant to translation. Foreigners who tackle them in Japanese may at first be baffled, but the deeper they delve into the treasure house of modern Japanese literature, the more certain they are to be captivated by the discovery of just how perversely complex and generously all-encompassing a written language can be.

And to think that modern Japanese literature might never have existed! Its path was perilous. Only a precarious combination of historical conditions—conditions largely beyond the control of the Japanese people—allowed it to blossom. What else to call the rise of modern Japanese literature but a miracle?

FORGETTING THE ORIGINS

National literature, just like national language, is established through the forgetting of its origins. It is true in the case of modern Japanese literature as well. The new kind of Japanese, which was written by and read among intellectuals during the early years of Japan's modernity and was to become the medium of Japanese literature, was obviously different from the written Japanese circulating in everyday life. Reading it must have felt somehow awkward, foreign, and pretentious to ordinary people, like eating with knives and forks instead of chopsticks. Only in the mid-Taishō era did the language used in newspapers shift from the traditional literary style to the new *genbun itchi* style, prose that was closer to the spoken language. And it was probably well into the Shōwa period that this new style of written language, through compulsory education, newspapers, and magazines, no longer seemed foreign even to people whose lives had nothing to do with universities: farmers, factory workers, shop owners.

As the written language that ordinary people used in writing diaries and letters became more similar to the new language, and as that new language became the norm, the origins of modern Japanese literature itself—the fact that it was initiated through acts of translation by bilinguals who had studied Western languages in universities—were quickly forgotten. Some people today may know that Akutagawa Ryūnosuke (1892–1927), who wrote in a particularly modernistic style, read an astounding amount of English at an astounding speed: he is rumored to have finished *War and Peace* in English in just four days. But few realize that Ozaki Kōyō (1868–1903), known for an ornate, "reactionary" style reminiscent of Genroku-era literature, was no less avid a reader of novels in English. It thus caused a stir in 2000 when his most famous work, *The Gold Demon* (*Konjiki yasha*, 1887), was proved to be an adaptation of an American dime novel.[8] How many are aware that Nakazato Kaizan (1885–1944), known for his long Buddhist novel *Daibosatsu tōge* (Bodhisattva pass, 1913), was an avid reader of Victor Hugo in English translation? Or that Osaragi Jirō (1897–1973), author of the swashbuckling Kurama tengu series (1924–1959), started writing to pay off his debt to Maruzen, a bookstore that specializes in imported books?

To reflect back on the origin of modern Japanese literature is itself incompatible with the "ideology of national language," which claims that national literature, written in one's own language, is an outpouring of the writer's inner soul, a direct expression of what he or she saw, felt, and imagined. No deliberate suppression was needed. Rather, forgetting the origins of modern Japanese literature was an unconscious process that ended inevitably in obfuscation and oblivion. The process accelerated as the spoken and written languages converged. The normative spoken language, initially forced on people through compulsory education in the Meiji period, began to spread uncoerced with the proliferation of radios and later television sets; it spread rapidly from living room to living room, over mountains and across rivers and prefectural borders. It is no wonder that the Japanese people came to feel as if their language was something they were born with and came to embrace their national literature as a natural manifestation of who they were.

Being bilingual no longer mattered. Many fine works—masterpieces, some of them—began appearing from writers who could not be considered bilinguals. Monolingual writers eventually became the majority.

The triumph of the Japanese language as truly the people's language could not be better exemplified than by a longtime best seller first published in 1958: Yasumoto Sueko's *Ni-anchan* (My second brother, 1958). The diary of a preadolescent ethnic Korean girl, it depicts her everyday life with her three siblings in a Kyushu mining town. Though orphaned and destitute, the four of them help one another to somehow complete their schooling, her older brother even managing to be often at the top of the class. The style is simplicity itself. "One should write as one sees and feels; therefore, even those who have not read much can also write"—that is the view of language underpinning the ideology of national language. Such a view of language ends up flooding the world with pap, but it sometimes also allows a child with a beautiful mind to produce a gem. The power of the ideology of national language reached an apex, in Japanese, in writing by this girl of Korean nationality. Having read *Ni-anchan* over and over during grade school, as an adult I have kept questioning whether my own writing could possibly move the reader with similar force.

Indeed, the one hundred years since the Meiji Restoration were years in which modern Japanese literature spread to, and blossomed in, every corner of Japan. These were years when public education expanded and literacy grew, even among the poorest of the poor. They were also years when books became more and more affordable, including translations. Western-style leather-bound books were once a symbol of wealth, but by the end of the Taishō period, cloth-bound, mass-produced books that sold for only one yen per copy became popular in multivolume collections. Literary collections appeared in quick succession and in all sorts of variations, from Japanese novels to translated novels, for young adults or children or even aimed specifically at girls, like the set I read avidly as a child. Paperback versions followed, making a literary masterpiece as affordable as a bowl of noodles.

Japanese, moreover, were fortunate to enjoy a century of peaceful daily life, fecund ground for literature to flourish. Although the country turned other nations into battlefields and pillaged them in war, not until the end of World War II did its own land come under fire. Even after total defeat in World War II, Japan eventually enjoyed not only peace but also rapid economic growth. The number of people who attained higher education further expanded, books became even more affordable, and multivolume collections of all kinds circulated. Virtually the entire population read literature madly, not only Japanese works but a wide array of world classics by everyone from Strindberg to Borges. Japan became a nation so literary that it would have been the envy of all literature-loving people of the world—if only they had known! (Japanese literature finally attracted the world's attention in 1968, exactly one hundred years after the Meiji Restoration, when Kawabata Yasunari was awarded the Nobel Prize in Literature.)

Reading engenders the desire to write. The notion of democracy that Japanese people eagerly embraced after World War II gave further impetus to that desire: every individual should be able not only to read but to *write* fine literature. More and more venues opened so that anyone could become a writer who so desired and was not totally devoid of talent. Aspiring writers from all walks of life got together and self-published coterie magazines called *dōjin-shi* (literally, "magazines for the like-minded"), usually cheaply printed on flimsy paper. These sprang up like mushrooms after the rain. Established publishers with their own monthly literary journals featured not only renowned authors but also those just making names for themselves. Authors awarded newcomer prizes gained full recognition as writing professionals on winning the prestigious Akutagawa Prize; after that, by continuing to receive a succession of yet more important prizes, they went on to gain expert status. Literary awards proliferated until literally hundreds of them existed, covering every conceivable genre and age-group. In time they spread a wide and tight-knit net over the country that generously rewarded every literary talent, however slight. The ideal world where every individual is both a reader and writer of literature had already materialized in Japan, well before the advent of our "utopian" Internet age of blogs and fan fiction. Yet, however idyllic that world may have been, underneath the surface modern Japanese literature was indeed, in the words of Professor Hirota, "headed for a fall."

6. ENGLISH AND NATIONAL LANGUAGES

IN THE INTERNET AGE

THE PHRASE "THE END OF LITERATURE" IS NOW A CLICHÉ. AND IT HAS BEEN A CLICHÉ, NOT ONLY IN JAPAN BUT ALL over the world, for half a century if not longer. Yet in recent years, voices bewailing the end of literature are gaining new urgency. Fewer and fewer people read literature deserving of the name; even the classics, novels once considered must-reads, are increasingly shunned. In this chapter I will start by departing from Japan to examine what the end of literature might mean for all concerned.

Laments about the end of literature can no longer be dismissed as the pastime of old fogies who have nothing better to do than reminisce fondly about "the good old days." These laments come amid three significant historical changes that have indubitably weakened the status of literature: the advancement of science, the diversification of cultural goods, and the spread of mass consumer society. These factors affect people's behavior where literature is concerned—their literary reading habits—now as never before.

Let us begin with the advancement of science. Today, people who wish to explore the eternal question that haunts the human race—what is a human being?—are turning increasingly to the latest scientific advances, particularly in fields such as genetics and brain science. The more personal question—who am I?—can also be answered to a significant degree with a DNA test or a brain scan. Scientists can objectively measure our likelihood of becoming an alcoholic or our sensitivity to others' pain. The growing importance of science is manifest in universities around the world that are relentlessly downsizing the humanities, especially literature.

Second is the diversification of cultural goods. By "cultural goods," I mean products that function at once as art and entertainment. At one time, seeing famous paintings and sculptures entailed traveling long distances, listening to music meant attending live performances, and only city dwellers could enjoy the theater regularly. For most people, by far the most accessible cultural goods were books, especially novels. Printed books gradually fulfilled their potential as mass products and came to be widely spread among the population. In retrospect, the golden age of national language and of the novel, from the latter half of the eighteenth century to the beginning of the twentieth, was the time when novels monopolized the market of cultural goods.

Within the last hundred years, however, new technology has led to the emergence of other mass-produced cultural goods. In the first half of the twentieth century came records, radio, and film, followed by television, videos, CDs, DVDs, video games, music downloads, streamed videos, and more. Particularly significant as cultural goods competing with novels are films and television dramas. In addition to stimulating our audiovisual senses, these cultural goods explore the meaning of human life and thus, like novels, address the question of how one should live. Dethroned, the novel has become merely one of many affordable mass-produced commodities.

All this was compounded by the emergence of the third factor, a mass consumer society. Ever since the written language became a cultural good that circulates in the form of books, every book has had two different values. On the one hand is its "intrinsic value"—how it enriches humanity in the long run—and on the other hand is its "market value." Even the Gutenberg Bible, as Marshall McLuhan and Benedict Anderson so rightly inform us, circulated not only as a sacred text but also as the first "mass-produced industrial commodity."

In a mass consumer society, the relationship between those two values becomes more and more arbitrary, for when it comes to affordable cultural goods, what sells is simply what the greatest number of people prefer. Someone who passionately loves a certain tea bowl favored by Sen no Rikyū, the famous seventeenth-century tea ceremony master, will probably have to settle for one that resembles it. Rikyū tea bowls are only for museums. But when it comes to affordable cultural goods, those replicable on a mass scale, things are different. Fans of Maria Callas's rendering of "O mio babbino caro," say, or Dean Martin's "Mambo Italiano" don't have to consult their wallets and resign themselves to buying a recording of somebody else singing it instead; all are equally affordable. People who choose differently do so not in resignation but out of preference. In the case of affordable cultural goods, sales are a direct reflection of consumer preference. And obviously, what sells the most does not necessarily reflect genuine discernment.

Art is not democratic. Art is sublime.

As consumerism increases, the disconnect between intrinsic value and market value only becomes more pronounced. In a full-fledged mass consumer society, information itself, along with cultural goods, becomes inexpensive—indeed virtually free, and thus ubiquitous. Everyone—rich or poor, aristocratic or common, highly educated or sadly ignorant—shares more or less the same information through the mass media, from newspapers to viral videos. In such a society, everyone, perhaps even royalty, forms part of the masses and ends up contributing to the craze and whirl of the mass phenomenon. Consumers inevitably know what book others are buying, knowledge that often prompts them to rush out and buy the same book, which, in turn, prompts still others to do the same. If this chain reaction gains enough momentum, it can trigger a mass phenomenon in which some books sell at an explosive rate—like the Harry Potter series.

A number of factors combined to make the Harry Potter series an unprecedented global marketing success. For one thing, the series was written in English. For another, it became a best seller in the United States. And it is certainly a product with its share of charm. Yet none of this can really explain why the books became the biggest sellers in history, sought by everyone from English aristocrats with libraries built up over generations to families in the burgeoning Asian middle class purchasing a children's book for the first time. Only the snowball effect characteristic of a mass phenomenon can adequately explain the worldwide lightning success of the Harry Potter books.

Theoretically, a book that becomes such a global phenomenon might be of any quality. It might even be a fine work of literature. More likely, it will leave much to be desired, for to spawn such frenzy, it must reach precisely those people who are not in the habit of reading. The sight of stacks upon stacks of best-selling books whose market value far outstrips their intrinsic value makes discriminating readers viscerally aware of the end of literature.

AND YET IT IS UNLIKELY THAT LITERATURE, BROADLY DEFINED to include works of philosophy and religion, will ever come to an end. None of the historical changes that have weakened literature can possibly end it.

The advancement of science will never bring about the end of literature. It will only clearly define the realm beyond which science cannot provide answers and the realm that literature takes on as its proper task: the realm of meaning. Science may explain how humans came into being, but it has no answer to the slippery question of how humans should live. Only literature makes it possible to pose such questions in the first place. And if there is no answer, only literature can point to the impossibility of ever finding one.

Second, even if literature becomes just one of many inexpensive cultural goods, it will not come to an end. Most of us find it rather ridiculous that there are people who, after seeing a film, would eagerly pick up a "novelization" of the film. There are even people who, after seeing a film based on a novel, would pick up not the original but the novelization. Such an act seems like a profanation of literature, but it is just the opposite. It proves that however unsophisticated readers may be, there are still things they want to understand through written words, still pleasures they know they can gain no other way. Reading offers levels of understanding and dimensions of pleasure that other media simply cannot.

Finally, even amid accelerating mass consumerism, literature will not come to an end. Plenty of people are and will continue to be born with an ability to appreciate good art if given the opportunity, and the same holds true for literature. No matter how many dime-a-dozen books inundate the market, there will always be those people who want to read good literature— "the Happy Few" in the words of Stendhal, one of my favorite novelists.

Nonetheless, what is troubling, what seems ominous even, for those of us whose mother tongue is not English, is that we have entered the age of English. One or two hundred years from now, what will have become of literature in other languages? Entering the age of English means reentering the linguistic double structure of the universal and the local that covered different regions of Earth before the emergence of national languages. But this time, English will be the one and the only universal language—and will remain so for a long time.

THE INTERNET

This is perhaps a good juncture to bring the Internet into our discussion. We cannot talk about the reemergence of the linguistic double structure without taking into consideration the advent of this technology. With the rise of the Internet, the English language has further secured its status as the universal language par excellence. This is not to say that other languages will eventually disappear from the Internet. Far from it. When the U.S.-invented technology made its first appearance, only English circulated on the Web, yet soon all manner of languages joined in. Among them were some that had been denied their rightful place in the world—languages suppressed by the nation-state, languages overshadowed by neighboring powerful languages, even languages on the verge of extinction because they had no written form. The Internet made it possible for all those obscure languages to circulate, making people embrace the new medium as a tool for multilingualism. There is no contradiction between the dominance of English on the Internet and the diversification of languages that circulate on the Internet, for English and other languages circulate on different levels.

Let us imagine a library that allows us to access all existing texts in the world—a Library with a capital L. Since the founding of the ancient library of Alexandria in the third century B.C.E., humanity has long dreamed of a library that would contain all the books of the world—an ultimate Library to store all of human knowledge. Thanks to the Internet, that dream is now being realized. Tools like scanning, search engines, and cloud storage are enabling the Internet to whisk us to an age in which, at almost no cost we can instantly access any and all texts that have been turned into digitized data—in fact, all cultural heritage. All we need is a screen. We humans are an ungrateful lot who quickly attune ourselves to new technological worlds; thus the idea of the Library no longer fascinates us. Yet when it first came into being nearly ten years ago, it was received with much excitement. People were agog and eagerly discussed what it would be like to live in this new world, a paradise of knowledge, a utopia of information.

On May 14, 2006, the *New York Times Magazine* carried a long and much debated article called "Scan This Book!" dealing with the Library, which author Kevin Kelly, a founder of the computer magazine *Wired*, calls the "universal library." While the second half of the article takes up copyright issues expected to emerge when the Library actually materializes, the first half is an enthusiastic depiction of how rapidly it is evolving and how wonderful it will be when completed.

According to Kelly, the human race took its first step toward establishing the Library in December 2004, when Google announced that it would collaborate with five principal libraries in the United States and Britain to digitize all the books in their collections, place them in a single database, and make them accessible from anywhere in the world. This project is officially called the Google Book Search Library Project, but here I will call it simply the Google Library Project. Two years later, at the time of the article's publication, Stanford University Libraries had already scanned eight million books, using a state-of-the-art robot made in Switzerland, at the rate of a thousand pages per hour. Other universities and companies had begun similar projects. Carnegie Mellon University was shipping its books to China and India to have them scanned there; Amazon had already scanned several hundred thousand books. Today, millions of books throughout the world are being scanned and digitized without cease.

Kelly says the Library will eventually carry not just books but also newspapers and magazines; reproductions of visual arts such as paintings, sculptures, and photographs; not to mention films, music recordings, radio and television programs, commercials, and of course personal videos. Also included will be Web pages or blog posts that no longer appear online. The list of items that will enter the Library is limitless, and here is how Kelly portrays this information utopia:

> From the days of Sumerian clay tablets till now, humans have "published" at least 32 million books, 750 million articles and essays, 25 million songs, 500 million images, 500,000 movies, 3 million videos, TV shows and short films and 100 billion public Web pages. All this material is currently contained in all the libraries and archives of the world. When fully digitized, the whole lot could be compressed (at current technological rates) onto 50 petabyte hard disks. Today you need a building about the size of a small-town library to house 50 petabytes. With tomorrow's technology, it will all fit onto your iPod. When that happens, the library of all libraries will ride in your purse or wallet—if it doesn't plug directly into your brain with thin white cords.

Needless to say, all information will be interlinked. With the swipe of a finger, you will be able to link to everything ever written about "petabytes," and then with another click, link to everything written on everything you encountered in the course of learning about petabytes. (The Internet informs me that a gigabyte is 2^{30}, a terabyte is 2^{40}, and a petabyte is 2^{50}.) Thus the chain of information expands infinitely—an idea already familiar to us.

Meanwhile, new technologies that make the Internet even more useful and interesting pop up almost daily; the Internet is now almost like a part of our natural environment. The same is true with the notion of the Library. It now seems only too logical that such a Library should exist. Yet there is one consequence of these developments that Kelly does not properly examine: how people's way of accessing the Library will further affect our use of language. I will not discuss the controversial issue of intellectual property that he raises. Nor will I discuss how easy it has proved to be for some governments to abuse the power of the Internet by boldly blocking certain information or secretly invading people's privacy. What I want to do is to refocus our attention on the question of written language.

Kelly is full of enthusiasm as he discusses the revolutionary nature of what he calls the universal library. Until now, those with easy access to a library of any scale have been privileged, often the residents of college towns or big cities. But no more: "[U]nlike the libraries of old, which were restricted to the elite, this library would be truly democratic, offering every book to every person." Once the universal library is realized, those who benefit the most will be the underprivileged—Kelly calls them the "underbooked"—billions around the world who do not have access to books in their physical form. "It is these underbooked—students in Mali, scientists in Kazakhstan, elderly people in Peru—whose lives will be transformed when even the simplest unadorned version of the universal library is placed in their hands." All this sounds quite wonderful. Yet a critical question has not been asked.

In what language, really, will these people, "students in Mali, scientists in Kazakhstan, elderly people in Peru," access this universal library? In Kelly's long article, there are only two places that touch on the question of language. And both of them simply mention that the universal library will contain "all languages." Kelly's goodwill toward the underbooked is admirable, but here again, I am astounded by the naïveté of someone highly intelligent whose mother tongue is English—someone who is not condemned to reflect on language.

To be sure, one day the Library will come to contain "the entire works of humankind, from the beginning of recorded history, in all languages, available to all people, all the time." Yet when Kelly wrote these words, it is unlikely that he meant literally that we will all be able to access the "entire works of humankind" by reading "all languages." More likely, he just assumed that the universal library would include all the languages that people, including the underbooked, could read, and stopped there.

Yes, no matter what your native tongue is, the Library/Internet allows you to see human pictorial, sculptural, and architectural accomplishments around the world: cave paintings in Altamira, statues in Angkor Wat, a mosque in the Alhambra. It also allows you to listen to musical accomplishments from Gregorian chant to the gamelan to Gershwin. People can all appreciate, to varying degrees, whatever appeals to their own visual and auditory senses. Language, however, is a different matter. Unless people can read it, written language is meaningless—a mere collection of dots and squiggles. Even if the universal library were to materialize tomorrow, people could use it to enter only the library of the particular language they can read. The Library will hold a great number of isolated libraries walled off by tall barriers of language. The towering exception will be the library in the English language—a library accessible not only to native speakers but also to a growing number of bilinguals for whom English is an "external language." It is inevitable that the English library will function on a different level from all the rest.

The virtually unfathomable naïveté of those whose mother tongue is English is further revealed in Kelly's reference to a similar project that is concurrently taking place in China. From the way Kelly describes the Chinese project, it seems as if the two great powers of the twenty-first century are engaged in a similar adventure. Yet their situations are quite different if you think twice about it. According to Kelly, a Chinese company called Superstar has already scanned all the books from two hundred libraries in China; this includes "1.3 million unique titles in China, which [Superstar] estimates is about half of all the books published in the Chinese language since 1949." Chinese libraries may have quickly accumulated an impressive number of books from abroad in recent years, but given the country's history, one could hardly expect these libraries to be comparable to those that participated in the Google Library Project from the outset: the libraries of Stanford, Harvard, Michigan, and Oxford, as well as the New York Public Library. Moreover, a preponderance of the books will be in Mandarin—the language with the greatest number of speakers, but not a universal language. As for "1.3 million unique titles" published in Mandarin *since 1949*—that is, since the establishment of Communist rule—what can we say? The Google Library Project will likely result in a library accessed by bilinguals from all over the world, including China. In contrast, it is all too evident that Superstar will become a library used by hardly anyone other than the Chinese—or scholars who specialize in China.

Moreover, in the age of the Internet, when it comes to making a library useful for those who seek knowledge, content is only half the story. The English-language library, which may already be the world's richest, will grow still richer as an increasing number of nonnative speakers begin to write in English. But this utopia will also be a nightmare of flooding information. Science may one day extend the average human life expectancy to 120 years, but even so, human life is ephemeral. Given our limited time, we need to know what books are more worth reading than others. For seekers of knowledge, the question is urgent. The Library will therefore have to excel in its rating system, its ability to inform users which are the "texts to read."

Unlike Latin, English has the double function of being at once a universal and a national language. As in libraries of other national languages, most items that enter the English-language library via the Internet probably will be no more than "chats." Yet the English library, as the library of a universal language, will be accessed by seekers of knowledge from all over the world. Hence the imperative for it to come up with a rating system of the highest rigor, one of a completely different order from a mere popularity contest. Such a ranking system will have to renew itself continually; a ranking system of ranking systems will thus also have to emerge. English-language readers, whether bilinguals or English-only monoglots, will then be able to enjoy an unparalleled feast.

Wait, an idealist might say. Just because someone is a non-English-reading monoglot, that is no reason for him or her to be deprived of access to the English library with all its advantages; in fact, we can make the Internet truly open to the world: we can make it possible for *all people to read all languages.* The logical solution, our idealist will say, is machine translation of natural languages. The task has proved to be far more difficult than originally envisioned, but people's efforts are slowly bearing fruit. Computer translation will no doubt become increasingly useful in the future, especially for translations between related languages. To think, however, that it will someday replace human translators is just as unrealistic as to think that the spread of audiovisual technology will someday make live musical performances passé.

Machine translation will always have severe limitations. When I consider the distance that separates English and Japanese, I can think of any number of reasons why asking a machine to bridge it would be like asking the sun to rise from the west. Let me just name two fundamental obstacles to machine translation of literature. First is the rhetorical function of language, a function that is essential to all natural languages and can be best summed up as "saying one thing and meaning another." Whether a phrase is used rhetorically can be determined only by understanding the author's intended meaning in context. "How can you translate with a machine?" an author might write. Is he asking a straightforward question? Or is he scoffing at the impossibility of machine translation? An automatic translation machine cannot be trusted to come up with a translation of that sentence in which the authorial intention is clear. Second, and perhaps even more important, a text that is translated by a machine simply cannot provide pleasure for the reader, and a text devoid of pleasure for the reader is simply not a real text. No one would actually *read* it.

However sophisticated machine translation becomes, it is unlikely that any translation device will hinder the increasing circulation of English as the universal language of the Internet. Added to this is the fact that English is the universal language of Internet technology itself: it is its *metalanguage*. People from all over the world inevitably find it easier to use English when communicating about the Internet.

FROM ACADEMIA TO LITERATURE

The dominance of English is most keenly felt in academia. There was no behind-the-scenes agreement among scholars of the world, nor was there any conspiracy on the part of native English speakers. Rather, the very nature of scholarship is gradually and inevitably unifying academic language into English. That various disciplines have become increasingly mathematicized in recent years is accelerating this shift even further.

Of the universities in the English-speaking world, top American universities today are in a class all their own. With its history as an immigrant nation, the United States has drawn talented scholars from the world over. Of the twenty universities reputed to be the world's best, seventeen are in the United States; 70 percent of Nobel laureates have taught or are teaching in American universities. The spread of the Internet, however, will bring about a change in the opposite direction, for there will be less need for scholars to be physically concentrated in English-speaking regions. Already some American universities are building branch campuses overseas in non-English-speaking regions, while top universities in those regions are beginning to conduct some of their courses in English. Just as universities scattered around Europe once became centers of learning through Latin, so now universities scattered around the world are on their way to becoming centers of learning through English.

The shift to English is naturally taking place at a much faster pace in the natural sciences. Yet, given the nature of scholarship, this linguistic shift is inevitable in other fields as well, such as the social sciences and humanities— two fields in which the permeation of English is sometimes already visible. This change will entail unexpected consequences, making even "sacred texts" in academia circulate in English.

Going back to the difference between "textbook" and "text," and the two kinds of "truths" existing in the world, Aristotle, as mentioned before, continues to be read today precisely because his writings are also texts that cannot be reduced to a textbook. To understand Aristotle, one must ultimately go back to his texts. In years to come, specialists in Greek philosophy will surely continue to read Aristotle in Greek. Yet as more scholars in social sciences and humanities begin to write in English, they will increasingly quote Aristotle in English from the translations they think are the best, making these translated texts circulate as new authoritative texts. The oldest extant text of the New Testament is in Greek, the universal language of the Mediterranean civilization at the time, but when the New Testament spread to western Europe, it did so as a Latin text. Similarly, Buddhist scriptures were originally handed down in Pali and Sanskrit, the universal languages of India at the time, but they spread in the Sinosphere as Chinese texts. Such is the power of the universal language, then and now. A growing number of canonical texts will begin to circulate in English in academia.

And there is no reason that what is already taking place in academia should not gradually affect how we look at our ultimate text—our literature. At some point in history, humans created national languages. With the arrival of an age that celebrated national languages, people began to look up to literature and see it as a conveyer of higher truths than scholarly knowledge. Today that age may be coming to an end. We who have learned to read and write *in our own language* are no longer what we were. We have become deeply attached to reading and writing in our own language. Nonetheless, when one's own language circulates concurrently with a universal language in society, and when it is apparent that the latter is gaining force, an ever greater number of knowledge seekers will become bilinguals. In the process, how these bilinguals engage with their literature will inevitably be affected, which in turn will inevitably affect their literature—and their language. For the fall of language is first set in motion when these bilinguals unknowingly begin to read English and their own language on two different levels.

Let us bear in mind the essentially asymmetrical relationship between the act of reading and the act of writing. Writing in an "external language" requires an effort that most people would find too burdensome; most people have other business to attend to besides learning how to write in English. These bilinguals will continue to write e-mails and blogs in their own language. The fall of a language is set in motion when such people *begin to take more seriously what they read in English*. It is set in motion when, for example, they turn to English-language media to learn about critical international events—they may or may not be conscious of the Anglophone bias there—and use the media of their own country only to find out the results of home sports games or follow home celebrity gossip. It is set in motion when they hurry to order a heavyweight English-language book attracting media attention before it comes out in translation, while neglecting fine books written in their own language. (Watching American or British television dramas rather than their own is not unconnected to this process.) Finally, it is set in motion when, because they have gradually become accustomed to making light of what is written in their own language, bilinguals start taking their own country's literature less seriously than literature written in English—especially the classics of English literature, which are evolving into the universal canon.

A vicious cycle then begins. The more palpable this trend becomes, the more non-English writers would feel that writing in their own language will not reach the readers they are aiming for. To make matters worse, this would be correspondingly truer for writers who take their writing seriously. Without a trusted readership, those writers would have less and less incentive to write in their own language, and there would be fewer and fewer texts worth reading in that language. Through the process of negative selection, writers who continue writing in their own language would be those whose books do not deserve to be called texts. They would write books that are read one day and forgotten the next. This cycle, once it began, could only gain in force. Not only bilinguals but true readers of literature—not mere consumers of books—would eventually cease to expect their own language to bear the intellectual, ethical, and aesthetic burdens it once did.

Literature in the broad sense of the term will never come to an end. Yet now in the age of English we face the possibility that, depending on how people treat their national languages, some countries' literature may witness a gradual fall. What was once a national language may be reduced to nothing more than a local language; a national literature, to nothing more than a local literature that no discriminating person takes seriously.

SŌSEKI: WHAT IF HE WERE ALIVE TODAY?

A sad fate might be in store for someone like Natsume Sōseki in the age of English.

In the past, when Europe's three principal national languages still circulated as universal languages, Japanese scholars in the humanities faced a huge

linguistic challenge. Many felt pressured to learn all three, as if they themselves were European—this on top of reading Chinese, their legacy from the
past. Some even went so far as to learn Greek and Latin in an attempt to capture the soul of Europe. And yet Japan's immense physical and psychological
distance from the West, combined with the "ideology of national language,"
meant that hardly any of them attempted to write in Western languages. The
state of academics that Sōseki portrayed in *Sanshirō* did not change in essence for nearly a hundred years, although the phenomenal accumulation
of translations greatly lessened the need to read original texts quite as avidly.
Forced to be content with translating and introducing new Western scholarship to their compatriots, Japanese scholars would cross the ocean once in
their lifetime to visit the Western scholar whose works they had studied, have
their photograph taken next to him all smiles, shake the great man's hand,
and return to Japan.

Now in the age of English, Japanese scholars are finally free from the pressure of modeling themselves after multilingual European scholars of the past.
Now a single foreign language—English—will do. Even scholars in the humanities have finally begun to write in English, rare though the instances still
may be. For the first time, this small number of scholars is making a transition from being mere translators on the sidelines to being real players in the
game: what they write can finally enter the chain of the world's "texts to read."
The transformation now taking place within Japanese academia is still largely
ignored by the general public, but in time it will likely be too obvious to miss.
Even when writing about Japan, the more important the subject, the more
meaningful it will be to write in English.

This is not necessarily good news for either the Japanese language or the
Japanese people.

History is full of irony. A century and a half ago, Japanese universities
served as major institutions for translation and transformed the Japanese language into a suitable vehicle for the pursuit of scholarship. Today, in the age of
English, universities are inviting back foreigners to give courses in English. In
some instances, even Japanese professors are being assigned to give courses
in English. Within the top echelons of academia, Japanese is slowly turning
into a second-class language.

A new challenge, no less frustrating than the previous one, awaits Japanese scholars in the humanities. For the difficulty of writing in an "external language" is proportionate to how different that external language is
to one's mother tongue. It is no easy task for a Japanese scholar to write a

"text" in English, one that conveys truths irreducible to and irreplaceable by "textbooks."

What of the unusually gifted scholar? Let us reimagine Natsume Sōseki as our contemporary and try to envision the path he might follow if he were born today. First, let us establish his credentials as a passionate seeker of knowledge. Like Fukuzawa Yukichi—who hardly slept properly while learning Dutch, who grasped the importance of electricity as soon as he saw an entry on it in a Dutch book, who had the grit to start all over with English as soon as he saw the uselessness of Dutch—Sōseki was a knowledge seeker of the first rank. He truly wanted to know everything there was to know. His two-and-a-half-year stay in London gave him for the first time in his life unlimited access to newly published books in English, and hence to the most recent research in diverse fields. He concluded soon after his arrival that attending classes was a waste of time; he spent nearly all his money buying books, shut himself up in a rented room, and devoured them. It was during this time that his ideas for *Theory of Literature* were first taking shape. Believing that the treatise would be his magnum opus, he felt an obsessive need—a need bordering on madness—to be updated on every conceivable subject.

Here is how he explained his project to his father-in-law in a letter from London: "I will begin with the question of how one should perceive the world and then go on to the question of how one should interpret life, addressing its meaning, purpose, and dynamics. I will then discuss what enlightenment is and analyze the elements that constitute enlightenment. I will then discuss how these elements combine and develop to shape the evolution of literature."[1] To do so, he declared he would have to be versed in "philosophy, history, politics, psychology, biology, and theories of evolution."

When translated into English, the grandiosity of what Sōseki is trying to achieve sounds a bit comical. But the original is written in one heavily Sinicized sentence, full of Chinese characters, befitting such grandiosity. Anyone who reads the lines cannot but be struck by Sōseki's impassioned craving for encyclopedic knowledge. The thought of returning to Japan, becoming a language teacher, and not having "the leisure for thought or the time for reading" was repugnant to him, he goes on to say. He even "sometimes dreamed that he found ten thousand yen on the street and *built a library* and wrote a book in it" (emphasis added). When I read Sōseki's letters and diaries from his London years, what comes to mind is an image of a man from the distant Orient sitting alone in a poorly heated room, on fire with aspiration, reading book after book after book. He was eventually called back to Japan because of the rumor among his fellow countrymen that excess studying had driven him over the edge.

Sōseki's passion for knowledge was not limited to literature or the humanities. Again like Fukuzawa—and unlike most novelists—he had the makings of a fine scientist. He had a lifelong friendship with the distinguished physicist Terada Torahiko (1878–1935), who is said to have been the model for the physicist Nonomiya in *Sanshirō*. In fact, the scene in which Nonomiya talks about his experiments on the pressure of light in his cellar-like laboratory was something Sōseki invented after hearing Terada describe the activities of researchers on the frontiers of science. In his essay "Natsume Sōseki sensei no tsuioku" (Memories of Natsume Sōseki), Terada expresses amazement that Sōseki was able to grasp the essence on one hearing: "The novel portrays with remarkable reality an experiment that Sōseki had only heard about but never seen. I think this [ability] is quite rare among Japanese writers."[2] In other scenes in *Sanshirō*, we see scientists debate about melting quartz threads in the flame of an oxyhydrogen blowpipe, about the Scottish physicist James Clerk Maxwell (1831–1879) and the Russian physicist Pyotr Lebedev (1866–1912), and about how "the pressure of light is proportionate to the square of the radius, but gravity is proportionate to the cube of the radius, so the smaller an object is, the less gravitational pull and the stronger the effect of light-pressure on it." These and scenes from other of his novels give us a glimpse of Sōseki's command of scientific concepts and his potential as a scientist.

As a seeker of knowledge par excellence, as someone with a scientific bent, and as a man driven by ambition, both unworldly and worldly, what would Sōseki have done if he had been born today? Let us assume that as he grew up, he would again decide to become a scholar. His scientific curiosity, hand in hand with his ambition to make a name for himself, might well have led him to become a scientist. He would then be writing articles in English, the universal language of academia, especially science—articles filled with mathematical formulas. Today, the international prominence of Asians is well recognized in all fields of science, from mathematics and physics to biology, engineering, and medicine. Sōseki, too, might have come to be known as a world-class scientist. Yet suppose he was not content to write scientific articles, which, however brilliant, can ultimately be replaced with a "textbook"? Suppose he aspired to work in the field of humanities and write texts in English so that his writings might enter the world's chain of "texts to read"? How would he fare?

Probably not very well, I'm afraid. Our fictional Sōseki would still be Japanese, an East Asian, and not Indian, for example. Thanks in large part to India's colonial past, many Indian nationals and ethnic Indians are now recognized not only as fine scientists but also as fine writers in English. That Hindi, Bengali, and Urdu all belong to the Indo-European family of languages, as does English, may also have something to do with it. Yet as far as the world knows, East Asians—Chinese, Koreans, and Japanese—are a race of people who have brains only for mathematics. This is mainly because, to a degree that Westerners can scarcely imagine, writing a good text in English is a nearly impossible task for those whose mother tongue is so distant. Our Sōseki may attempt to write texts in English, but the chance of those texts entering the world's chain of "texts to read" will be slight. If he decides to persevere in his attempt, he will probably spend much of his precious time wrestling with the English language; cursing his mother tongue, so distant from English; and envying those more fortunate. To be sure, the actual Sōseki was not a happy soul, but a Sōseki who struggled to write literary works in English would have been even less so.

And yet, however frustrating writing in English might be, would a man of Sōseki's caliber today take to writing literature in Japanese? Would he do what Sōseki did over a hundred years ago—walk away from a prestigious teaching post to concentrate on writing novels in Japanese? What in the current Japanese literary scene would allure a modern Sōseki?

THE JAPANESE LITERARY SCENE TODAY

Today, if one goes into a Japanese bookstore and looks around, it is evident that Japanese as a written language is alive and well. Over seventy-five thousand new titles are published yearly, a robust number. A century and a half after Western languages first began to be translated into Japanese, concepts that were once foreign but critical in understanding and building a modern nation are now an integral part of the language, and the quality of Japanese that circulates in newspapers and magazines may be higher than ever before. The state of Japanese literature, however, is a different matter. In any mass consumer society, literature that circulates widely is seldom deserving of the name. It is the same in Japan—with one difference: the degree to which the status of literature itself has fallen in people's minds. If the word "literature" still evokes some respect, it is only because it is associated with the works of earlier writers who made Japanese literature a "major literature." In the past,

Japanese people were avid readers of literature, including works in translation. Compared with that in other countries, the national reverence for literature perhaps bordered on the extreme. But now it is the national indifference to literature that borders on the extreme.

Today, Japanese seekers of knowledge still read books, but hardly any literature—not even the modern classics. The younger they are, the truer this is. They read books in Japanese when they want to know about alternative energy, say, or the latest discoveries in brain science, or what's taking place in the world of Islam. They also read books in Japanese on issues like the aging country's pension system and possible correlations between the sliding economy and the suicide rate. It's as if knowledge seekers already sense that Japanese literature is turning into a literature of the local language—a local literature. Perhaps because they have lost interest in Japanese literature, their interest in literature of any kind has also waned, and even translations of Western literature, once so popular, languish unread. Translations do continue to be read, but the vast majority of them are nonfiction, and from English.

The demise of literature in Japan began sometime early in the 1970s, as members of the postwar generation (who, as we shall see in the next chapter, were steadily cut off from prewar society) first began writing. That is, the demise of Japanese literature began long before the unquestioned advent of the age of English and the steep decline of print media brought on by the Internet. Collected works of literature had already become a thing of the past, as had coterie magazines. Some of the major literary journals had also begun to disappear. *Shinchō*, the oldest and most prestigious of those journals, with a history of more than one hundred years, is one of the few still in circulation, but its numbers have plummeted from a peak of 100,000 immediately after the war to fewer than 10,000 now—many of which are sent out as complimentary copies.

A striking manifestation of this demise is the dwindling number and prestige of literary critics. In the past, someone like Kobayashi Hideo (1902–1983) was all but deified, with photographs of his distinguished face appearing everywhere from literary journals to magazines to newspapers. He and his fellow critics not only wrote books and articles but gave public talks, alone or in pairs or threes, speaking of Japanese literature in the context of world literary trends. Yet for decades now, seekers of knowledge have had little interest in discussing Japanese literature. And who can blame them? Aside from genre fiction such as historical novels, detective stories, and science fiction, representative works of today's Japanese literature often read like rehashes of American literature—ignoring not only the Japanese literary heritage but, more critically, the glaring fact that Japanese society and American society differ. One hundred years from now, readers of those works will have no idea what it was like to live in the current Heisei period (starting in 1989) of Japan. Though well received in the global market, such works contrast starkly with Sōseki's writings, which have an uncanny ability to transport readers back to the Japan of the Meiji and Taishō periods. The idiosyncratic and inventive style of Sōseki's texts makes them nearly impossible to translate, so they are little appreciated outside the country, although highly regarded by foreigners who read them in the original. Compared with Sōseki's works, works of contemporary fiction tend to resemble global cultural goods, which, like Hollywood blockbuster films, do not require language—or translation—in the truest sense of the word. No wonder Japan's best and brightest have turned their backs on literature.

Let me ask again: Today, would a man of Sōseki's caliber even try to write novels in Japanese? I know this may sound ungracious to the many writers of Japanese fiction active today, myself included, but I strongly suspect that he would not. How literature suffered such a sharp loss of prestige in Japan, we will explore in the final chapter.

7. THE FUTURE OF
NATIONAL LANGUAGES

W HAT WILL BECOME OF ALL THE NATIONAL LANGUAGES
THAT ARE NOT ENGLISH?
This is our ultimate question. And the answer depends ultimately on what each population—and the government of that population—wants to do with its language in this age of English. Theoretically, the optimal solution for a nation to survive and thrive in this age might be to turn every citizen into a bilingual. This new bilingualism would have to differ from premodern bilingualism in two essential ways. Before, only a limited number of the cultural elite were bilingual, and only the universal language was taken seriously. Now everyone would be bilingual and would take his or her own language seriously, respecting its heritage. English would be the vehicle of much scholarly writing, yet not only literature but scholarship too would flourish in the indigenous language, including translations from other languages. Citizens of such an ideal nation would also learn other foreign languages to counterbalance the hegemony of a single language as a means of international communication. Blessed would be the fate of national languages if every nation could achieve such linguistic virtuosity. In practice, however, for most nations, realizing such a goal—even imperfectly—is nearly impossible.

More likely, each nation will be conflicted between encouraging English fluency and protecting its own language. All non-Anglophone nations will be affected by this conflict, each in a different way. Moreover, the asymmetry between Western and non-Western languages will inevitably come into play as we try to picture what the future holds for various languages.

Of the Western nations, those best suited to attain the new kind of bi-lingualism are the Scandinavian countries, the Netherlands, and Germany—their languages being Germanic, as is English. In the Scandinavian countries and the Netherlands, the younger generation is already more or less bilingual because of public education systems that emphasize English acquisition from an early age. Germans as a whole straggle, Germany being a much more pop-ulous country and thus linguistically self-sufficient, but generally those who are educated are bilingual. However, linguistic affinity with English may be a mixed blessing. There is a risk that the population might eventually become more attuned to contemporary Anglophone culture than to its own heritage. Because writing in English comes easily for users of Germanic languages, more and more writers might even be tempted to write novels, poems, and plays in English with a world audience in mind. And English words and grammar could infiltrate the language with ever greater ease.

Western nations using non-Germanic languages such as Greek and the Slavic and Romance languages, for example, naturally lag far behind in bilin-gualism. The awkward English of the French is a century-old cliché. Never-theless, a shared history of Greek and Latin borrowing and intertranslation makes even those languages—including non-Indo-European languages such as Hungarian and Finnish—vulnerable to the mixed blessing that haunts the Germanic languages.

The prospects for major European languages, nonetheless, are not too dis-mal provided people's will to preserve their language is strong—as it actually is among the French, for one. When I think of the future prospects of these languages, I cannot help recalling my childhood experience of reading with wonderment the literature of various European countries, albeit in Japanese translation. While English will no doubt long reign supreme as the language of scholarship, and the fate of minor languages remains precarious, the world may well continue to be blessed with fine works of literature in the major languages—or, at least, I dearly hope so.

Non-European languages face predicaments that are necessarily more varied and more uncertain, however similar the underlying conflict may be. First of all, though the fact is not obvious to most people in the West, many non-Western languages do not yet function as national languages. A nation must have a strong national language (or languages) even to begin aiming at the new kind of bilingualism; yet many nations—mostly former colonies, protectorates, or mandates of European powers—do not have a function-ing national language despite having earned their independence well over half a century ago. Most often, this is because numerous regional or ethnic languages are spoken in one nation. The "national" boundaries that Western powers drew in the past simply disregarded local linguistic diversity. Tension exists not just between the former colonial power's language and the nation's own but also among the different local languages. Nationalism impels the people in such nations to have a unifying national language. Yet because they never spoke the same language to start with, they often resist what the authorities declare to be their country's national language. English or French thus ends up circulating as the lingua franca of government, higher education, and interregional commerce. As a result, while indigenous poetry may flourish, prose often fails to reach a level of sophistication high enough to satisfy the truly cultivated.

India's case is well known. After more than 150 years of British rule, the independent government sought to dispose of English and gradually replace it with Hindi, making Hindi the country's sole national language. Non-Hindi speakers resisted. Violence even erupted. The central government was forced to give more than twenty other languages official regional power while allowing the continued use of English. The current policy is confusing. The government is trying to encourage the spread of Hindi as India's national language while remaining under obligation to strengthen regional languages as well. Moreover, all this effort at multilingualism naturally does not stop middle- and upper-class parents from sending their children—society's future elite—to private schools where the classes are taught in English. Will the day come when Hindi becomes India's true national language? Or will the other major regional languages—Bengali, Gujarati, Tamil, Telugu, Urdu—each come to function alongside Hindi as one of many national languages? Poetry will certainly continue to be written in these languages. But will Indian intellectuals ever start using them rather than English to write serious prose or to pursue scholarship?

Not all non-Western countries espouse Indian-style multilingualism. The Philippines, for one, is heading in the opposite direction. In the centuries of Spanish rule (1521–1898), Spanish was its official language. Then when the United States took over the country in 1898, both Spanish and English became official languages. The Philippines gained independence in 1946, and finally in 1973, well over a quarter of a century on, its constitution declared Filipino the country's national language. English, which is still widely used, remains an official language alongside Filipino, but the nation's current policy is to turn Filipino into a true national language, not just a nominal one—a policy disputed by many because "Filipino" is merely another name for Tagalog, a dialect spoken by less than one-third of the population. Moreover, owing to the English-centered public education system implemented by the United States in the past, the majority of the population still has a working knowledge of English. Given that most Filipinos can handle English fairly well and it remains the language of choice for the elite, will the government continue devoting resources to turning Filipino into a true national language in the age of English, especially if the effort means making Filipino people less attuned to English?

Most former colonies in sub-Saharan Africa face a situation even more inimical to the creation of a national language. Though saddled with a plethora of languages, they face pressing problems stemming from war and poverty that leave little room for language policy debates. That said, the spread of Swahili, initially promoted by colonial powers baffled by the multiplicity of tongues, is showing some success. Swahili is now an official language in some states and is slowly turning into the lingua franca of East Africa. It is nonetheless a second language for most people who use it and still has a long way to go before it becomes a true national language.

Clearly, people in nearly all former European colonies in sub-Saharan Africa still live within the linguistic double structure that characterized premodern society: the language of their former colonial power is the universal language used by a relatively small number of bilingual elites, while their own languages are local languages used by a monolingual mass. The ideology of national language is strong, and, among writers, there is constant tension between writing in the universal language and writing in the indigenous language. The world-famous Kenyan writer Ngũgĩ wa Thiong'o (b. 1938), who recalls in his essay "Decolonising the Mind" that "one of the most humiliating experiences was to be caught speaking Gĩkũyũ in the vicinity of the school,"[1] has switched from writing in English to writing in Gĩkũyũ. What will be the future linguistic policies of former British colonies in sub-Saharan Africa? Will these nations continue to allocate resources to building their own languages? Even if they do, will members of the ruling class ever stop sending their children to elite schools to ensure that English becomes their first written language? And what of the former French colonies in Sub-Saharan Africa? Will they keep French as an official language or will they veer away from it like the former French protectorates in Southeast Asia—Vietnam, Cambodia, Laos—and become more intent on adopting English? What will be the fate of their national literatures?

TEACHING JAPANESE IN JAPANESE SCHOOLS

Despite this unpredictability that casts a shadow over non-European languages as a whole, many of them—including Mandarin, Korean, Vietnamese, Thai, Turkish, Hebrew, and Indonesian—are now full-fledged national languages with a flowering national literature. Others, like Arabic, boast a vigorous literary tradition not limited to one country. Yet perhaps no non-European language has been as historically fortunate as Japanese, as we have seen. Even so, remarkably, Japanese people themselves are undoing this historical good fortune. To clarify this perplexing situation, I will begin by tracing how Japanese people have mistreated their language since the end of World War II. And to do so, I must first put into words something that most readers of this book will find only too obvious: the importance of a literary canon.

People in Western countries generally share a pervasive belief that their own country's literary canon should be read and passed on to the next generation. By "literary canon," I mean not works that have already been relegated to the domain of specialists but works written since the rise of the national language—works that the populace can read without great difficulty and that they return to frequently, even maintaining a constant, lifelong dialogue with them. This is why in Western countries compulsory education in the national language has two aims: the attainment of reading and writing proficiency and the appreciation of the canon. Of course, just which works constitute the canon is a matter for debate, with calls for more female authors, more nonwhite authors, more foreign authors, and so on. Dissenters even question whether there should be any such thing as a canon in the first place. This is especially true of Americans, who, without any real need to defend their culture or language, can afford to challenge conventional wisdom. Still, the vital premise stands: Westerners basically believe that having students acquire not just reading and writing skills but familiarity with the canon, cherished works of literature written in the national language, ought to be the basis of education in the language arts, even in junior high and high school.

Today, when information a week old appears ancient, this approach to education may seem quaint. But the concept of transmitting national cultural heritage remains a cherished notion in the West, and educators engaged in the activity still focus chiefly on literature—the written word—before painting, music, dance, and other arts. Our written language is our ultimate spiritual homeland. We can no longer speak as naïvely as before in this age of swelling immigrant populations of "native literary heritage"; and yet I would submit that the reason for the deep connection among native speakers of the same language is simply that they read and are in dialogue with the same classics, however tangentially. And in order for the transmission of cultural heritage to occupy an important place in compulsory education, the entire nation must share that basic understanding.

Sadly, the Japanese nation does not.

The concept of a canon does exist in Japan. With the spread of the "ideology of national language" in the Meiji period, the government led the way, assisted by scholars, in defining the canon of premodern Japanese literature. Works written in Chinese, previously held in high regard, were eliminated, and a selection of works dating all the way back to *Ten Thousand Leaves* was newly enshrined. The modern canon was established in a more spontaneous way, without the government stepping in, as society matured and publishers began competing to put out literary anthologies; works by Natsume Sōseki, Tanizaki Jun'ichirō, Higuchi Ichiyō, and others emerged as the greatest modern classics. By the beginning of the Shōwa period, all educated Japanese were well versed in those works as a matter of course. But after World War II, the belief that such classics constitute a heritage to be read and passed on to each new generation gradually faded from society.

The little emphasis given to the modern canon of Japanese literature shows most blatantly in the astonishing paucity of the school curriculum for the study of language arts. In 2008, after seeing children's learning abilities fall year by year, the Ministry of Education undertook a sweeping revision of class hours.[2] A glance at the new distribution of class hours for the third year of junior high school (the final year of compulsory education) shows that English, mathematics, and social studies all increased from three hours per week to four, with science doubling from two hours per week to four. Only the study of Japanese remained unchanged, at three hours per week. Why? Why not have pupils devote at least four or five hours a week to the study of their own language and literature, as in Western countries?

Roughly nine of every ten Japanese children graduate from high school. High school education is thus almost part of compulsory education, but the Ministry of Education has less say over the high school curriculum, and individual schools have more freedom. One might suppose, then, that the number of hours devoted to instruction in Japanese language and literature would increase—but the reverse is true. Some high schools get away with allocating seven hours a week to English and only two to Japanese. Not only that, most colleges and universities do not require students to take any course that would be equivalent to, let us say, "English 101" in the United States. Even at the elite University of Tokyo, where students are required to take at least three semesters of English, it is possible—it is, in fact, normal—to graduate without having taken a single semester of Japanese.

What is still more astonishing is the meager content of junior and senior high school textbooks for courses in Japanese language arts. These textbooks are not made by the Ministry of Education; rather, various private companies make them, and those that win the ministry's approval are used in schools. They are all pretty much alike, but the ones used most commonly in junior high schools, with over 60 percent of the market share, are put out by a company named Mitsumura Tosho. Let's take a look at its 2013 textbook for the ninth grade, the final year of compulsory education. Bear in mind that this textbook covers not a semester but an entire year's curriculum.

The textbook itself is gorgeous, full of color drawings, photographs, and diagrams, but it is a mere 1.25 centimeters (0.5 inch) thick. The print is big, as if for a children's picture book. Of the total 301 pages, there are only 115 pages of actual readings—and I am being generous in the count. The longest work is, for some reason, a 12-page short story by Lu Xun (1881–1936), the father of modern Chinese literature, translated from the Chinese. The next longest is 8.5 pages. Most of the reading materials are excerpts. Besides fiction, there are essays on science, newspaper articles, and such. Three little-known poems are also included. The remaining two-thirds of the book consists of practice in writing Chinese characters, exercises for vocabulary acquisition, and grammatical explanations. Mixed in with these are inane suggestions on topics like "how to speak effectively," "how to write persuasively," and "how to read purposefully," with colorful illustrations. A literate teenager could easily read the entire textbook in one sitting.

As astonishing as this lack of substance is the total lack of commitment to the idea of introducing the modern literary canon. Dead authors and living are jumbled together, and the living vastly outnumber the dead: of sixteen passages of prose and free verse, eleven are by living authors, and of the remaining five, two are by authors recently deceased. Of works in the canon, only a short story by Mori Ōgai (1862–1922) would qualify. Toward the end of the book is a six-page section on masterworks of ancient and modern literature, introducing pre-Meiji and post-Meiji works in no particular order. From Sōseki, there are *six lines* taken from his novel *Grass Pillow*. That's all.

High school textbooks do no better at introducing the modern canon. By far, most of the selections are from currently popular contemporary writers. And in junior and senior high alike, *students are never required to read a single work of literature* other than their textbook. Textbooks do contain sections with recommendations for further reading, but here again, works by popular contemporary writers are greatly in the majority.

To repeat, the sad truth is that assigning any book of Japanese fiction—let alone a modern classic—to be read from first page to last never happens in any Japanese classroom from primary school through college, with the possible exception of college classes for literature majors. My own experience long ago as a student in the American public school system was vastly different. At one time or another, I was placed in every level of the streamed classes, from what the students called the "dumb class" to the regular class to the honors class. Only in the "dumb class" did we use a textbook. In the regular class, we read Shakespeare and Dickens as a matter of course, and in the honors class, where we were expected to learn the fundamentals of Western culture, we also read Greek mythology and the entire *Odyssey*. This was long ago, as I say, and whether education in language arts is still this orthodox in the United States, I wouldn't know; but I strongly doubt that things have reached the point where a person could complete compulsory education without having read at least one play by Shakespeare.

WORLD WAR II AND THE JAPANESE LEFT

Why has education in Japan not taught the canon of modern Japanese literature? Why has the Japanese language not been treated with due respect? Behind the surface reasons lie deeper reasons, with still deeper reasons beyond; no simple explanation is possible, but I would like to start by illuminating the postwar intellectual scene in Japan, where the phenomenon began.

Every country has its right wing and left wing, but anyone reading about Japan in the English-language media would have little idea that there has been a strong left wing in Japan since World War II. News items about Japan in the English-language media generally treat topics relating to the economy, popular culture, or, in recent years, the Fukushima reactor disaster. Moreover, the presence of the Japanese right wing is regularly noted. Rightists' shameless deeds and words unfailingly make headlines. Yet the continual coverage from such an angle gives a skewed view of Japanese society, which certainly has its own share of zealots, but no more so than other countries. What is nearly totally suppressed in the English media—and probably in most foreign media—is the significant role played by Japanese leftist intellectuals. This utter lack of interest displayed by the world about the presence of the Japanese leftist intellectuals cannot be dismissed lightly as mere indifference. People generally seek coherent narratives that do not upset their worldview. For foreigners, Japanese people "have to be" basically traditional or even reactionary, surrounded though they may be by every latest gadget; anything that does not fit this fixed view disturbs the narrative and so gets left out. But from the end of World War II until recently, Japanese intellectuals were predominantly left-wing—far beyond just liberal. Any who were not were automatically labeled "reactionary" to distinguish them from the majority.

In the twentieth century, Japan plunged into a reckless war and was defeated. As a result, Japanese intellectuals—everyone from students at elite universities to primary and secondary schoolteachers, university professors, writers, and editors—turned against all that represented the Japan of the past and their "tainted" cultural heritage. On fire to create a new Japan, they embraced Marxist ideology and swung in unison to the left, as often happens in impoverished developing countries; many of them became members of the Communist Party. During and following the Occupation (1945–1952), while the Japanese populace wholeheartedly and unabashedly embraced all things American, these intellectuals saw the United States as a corrupt capitalist nation. Based on Marxist historical materialism, they envisioned a Communist or socialist country as the final, ideal stage.

The most influential among these leftists were naturally "public intellectuals" (*bunkajin*) who published their writings in the country's two most prestigious venues: the publisher Iwanami Shoten and the newspaper *Asahi Shimbun*, which claims to have a circulation of 7.5 million, second only to the *Yomiuri*. The Japanese reading public revered these public intellectuals as postwar spiritual guides. Though their influence began to wane as the years went by, even in the 1970s and early 1980s being intellectual meant being left-wing. University faculties of political science, history, and economics continued to be dominated by Marxist ideology. (To this day, *Das Kapital* is taught in utter seriousness at many Japanese universities.) What dealt a major blow to the status of these intellectuals was the fall of the Berlin Wall in 1989. But by then, the damage done to modern Japanese literature and the Japanese language was all but irreversible.

THE AMERICAN OCCUPATION AND THE MINISTRY OF EDUCATION

History sometimes serves up unexpected farces. Japan's leftist intellectuals staked everything on two principles: pacifism and egalitarianism. Their devotion to the former is certainly understandable. But their trumpeting of the latter was not only because egalitarianism forms the basis of leftist thought. It was also because they saw the military and government elite as the perpetrators of World War II, and the common people in Japan and other countries as the war's victims. In other words, to sever Japan as completely as possible from its imperial past, they were fiercely against patriotism and elitism. Just as the word *collaboration* was tainted in postwar France, so in postwar Japan the words "patriotism" and "elite" became tainted, used only in a pejorative sense. The situation turned farcical because their antiestablishment stance led Japan's leftist intellectuals to side unawares with the language policy proposed by the very Occupation forces—and the Occupation-controlled Japanese government—that they regarded as their enemy. This led them ultimately and ironically to also side unawares with the Ministry of Education, with which they were constantly fighting when it came to interpretations of the country's recent history, but with which they happened to share similar views when it came to the question of language.

The leftist intellectuals, the Occupation forces, and the Ministry of Education agreed on one thing: that written Japanese should espouse phoneticism. The intellectuals' equation of egalitarianism and antielitism led them to believe that all Japanese people were potentially not just readers of books but writers, and only the difficulty of the language stood in their way. Anyone who is born and grows up in Japan can speak the language, they reasoned; therefore, if the written language were made easier to reflect the spoken language more closely, then everyone, no matter how far removed from books his or her daily life might be, could write—the rice farmer and the factory worker no less than the literary lion. In their idealism, these leftists wound up sharing the same goal, in principle, as the occupying forces, who, taken aback by the mysteries of the incomprehensible signs all around them, were calling for the complete romanization of the Japanese writing system. They thus also wound up sharing the same goal as the Ministry of Education, which, from its inception in Meiji, was a citadel of phoneticism.

The United States Education Mission to Japan arrived in March 1946, seven months after the end of the war. The mission, which played a decisive role in reforming Japan's public education system, ended its brief stay with a declaration confirming the opinion of the general headquarters (GHQ) of the American Occupation forces that the best thing to do with the Japanese language would be to romanize it. It was as if the Ministry of Education had heard a resounding voice from above, confirming the legitimacy of its cherished belief in phoneticism. As a step in simplifying and modernizing the Japanese language, at the end of that year, just over a year after the country's surrender, the ministry unilaterally enforced three language "reforms" through compulsory education and the mass media: the number of Chinese characters to be used was restricted, the form of many characters was simplified, and the traditional kana orthography was altered to reflect pronunciation more accurately.

When print language is established, it is only natural that the written language should somehow regulate itself to meet the demands of the market. Governmental intervention may also come into play, depending on circumstances. In Japan, it made sense to put limits on the number of Chinese characters used in official documents and media and to simplify the most frequently used ones in some logical way. Likewise, it made sense to alter the use of kana to fit the modern language. But spurred by the declaration of the GHQ and the United States Education Mission, the Japanese Ministry of Education acted with inappropriate haste and unforgivable cavalierness, implementing drastic change before anyone realized what was happening. Out of a pool of tens of thousands of Chinese characters, the ministry limited the number for everyday use to 1,850— without consulting experts, let alone seeking public opinion. (The number may still seem huge, but the reader should bear in mind that learning Chinese characters is akin to learning vocabulary.) Further, those characters were simplified in a haphazard way, taking out a line here and a dot there, as if it didn't matter that omitting a single stroke can sever a character from its semantic roots. Perhaps most damaging was the switchover to phonetic kana, which obscured the roots of a wide array of words. In English it would be almost as bad as enforcing a new spelling of philosophy as "filosofee."

Then, in August 1948, to establish how detrimental the use of Chinese characters was to Japanese literacy, a nationwide survey was conducted under the orders of John Pelzel, an officer in the Civil Information and Educational Section of the GHQ. The survey was extensive, testing a random sampling of 16,814 men and women ages fifteen to sixty-four. Given its long-standing espousal of phoneticism—the first minister of education was Mori Arinori, who had recommended adopting English as the national language—the Ministry of Education would likely have had no objection to implementing romanization if the GHQ had insisted, however impractical and ultimately impossible that course might have been. But unexpectedly, the results demonstrated no such need: a mere 2.1 percent of those tested proved to be functionally illiterate.

Pelzel apparently found this outcome hard to accept. One day, he summoned to his hotel room a budding linguist named Shibata Takeshi, who had helped conduct the survey, and asked him point-blank to rewrite the results. Though a strong lifelong supporter of romanization, Shibata refused on the grounds that "as a scholar" he could not do such a thing. Pelzel did not force the issue. And so, with this brief conference in a hotel room, where two men talked sitting on a bed side by side, the country was spared the fate of adopting romanization—at least for the time being.³

The survey results did not halt the movement to switch to the Roman alphabet. Romanization remained an ultimate goal of the Occupation's GHQ and a goal considered well worth pursuing by the Ministry of Education, which had direct control over Japan's language policies. And since the Ministry of Education was solidly in favor of phoneticism, the movement continued to gain steam even after the departure of the U.S. forces. A new National Language Research Council was established to explore the merits of such a change, and school curriculums were redesigned to increase the number of school hours devoted to writing Japanese in *rōmaji*, Roman letters. On top of all this, the emergence of the typewriter, ubiquitous in American films and television dramas as a symbol of modern times, added urgency to the debate: those in favor of romanization threatened that unless the Japanese abolished Chinese characters forthwith, they would be left behind in the dust, unable to use that epitome of modern civilization. The debate over how to do this went on for years; as at the dawn of Japan's modern era, not only those in favor of romanization but proponents of various phonetic writing styles (hiragana, katakana, or some brand-new form of writing yet to be invented) all strenuously made their case.

"REACTIONARY" INTELLECTUALS

In retrospect, it seems almost bizarre that the hastily implemented changes and ongoing push toward romanization aroused no opposition at the time. But those who were aware of what was happening to the Japanese language— the media that had to use new printing and the schoolteachers who had to teach a new way of writing, not to mention the editors involved in drawing up new textbooks—consisted of virtually all those who had swung left after the war. People who might have had qualms voiced no protest, perhaps because they dared not. Most disturbing in the face of such governmental control over the language was the silence of public intellectuals—the nation's "spiritual guides," those who could have spoken out and been heard. As writers themselves, not all of them could have been insensitive to the government's tampering with the written language as they knew it. Behind their silence lay the unpleasant historical fact that the Japanese Empire left muddy footprints in Asia, including forcing the Japanese language on its colonies in Taiwan and Korea—something we shall come back to later.

The first public intellectual to speak up against phoneticism was Fukuda Tsuneari (1912–1994), a scholar of English literature and respected translator of Shakespeare whose name came to be preceded with the derogatory label "reactionary." In 1958, more than ten years after the changes had been implemented, Fukuda began publishing a series of journal articles that informed the Japanese reading public for the first time of the offhand manner in which the Japanese language had been tampered with. Then in 1961, several writers who had participated in the National Language Research Council quit, declaring publicly that the council was stacked in favor of phoneticism and there was no point in continuing the debate. This made headlines. The following year, the committee on romanization was disbanded. And in 1966, the head of the council, Education Minister Nakamura Umekichi, held a news conference laying out for the first time in Japan's modern history an official policy on what the written language should be: a mixture of Chinese characters and Japanese kana. This declaration must have come as a surprise to the general public, most of whom were unaware that these debates were going on and never dreamed that their language could be written otherwise. And so—exactly one hundred years after Maejima Hisoka's petition to the shogun to eradicate Chinese characters—the issue was finally laid to rest.

All this is mere orthography, you may say. But it is not mere orthography. Fukuda's articles, which came out in book form in 1960 under the title *Watashi no kokugo kyōshitsu* (My Japanese language classroom), place special emphasis on how irrational and impossible it would be for the Japanese language to adopt a strictly phonetic writing system. In this, he was absolutely right. For one thing, the enormous prevalence of homophones among ideogram compounds, which are most often used for abstract concepts, makes abolishing Chinese characters out of the question. Depending on the characters used, the word *seikō*, for example, has a multitude of totally unrelated meanings, including "success" (成功), "precision" (精巧), "starlight" (星光),

"propensity" (性行), and "sexual intercourse" (性交). Fukuda's discussion, however, concentrates on something less obvious to the Japanese public: the loss they suffered through kana reform.

With great erudition, love of Japanese, and concern for his country, as well as a puckish wit befitting a scholar of English literature, Fukuda describes how phonetic kana notation confused the Japanese language and dulled people's awareness of word roots. He writes, "Words are not tools for the transmission of culture; they *are* culture. They are our very selves."[4] To linguist Matsuzaka Tadanori, a member of the council who espoused romanization, he issues this challenge: "Mr. Matsuzaka, come to your senses. Does writing exist for the typewriter, or the typewriter for writing?" Little did he know that the invention of the computer would one day make this argument obsolete— and prove him right in his assertion that technologies exist for humans, and not vice versa.

Fukuda ends his book with these words:

And so during the postwar confusion, a time when people's attention was fixed on food and clothing with no room to spare for other matters, the orthodox notation that so many scholars of the past had sweated blood to defend was hastily overturned—a truly lamentable, irretrievable turn of events. Moreover, people went right on jabbering about tradition and culture, while disdaining the *words* on which tradition and culture depend. What tradition, what culture, pray tell? Now I see, this is what it means to lose a war.[5] (Emphasis in original)

Even now those final words, "Now I see, this is what it means to lose a war," wring my heart.

Chinese characters per se luckily survived. The cap on the number of characters designated for everyday use was eventually raised from 1,850 to 2,136. Yet the simplification of these characters and the phonetic use of kana remain unadjusted and haphazard to this day.

What is crucial to realize is that these so-called reforms did not merely impoverish the Japanese language but also, by altering the written language that until then everyone had been able to read, created a needless cultural gulf— unlike the previous one (see chapter 4), which was necessitated by the force of history. The year 1946 was the watershed: generations born after that were increasingly exposed to the new, poorer orthographic style and gradually became reluctant to read anything written before the changes unless it was rewritten in that style. In this way, Japan began to produce generations for whom reading anything prewar in its original form is increasingly a struggle. Older, premodern texts have of course become even more remote.

What an utter waste! The books I read from around age twelve (when, as I have mentioned, my father was transferred to New York and our family went there to live) belonged to an early anthology of modern Japanese literature we had around the house. I devoured them without even realizing that they were written in traditional style. They did not strike me or my sister, who wasn't as much of a bookworm, as particularly hard going. But back in Japan, the number of people who had scarcely laid eyes on anything but the new Japanese was steadily increasing.

WRITTEN LANGUAGE IS A MERE REPRESENTATION OF THE SOUNDS of spoken language: this mistaken assumption underlying the belief in phonetic writing reflects a view of language that inevitably arises in cultures using a phonetic alphabet. The French philosopher Jacques Derrida (1930–2004) gave the name "phonocentrism" to this view, which he saw as a Western ideology and around which he developed a critique of Western metaphysics. Phonocentrism places higher value on spoken language as being more primary than and thus superior to written language, which it conceives as necessarily corrupting the original intention of the Subject—the center of meaning.

The problem is, the introduction of Western ideology into a non-Western context often does unimagined harm. Transported to a different culture, thought often loses its subtlety and can even rampage like a wild beast. The damage inflicted on the Japanese language by postwar revisions arose because belief in the superiority of phonetic notation was in fact a mark of utopianism imported from the West. Touting primitive communism, egalitarianism, and the Self freed from the shackles of the past, this utopianism wreaked cultural havoc even in the West. But in the non-West, it wreaked havoc of an entirely different order of magnitude. China's Cultural Revolution saw invaluable cultural treasures wiped from the face of the Earth and book lovers strung up and humiliated. Cambodia's Khmer Rouge massacred the entire literate population. Though it may sound extreme to speak of Japan's postwar language revisions in the same breath with such atrocities, they all arose from similar utopian dreams. The Chinese revolution took place under one-party rule, and the Khmer Rouge massacres were a ripple effect of years of colonial rule followed by a corrupt regime and the Vietnam War; yet in postwar Japan, during a time of peace, prosperity, and freedom of speech, mindless actions of the country's leaders, both political and intellectual, produced a generation increasingly estranged from its rightful literary heritage.

LINGERING GUILT, OVERCONFIDENCE, AND SELF-DOUBT

From here, let us start delving deeper into possible reasons why the Japanese language has suffered such undeserved treatment at the hands of the Japanese people themselves.

It is not that Japanese people are uninterested in their language. On the contrary, they often fret that the younger generation in particular is making a hash of it. Bookshops overflow with books on the proper use of honorifics and other language-related topics. Coffee-table magazines aimed at women are incessantly putting out special issues devoted to "beautiful Japanese"— much the same way they feature innocuous topics like "the aesthetics of Japanese lifestyle" or "the health benefits of Japanese cuisine." There are television quiz shows on language usage. Many people fascinated by Chinese characters, including children, are taking examinations to test their ability. But giving serious thought to their language from a world-historical perspective is a different matter.

One reason lies in Japan's relatively recent history. As mentioned earlier, because the Japanese language was forcibly imposed on Taiwanese and Koreans, Japan's imperial past still makes many Japanese, especially intellectuals, feel a need to feel guilty. The fall of the Berlin Wall finally freed any intellectuals from the fetters of the left, allowing them to begin trying to come up with a more balanced understanding of their past: rather than looking on the nation's path from the Meiji Restoration to World War II as an inexorable slide into evil, it became possible to take a positive view of Japan's successful modernization—quite a natural view to take, when you think of it—without being automatically labeled "reactionary." Nonetheless, inhibition persists when talking about the Japanese language. Anyone who calls for people to value the language that evolved through that same process of modernization is still automatically labeled reactionary, or worse, right-wing. And until very recently, to suggest that Japanese are lucky to have such a rich heritage of modern literature was in a real sense taboo.

Yet, there is a second, underlying reason that Japanese have never given serious thought to the need to protect their linguistic and literary heritage.

I am referring to Japan's geographic location, which, as we have already discussed, has conferred great advantages. Because Japanese people have never suffered any foreign invasions, they have always viewed their language and culture as givens that nothing can ever take away. To them, Japanese language and culture are inseparable from themselves, eternally safe as long as they, the Japanese people, exist—as if the historical constructs of Japanese language and culture were permanently embedded in Japanese DNA. This naïve overconfidence is ubiquitous even among those in a position to actively defend Japanese language and culture.

A recent example is provided by Kawai Hayao (1928–2007), a prominent Jungian psychologist who headed the International Research Center for Japanese Studies and then the Agency for Cultural Affairs, a special body under the Ministry of Education. As we shall see, there was a brief movement around the turn of the twenty-first century to make English an official language of Japan. A reporter for the *Asahi Shimbun* observed to Kawai, the appointed leader of the discussion, that some people criticized the idea on the grounds that to do so would wreak harm on Japanese language and culture. Kawai responded with supreme aplomb: "They're misguided. Nobody is saying English will take priority over Japanese. *Japanese language and culture will be just fine.* If Japanese language and culture are so frail that a little thing like this does them irreparable harm, then good riddance" (emphasis added).[6]

Or let us go back a little further in time and take the example of popular novelist Sakaguchi Ango (1906–1955), whose famous wartime essay "Nihon bunka shikan" (A personal view of Japanese culture) contains a pithy and sharply worded, if totally deluded, statement of his belief in the indestructability of Japanese culture. There is no need, he wrote, for the Japanese to cherish a building like the Hōryūji, a temple built in Nara in the first half of the seventh century and the world's oldest wooden structure: "If necessary we should tear down the Hōryūji and build a railway station. The glorious culture and traditions of our people would by no means be destroyed as a result. Even without the Hōryūji, Japan would go on."[7] Ango makes another declaration about the Katsura Imperial Villa, an architectural gem from the seventeenth century whose beauties were brought to the attention of the Japanese people by German architect Bruno Taut in the 1930s. According to Ango, "Taut had to discover Japan, whereas we have no need to discover Japan, for we are actually Japanese. We may have lost sight of our ancient culture, but it is impossible for us to lose sight of Japan." Since Ango wrote the essay during the war, his tone is defiant, yet his statement served only to reinforce the naïve overconfidence that Japanese have regarding their culture, and the essay continues to be extremely popular. What Ango and those Japanese readers who nod in agreement at his words do not realize is that other people around the world, by living through repeated foreign invasions, came indeed to "discover" their own countries. He concludes, "As long as the everyday life of the Japanese people is healthy, Japan itself will be healthy."

Like Ango, Japanese people took it as an article of faith that even if they destroyed their cultural treasures, they would never "lose sight of Japan." And what has been the effect of this cultural neglect on the Japanese cityscape? With no regulations on architecture apart from safety standards, the market drive to maximize floor area resulted in the wholesale destruction of old structures in favor of a motley assortment of commercial and office buildings of every shape, height, hue, and description; cheap blocks of stacked one-room flats; mismatched small residential developments; snakelike, twisting asphalt roads intersecting absurdly with elevated railroads; pedestrian overpasses with peeled paint where no one sets foot; a tangle of electric wires covering the sky like a spider's web—in short, unutterable ugliness. I, for one, cannot go for a walk without feeling waves of anger, sorrow, despair. The survival of the Hōryūji is cause for rejoicing, but ordinary street scenes have greater impact on our daily lives.

"Japanese language and culture will be just fine," Kawai blandly assured the nation, but a country's urban landscapes are part of its culture, too. Japanese culture was not, after all, "just fine." And, though Japanese people will not believe it, the language is not "just fine," either. The only reason they are so confident is that historically, thanks to the favorable geographic location of the Japanese islands, there was never any need to defend the language. Most ethnic groups around the world have had occasion at some point in their history to defend their language passionately from incursions by other groups. The language of every ethnic group on Earth arose accidentally in the course of history, without any intrinsic need to exist. But a language exposed to risk becomes a defining marker of ethnic identity, thereby gaining necessity and becoming the object of passionate defense by its speakers, who regard it as "our own language." A language that goes undefended will perish. Even if its written word is preserved in books, the books will go unread and so perish. Human history is also a history of war among languages.

Japanese people are now facing a situation without precedent since the birth of the Japanese language. The geographic isolation that long protected that language is a thing of the past in today's technologically advanced age.

"We have no need to discover Japan, for we are actually Japanese." So wrote Sakaguchi Ango, but what kind of people are "actually Japanese"? The Japanese language is not embedded in anyone's DNA. I know plenty of people overseas who are Japanese by blood yet cannot speak a word of the language. I know plenty of people even inside Japan who can speak the language yet can barely read a word of it. Can we say unequivocally that they too are "actually Japanese" and have not "[lost] sight of Japan"?

The third and final reason why I believe Japanese people have not prized their language is darker—and more tragic. However strange this may sound to Western ears, most people in Japan are skeptical as to whether their own language has true legitimacy. Yes, for a millennium and a half the Japanese language ranked below Chinese, as was only natural, since Japan was part of the Sinosphere. But people today hardly care about that long-ago era. At issue is the status of the Japanese language in the modern era. Despite their enthusiastic embracing of the ideology of national language, and despite the emergence of Japanese as a fully functioning national language, Japanese people remain unsure if their language is truly legitimate. Undergoing the "shock of the West" also meant seeing Westerners as model human beings and oneself as anything but, a bias that lingers to this day. Foreigners who visit Japan must find it incongruous that any of the faces featured in the advertising flooding the streets are Western. The bias extends to language: Western languages are seen as models for the whole human race to use. While taking justifiable pride in a vibrant literary heritage, Japanese people at some point, without even knowing it, became captive to the notion that only Western languages are valid. Various non-Western peoples surely share a similar sense of estrangement from their own language.

The use of Chinese ideograms naturally reinforced this pervasive self-doubt. Japan was by no means the only country to contemplate banishing ideograms outright after undergoing the "shock of the West." There have been movements to abolish ideograms even in China, the place of their birth. The same impulse spread throughout the Sinosphere. Abstract concepts derived from ideograms are even more prevalent in Korean than in Japanese, yet in North Korea the use of ideograms is prohibited, and even in South Korea they have all but disappeared, replaced in both countries by *hangul*, a phonetic script unique to the Korean language. Vietnam, where a still higher proportion of abstract words was originally written in ideograms, switched to the Roman alphabet in the first half of the twentieth century. Even without ideograms, Vietnamese and Korean have continued to function as written languages largely because their pronunciation is more varied and complex than that of Japanese, resulting in fewer homophones.

Just in the past twenty years or so, Japanese people have begun taking a more positive view of ideograms. During that time, it has become clear that China, while beginning to flex its muscles as a superpower, has no intention of abolishing its ideograms, albeit in simplified form for everyday characters. Furthermore, the technological revolution created by the computer has made ideograms far less inconvenient and antipopulist than before. More foreigners now willingly undertake their study. Though the tradition of classical Chinese writing may be lost, at least Chinese ideograms, with a history of over three and a half millennia, have gained a seat at the table. The human race has escaped the danger of losing its sole living set of ideograms.

But the mere acceptance of ideograms in the world is not enough to erase Japanese people's persistent self-doubts about their language. As we have seen, the man who later became Japan's first education minister called for the nation to adopt English. And as mentioned in chapter 2, the acclaimed novelist Shiga Naoya called for the defeated nation to abandon Japanese in favor of French. Even more surprisingly, ultranationalist thinker Kita Ikki (1883–1939), who would be executed as the brains behind the failed military coup of February 26, 1936, urged the nation to take up Esperanto. Since he was a socialist, perhaps his position should be no cause for surprise—and yet seeing an ultranationalist's name in conjunction with Esperanto is startling. Why did this political extremist advocate the adoption of an international language based on Western languages? Because he considered Japanese to be "exceedingly inferior." If Japanese people took Esperanto as their second language, then, he claimed, Japanese would "by the law of natural selection" vanish in fifty years. But there was more to his advocacy of Esperanto than this. In a book called *Kokugo to iu shisō* (The ideology of national language, 1997), written in Japanese, Korean sociolinguist I Yeonsuk quotes Kita as saying that should the Empire of Greater Japan spread to Russia and Australia, then forcing the language on those populations "the way we forced Koreans to use Japanese"[8] would never do. (With understandable wrath, she adds, "The Korean nation compelled to use this 'inferior' Japanese was a pathetic sacrificial lamb.")[9] In any case, it is striking that these three influential men—one a high government official, one a celebrated novelist, and one a radical enemy of the state—all saw Japanese as irredeemable and urged its abolition.

Even now, when economically Japan stands shoulder to shoulder with the West, Japanese people's pangs of perceived linguistic inadequacy linger unabated; if anything, they have intensified. Advertising is awash with the Roman alphabet (for Japanese brand names) and katakana (for expressions borrowed from English, French, Italian, Spanish, and more). Both styles are expressions of a deep-seated longing: *If only Japanese were a Western language!* The media are also infatuated by such words. And the Japanese government, instead of countering this trend by taking advantage of the superb word-building capacity of Chinese ideograms, goes happily along spewing out barely comprehensible "katakana English." Phoneme pairs often become indistinguishable, as with "major" and "measure" (メジャー) or "chip" and "tip" (チップ)—not to mention "free market" and "flea market" (フリーマーケット). Confusion mounts. One has to sympathize with the seventy-one-year-old male who, in June 2013, sued NHK, Japan's public television network, for mental suffering caused by the flood of incomprehensible loanwords.

In any case, the disquieting sense that one's native language is somehow illegitimate is one of many tragic consequences of the rupture with their native heritage that people in Japan and other non-Western countries have undergone in modern times.

"UNIVERSAL BILINGUALISM" IN JAPAN?

And so, having no faith that Japanese literature should be passed on, no history of protecting the Japanese language, and no conviction that Japanese is even a legitimate language to begin with, the Japanese people were thrust into the age of English.

How have they dealt with the situation? As in most other countries, the need to learn English has been felt more pressingly than ever before. But for the Japanese, the feeling that they *ought* to know English has become an irrational obsession, a paranoia that has spread across the nation like a plague. This is probably because most people, despite years of suffering from mandatory English courses in junior high, high school, and college, end up with little or no grasp of the language. A highly educated few can read it, but hardly anyone can speak it or write it. Feeling defeated, and blaming themselves for the defeat, ordinary people have succumbed to a kind of mass hysteria, convinced despite all evidence to the contrary that they can and must master the language.

For years, city streets have been plastered with ads for English conversation schools. Television commercials promise that if you just listen to *these* English-language materials, you'll soon be chattering away. Of Japanese podcasts accessed through the iTunes store in the education category on September 29, 2013, an astounding twenty-eight out of the top thirty were programs for learning English. Short-term stays abroad for the purpose of learning English are fast becoming de rigueur.

It was against this background that a movement arose in 1999 to make English the nation's second official language. The movement sought to transform the entire population into bilinguals through a totally new system of public education. Though much discussed in media at the time (along with reports that some Koreans were calling for Korea to do the same), the movement gradually fizzled out. Given that the Japanese have a perfectly fine national language, many thought the idea preposterous. Even those who did not oppose the idea itself thought its implementation too costly and thus impracticable.

However, unlike the nation's hysterical obsession with English, the sense of crisis underlying the movement to make English an official language had a clear motivation. At the center of the movement was a well-known figure named Funabashi Yōichi, a journalist stationed for years in New York as a foreign correspondent for the *Asahi Shimbun*. In 2000, he published a book entitled *Aete Eigo kōyōgo ron* (In spite of all, make English an official language),[10] which contains a devastating account of how the inability of past Japanese officials and politicians to express themselves in English or even to understand what was said to them led to an accumulation of diplomatic blunders culminating in World War II. Funabashi also cites more recent examples to show how lack of English mastery at international negotiation tables places Japan and Japanese companies in a highly disadvantageous position.

Now that we have entered the age of English and the Internet, Japanese people's helplessly poor English poses a greater potential threat to the nation than ever. International negotiations in English have become daily events. The Internet has ushered in continuous global publicity campaigns where information is creatively manipulated. What is well articulated in English on the Internet becomes "truth" the whole world believes in. *Fama volat*: rumor has wings. Or better, *fama crescit eundo*: rumor grows as it goes. And often rumors have no relation to the truth. Words can have a terrible power to turn white into black, and the more such treacherous words circulate, the more traction they gain. If Japan were subjected to a barrage of groundless verbal attacks, rebuttals in lame English, however numerous or earnest they might be, would serve no purpose. The only way to counter the attacks would be

to patiently state the truth in articulate, persuasive English. And for this approach to be effective, people with more than sufficient command of English
would have to exist on a certain scale. Backed by the intrinsic power of the
truth, well-crafted English circulating widely might well have power to per-
suade the world.

The sense of crisis underlying the proposal to make English an official language of Japan is thus quite understandable. Yet in addition to the objections
raised earlier, there is a major problem with this goal: proponents are intent
on making *all* Japanese people bilingual. They hold that the current system of
English education, with its abysmal results, needs to be changed drastically,
as by bringing in native speakers en masse. But as long as the goal is universal
bilingualism, such methods will never result in the high-level bilingualism
Japan now requires. The only realistic way to develop a cadre of skilled bilinguals is to head in exactly the opposite direction—that is, to give up on the
notion of universal bilingualism. This means abandoning once and for all a
principle held inviolable (at least on the surface) by the Ministry of Education
and the Japanese populace ever since World War II: the principle of egalitarianism. By giving special education opportunities to a select stratum, Japan
must choose a path it has until now shunned, a path it has seen as morally
wrong.

The national budget cannot be expanded indefinitely to accommodate
English education. Not every child is eager to learn English (in fact, English
is the most abhorred subject in Japanese schools). It makes no sense to spend
the nation's limited resources equally on those who do want to learn English
and those who do not. Those resources should be devoted to a limited pool
of talent, the government leading the way. That sort of training cannot be left
solely to market forces because doing so would make it accessible only to the
rich. Worse, doing so would diminish the likelihood of Japan's ever gaining
the bilinguals it truly needs. Without some guiding principle, the tenets of the
market will simply respond to consumers' demand for more English by creating people who speak English like Americans—a meaningless ability in and
of itself. Nor should Japan try to create mere government puppets. The bilinguals Japan truly needs are people capable of defending or criticizing their
own country as informed citizens. This requires, first and foremost, thorough
grounding in Japan and the Japanese language.

Japanese proponents of nationwide bilingualism often cite Singapore as
a model. (Scandinavians are also bilingual, but they look too different from
Japanese.) If Singaporeans, who look so much like us, are on their way to

achieving bilingualism, then so can we, they argue. Taking Singapore as a model, however, is ludicrously wrong-headed. Unlike Japan, Singapore—a multiethnic, multilingual, former British colony—needs a common language among its diverse population, which is part Malay, part Chinese, and part Tamil. And because it is a multiethnic country, it espouses multilingualism, encouraging people to maintain their ethnic identity by making it compulsory in public schools for children to master their mother tongue—or Mandarin, in the case of ethnic Chinese. This multilingual educational policy may make Singaporeans appear bilingual on the surface, but insofar as written language is concerned, they are in fact Anglophone. The language of instruction in primary and secondary education gradually involves more English, and it is totally English at the college or university level. (Some university courses in Malay, Chinese, and Tamil language and literature are available.) Singaporean writers write predominantly in English. Moreover, as some members of the younger generation are even beginning to use English at home, Singapore might end up becoming a true Anglophone country. To think of it as an ideal bilingual nation is to miss the basic assumption of the new bilingualism, which requires reading and writing proficiency in two languages.

People in the English-speaking world are so used to others speaking in English that they may perhaps have trouble understanding the monumental difficulty of achieving universal bilingualism, and the near impossibility of doing so for native speakers of non-Western languages. But what if all Americans, say, were required to learn Japanese at school—not just to speak the language but to read and write it as well? A little exercise of the imagination will show what fantastic effort it would take to achieve that goal. For Japan, universal bilingualism is not an option.

The Japanese government needs strong conviction to counter the mass hysteria that cries incessantly for more and more English. Above all, it needs to make it its mission to defend the Japanese language by giving it priority over English. One's identity derives not from one's nation or blood but from the language one uses; what makes Japanese people Japanese is not their nation or their blood but the Japanese language that they use.

PROTECTING JAPANESE

My proposals for language education are simple. First, concerning English education, teach the fundamentals so that all children acquire a basis for reading proficiency. The importance of being able to read the universal language circulating the globe in this age of the Internet can scarcely be overemphasized. Reading also provides the key to understanding elevated discourse. Then, have only those who wish to study further do so. For a select number, allocate special funds, whether government or private, to develop the cadre of bilinguals that Japan needs. That's all. (The only thing I might add would be to encourage the study of other foreign languages as well.)

Many Japanese would call such a policy elitist. They would protest, "Think of the feelings of the children left behind!" But children are stronger than that. Those who fear "elite" education also say it will lead to an economically stratified society. Look around, however, and you will see that the existence in Japan of a large middle class renders unlikely the opening of an economic gap between a chosen few and the rest. And, given the thorough education people already receive and the vast number of translated materials available, an information gap seems equally unlikely. Most important, consider what will happen if Japanese thinking does not change and such a policy is not adopted in the schools. Japan will not gain the bilinguals it so desperately needs, but that's not all. Little by little, before anyone knows it, fine prose writing will meet its demise as people take their own language less seriously in a vain attempt to "globalize."

This brings me to my second point. The Japanese language arts curriculum should be designed with one basic principle in mind—ensuring that the modern classics continue to be read. If that principle is upheld, the educational reforms I envision will inevitably follow: hours of Japanese language instruction in primary and secondary schools will increase. Students will read a number of works of modern Japanese literature from about a century ago, cover to cover. And in colleges and universities, they will deepen their familiarity with the modern canon.

Of course, I am not suggesting that other types of reading are unworthy. All of us, in the course of our lives, naturally encounter and enjoy all sorts of books, which is well and good—but for most people the world of fine literature is sadly remote. Education has to open doors that the home environment and the marketplace cannot.

These proposals will sound like mere common sense in most Western societies. However, for Japan, a non-Western country, returning to texts dating from the time of the formation of its national language would have far deeper significance. In the West, modern texts are bound culturally with earlier classical texts. However distant the age of Greek classics and the Bible, figures like Apollo, Hercules, and Venus, as well as Noah, Job, and Mary Magdalene, live on in today's literary works. But such is not the case in Japan. The new litera-ture that arose from what Sōseki called a "sudden twist" becomes more cut off from earlier literature with every passing day. Hence all the more reason to instill the habit of reading classics that date from around the time of that sudden twist, a seminal time when writers still privy to the nation's full liter-ary heritage drew excitedly on it to give birth to a new language and literature. If Japanese people could reconnect to those modern classics, then despite having twice lost sight of themselves as a nation in the upheavals of recent history, first during the Meiji Restoration and again in the defeat of World War II, they would be able to connect, however hazily, with the Japanese of their ancient forebears and sense that in the Japanese written word they have a true spiritual homeland.

Once the great Library comes into being, works will never go out of print. One day, it will be possible to access every work of literature ever published. But literature is not merely something to be stored. Its life is renewed through each act of reading. The richness of a national literature de-pends not on how many "texts to read" its library contains but on how much the average person reads them. Suppose that fifty or a hundred years from now in Japan, no one but specialists in the history of modern literature ever reads Sanshirō. It would be as if the miracle of modern Japanese literature had never taken place; as if back in the nineteenth century, Japan had become a U.S. colony after all.

Nor is that all. From a global perspective, defending the Japanese written language is something Japanese people owe not just to themselves but to the world. I say this with full awareness that it sounds bombastic. Yet only we Japanese, through our use of this unusual written language, are in a posi-tion to counter the widespread belief in phoneticism. As a spoken language, Japanese is not particularly special. But as a written language, it is: in mixing ideograms with two different sets of kana, it uses a method of notation unlike any other in the world. This is not to say that the Japanese language is special in its visual appeal. Even phonograms have visual appeal, as we all know. The Arabic script that adorns mosque fronts has solemn beauty, like a dancer mo-mentarily arresting her movement in the air. The Devanagari alphabet used in writing Hindi languages looks playful, like toy soldiers in a row. Even the Roman alphabet retains a strong visual aspect, as seen in the variety of type-faces available on any computer; a simple change of typeface can make the same sentence appear old-fashioned or modern. Such connections between visual effect and the production of meaning can occur using any set of signs, whether ideograms or phonograms.

However, *using different sets of signs to affect the production of meaning* is something on a different level altogether, something unique to Japanese. It does not happen in Chinese writing, which uses only ideograms. (For a brief time, during the Japanese Occupation and slightly beyond, Korean also was written by mixing the phonetic *hangul* and Chinese ideograms.) The shades of meaning that arise from using different sets of signs for different purposes occur whether the writing is done by brush in beautiful calligraphy or by ballpoint pen in a deplorably clumsy hand, whether it is set in Ming or sans-serif typeface. The semantic difference comes from something unrelated to such visual effects. It comes from writing the very same words, pronounced the very same way, but using completely different letters that belong to different systems. Again, the very existence of a written language using such a remarkable method of notation is a living counterargument to phoneticism.

Let us return to the opening lines of the short poem by Hagiwara Sakutarō that we examined in chapter 2:

> I should like to go to France,
> But France is far too far.
> So I shall don a new suit
> And roam where fancy leads.[11]

Here, much of the effect of the poem comes from writing the word "France" in hiragana, which is almost never used for foreign place-names: ふらんす. This device lends the lines an ineffable softness and suppleness appropriate to the "woman's hand." Write the same word in Chinese characters and the effect vanishes: 仏蘭西. Write it in katakana, the usual way of writing foreign place-names, and one is left with the ordinary, prosaic expression of an ordinary sentiment: フランス. No written language but Japanese can play with the production of meaning in this bewitching way. Don't tell the French, but the fall of written Japanese, with this striking capability that demonstrates the irreducible and fundamental difference between spoken language and written, represents a far greater loss to humanity than even the fall of the glorious French language.

Of course, to the rest of the world's inhabitants, the fact that Japan had a national language and a modern literature before any other non-Western country matters not in the least. The designation of Japanese literature as a "major literature" will be forgotten as other non-Western literatures become increasingly "major." Even the fact that written Japanese stands as a living counterargument to phoneticism will fade, once the theoretical pitfalls of phoneticism are grasped. But that all seekers of knowledge should use the identical language to think and to read and write is not a development to which humanity can remain indifferent. Reality is constructed by languages, and the existence of a variety of languages means the existence of a variety of realities, a variety of truths. Understanding the multifaceted nature of truth does not necessarily make people happy, but it makes them humble, and mature, and wise. It makes them worthy of the name *Homo sapiens*.

FINALLY, I WOULD LIKE TO POINT OUT THAT NOW IN THE AGE OF English, choosing a language policy is not the exclusive concern of non-English-speaking nations. It is also a concern for English-speaking nations, where, to realize the world's diversity and gain the humility that is proper to any human being, people need to learn a foreign language as a matter of course. Acquiring a foreign language should be a universal requirement of compulsory education. Furthermore, English expressions used in international conferences should be regulated and standardized to some extent. Native English speakers need to know that to foreigners, Latinate vocabulary is easier to understand than what to the native speakers is easy, child-friendly language. At international conferences, telling jokes that none but native speakers can comprehend is inappropriate, even if fun. If native speakers of English—those who enjoy the privilege of having their mother tongue as the universal language—would not wait for others to protest but would take steps to regulate themselves, what respect they would earn from the rest of the world! If that is too much to ask, the rest of the world would appreciate it if they would at least be aware of their privileged position—and more important, be aware that the privilege is unwarranted. In this age of global communication, some language or other was bound to become a universal language used in every corner of the world. English became that language not because it is intrinsically more universal than other languages, but because through a series of historical coincidences it came to circulate ever more widely until it reached the tipping point. That's all there is to it. English is an accidental universal language.

If more English native speakers walked through the doors of other languages, they would discover undreamed-of landscapes. Perhaps some of them might then begin to think that the truly blessed are not they themselves, but those who are eternally condemned to reflect on language, eternally condemned to marvel at the richness of the world.

NOTES

PREFACE

1. Mizumura Minae, *Nihongo ga horobiru toki: Eigo no seiki no naka de* (Tokyo: Chikumashobō, 2008), 59. All citations from Japanese works are translated by either Mari Yoshihara or Juliet Winters Carpenter unless otherwise indicated.

INTRODUCTION

1. Minae Mizumura, "Renunciation," *Yale French Studies* 69 (1985): 81–97.

2. FROM *PAR AVION* TO VIA AIR MAIL

1. Hagiwara Sakutarō, "Ryojō" (On a journey), in *Junjō shōkyokushū* (Amazon Services International, ASIN: B009IY9L0Y, 1925), Kindle ed.
2. Shiga Naoya, "Kokugo mondai," *Kaizō*, April 1946.
3. Minaé Mizumura, "La littérature moderne japonaise: Deux temps," in *Le Temps des oeuvres / Mémoire et préfiguration*, ed. Jacques Neefs (Saint-Denis: Presses Universitaires de Vincennes, 2001). Revised by the author.

3. PEOPLE AROUND THE WORLD WRITING IN EXTERNAL LANGUAGES

1. Benedict Anderson, *Imagined Communities: Reflections on the Origin and Spread of Nationalism*, rev. ed. (1983; London: Verso, 2006), Kindle ed. Quotations in this chapter are from this work unless otherwise noted.
2. Benedict Anderson, "Global Bases for Early Asian Nationalisms" (lectures presented at Waseda University, Tokyo, April 23, 2005). Slightly edited and revised, based on a transcript provided courtesy of Umemori Naoyuki. Also published in Japanese in Umemori Naoyuki, ed., *Benedict Anderson globalization wo kataru* (Tokyo: Kōbunsha, 2007).

3. Galileo wrote his later works in Italian, which was one of the first vernaculars to become a "print language."

4. THE BIRTH OF JAPANESE AS A NATIONAL LANGUAGE

1. Natsume Sōseki, *Sanshirō* (Amazon Services International, ASIN: B009IXLLU8, 1909), Kindle ed.

2. Higuchi Ichiyō (1872–1896) was one of the first women to write in the Meiji period. Despite her brief life of twenty-four years, her work is revered alongside that of modern Japan's greatest writers. It is not discussed in this book because her novels are thematically modern yet stylistically premodern. She was trained in writing *waka* poems, and her prose reflects that tradition; only her final work is written in the *genbun itchi* style.

3. Helen Craig McCullough, trans., *Kokin Wakashū: The First Imperial Anthology of Japanese Poetry* (Stanford, Calif.: Stanford University Press, 1985), 20.

4. Uchimura Kanzō, *How I Became a Christian* (1890; repr., Whitefish, Mont.: Kessinger, 2010), 57.

5. Ibid., 58.

6. Fukuzawa Yukichi, *An Encouragement of Learning*, trans. David A. Dilworth (Tokyo: Keio University Press, 2012).

7. Fukuzawa Yukichi, *The Autobiography of Yukichi Fukuzawa*, trans. Eiichi Kiyooka (1966; repr., New York: Columbia University Press, 2007), 206.

8. Ibid., 207.

9. Ibid., 207–8.

10. Katō Shūichi and Maruyama Masao, "Hon'yaku no shisō," in *Nihon kindai shisō taikei* (Tokyo: Iwanami Shoten, 1991).

11. Mori Arinori, *Education in Japan: A Series of Letters Addressed by Prominent Americans to Arinori Mori* (1873; repr., New York: Appleton, 2000), lvi.

12. Fukuzawa, *Autobiography*, 6. Quotations in this section are from this work.

13. Maruyama Masao and Katō Shūichi, *Hon'yaku to Nihon no kindai* (Tokyo: Iwanami Shoten, 1998).

5. THE MIRACLE OF MODERN JAPANESE LITERATURE

1. Natsume Sōseki, *Sanshirō* (Amazon Services International, ASIN: B009IXLLU8, 1909), Kindle ed. Quotations in this chapter are from this work unless otherwise noted.

2. Natsume Sōseki, *Theory of Literature*, trans. Joseph A. Murphy, in *Theory of Literature and Other Critical Writings*, ed. Michael K. Bourdaghs, Atsuko Ueda, and Joseph A. Murphy (New York: Columbia University Press, 2012), Kindle ed.

3. Sōseki, "My Individualism," trans. Jay Rubin, in ibid.

4. Sōseki, preface to *Theory of Literature*, trans. Michael K. Bourdaghs, in ibid.

5. Ibid.

6. Natsume Sōseki, *Shokanshū*, ed. Komiya Hōryū, Sōseki zenshū 28 (1956; Tokyo: Iwanami Shoten, 1980), 209.

7. Natsume Sōseki, "Gendai Nihon no kaika" (Amazon Services International, ASIN: B009IXK2EO, 1911), Kindle ed.

8. Hori Keiko, " 'Konjiki yasha' ni okeru hon'anteki sokumen," in *Ozaki Kōyō shū*, Shin Nihon koten bungaku taikei: Meiji hen 19, Geppō (Monthly report) (Tokyo: Iwanami Shoten, 2003).

6. ENGLISH AND NATIONAL LANGUAGES IN THE INTERNET AGE

1. Natsume Sōseki, "Gifu e no tegami," in *Shokanshū*, ed. Komiya Hōryū, Sōseki zenshū 27 (Tokyo: Iwanami Shoten, 1956), 168.

2. Terada Torahiko, "Natsume Sōseki sensei no tsuioku" (Amazon Services International, ASIN: B009AJFLHY, 1948), Kindle ed.

7. THE FUTURE OF NATIONAL LANGUAGES

1. Ngũgĩ wa Thiong'o, "Decolonising the Mind," in *The Norton Anthology of English Literature*, vol. F, *The Twentieth Century and After*, 8th ed., ed. Stephen Greenblatt, M. H. Abrams, Jahan Ramazani, and Jon Stallworthy (1986; New York: Norton, 2005), 2537.

2. In 2001, the Ministry of Education was renamed the Ministry of Education, Culture, Sports, Science and Technology.

3. Atsuji Tetsuji, *Sengo Nihon kanjishi* (Tokyo: Shinchōsha, 2010), 39–51.

4. Fukuda Tsuneari, *Watashi no kokugo kyōshitsu* (1960; Tokyo: Shinchōsha, 1961), 312.

5. Ibid.

6. Kawai Hayao, "Kokusai shakai de fukaketsu na 'shudan,' " in *Ronsō: Eigo ga kōyōgo ni naru hi* (Tokyo: Chūkō Shinsho Rakure, 2002), 51.

7. Sakaguchi Ango, *Nihon bunka shikan* (1943; Tokyo: Kōdansha, ASIN: B00J9Y95U4, 1996), Kindle ed.

8. I Yeonsuk, *Kokugo to iu shisō: Kindai Nihon no gengo ninshiki* (Tokyo: Iwanami Shoten, 1996), 251.

9. Ibid., 313.

10. Funabashi Yōichi, *Aete Eigo kōyōgo ron* (Tokyo: Bungei Shunjū, 2000).

11. Hagiwara Sakutarō, "Ryojō" (On a journey), in *Junjō shōkyokushū* (Amazon Services International, ASIN: B009IY9L0Y, 1925), Kindle ed.

SELECTED BIBLIOGRAPHY

I have kept the Selected Bibliography concise because this is not a book of scholarship in the usual sense of the term. I am indebted to all the books I have had the good fortune to encounter in my life, from the children's books I returned to again and again for pleasure to the tomes on literary theory I struggled through but now look back on with a sense of gratitude mixed with nostalgia.

Anderson, Benedict. "Global Bases for Early Asian Nationalisms." Lectures presented at Waseda University, Tokyo, April 23, 2005. [Also published in Japanese in Naoyuki Umemori, ed., *Benedict Anderson globalization wo kataru*. Tokyo: Kōbunsha, 2007.]

——. *Imagined Communities: Reflections on the Origin and Spread of Nationalism.* Rev. ed. London: Verso, 2006. Kindle ed.

Atsuji Tetsuji. *Sengo Nihon kanji shi.* Tokyo: Shinchōsha, 2010.

Fukuda Tsuneari. *Watashi no kokugo kyōshitsu.* 1960. Tokyo: Shinchōsha, 1961.

Fukuzawa Yukichi. *The Autobiography of Yukichi Fukuzawa.* Translated by Eiichi Kiyooka. 1966. Reprint, New York: Columbia University Press, 2007.

Funabashi Yōichi. *Aete Eigo kōyōgo ron.* Tokyo: Bungei Shunjū, 2000.

I Yeonsuk. *Kokugo to iu shisō: Kindai Nihon no gengo ninshiki.* Tokyo: Iwanami Shoten, 1996.

Katō Shūichi and Maruyama Masao. "Hon'yaku no shisō." In *Nihon kindai shisō taikei.* Tokyo: Iwanami Shoten, 1991.

Kin Bunkyō. *Kanbun to higashi Asia.* Tokyo: Iwanami Shoten, 2010.

Maruyama Masao and Katō Shūichi. *Hon'yaku to Nihon no kindai.* Tokyo: Iwanami Shoten, 1998.

Natsume Sōseki. "Gendai Nihon no kaika." Amazon Services International, ASIN: B009IXK2EO, 1911. Kindle ed.

——. *Sanshirō*. Amazon Services International, ASIN: B009IXLLU8, 1909. Kindle ed.

——. *Shokanshū*. Edited by Komiya Hōryū. Sōseki zenshū 28. 1956. Tokyo: Iwanami Shoten, 1980.

——. *Theory of Literature and Other Critical Writings*. Edited by Michael K. Bourdaghs, Atsuko Ueda, and Joseph A. Murphy. New York: Columbia University Press, 2012. Kindle ed.

Shinada Yoshikazu. "Kokumin kashū toshite no 'Man'yōshū.'" In *Sōzōsareta koten: Canon keisei, kokumin kokka, Nihon bungaku*, edited by Haruo Shirane and Suzuki Tomi. Tokyo: Shin'yōsha, 1999.

Suzuki Yoshisato and Chūko Shinsho Rakure Henshūbu, eds. *Ronsō: Eigo ga kōyōgo ni naru hi*. Tokyo: Chūō Kōrōn Shinsha, 2002.

Yamaguchi Nakami. *Nihongo no rekishi*. Tokyo: Iwanami Shoten, 2006.

INDEX

Daibosatsu tōge (Bodhisattva pass; Nakazato Kaizan), 154

Dangerous Liaisons, The (Pierre Choderlos de Laclos), 148

Danish language, 39, 93, 95

Dante Alighieri, 90, 116

David Copperfield (Charles Dickens), 104

"Decolonising the Mind" (Ngũgĩ Wa Thiong'o), 178

"Defense and Illustration of the French Language, The" (Joachim du Bellay), 91

Defoe, Daniel, 99, 136

de Man, Paul, 2

Derrida, Jacques, 189

Descartes, René, 91

Devanagari alphabet, 200

De Vulgari Eloquentia (On eloquence in the vernacular; Dante Alighieri), 90

Dickens, Charles, 104, 182

Diderot, Denis, 49

Divine Comedy (Dante Alighieri), 90, 116

dōjin-shi (magazines for the like-minded), 156

Don Quixote (Miguel de Cervantes), 116

Dostoevsky, Fyodor, 94, 104

du Bellay, Joachim, 91

Dutch colonialism and language, 50, 59–60, 127–31, 176

Dutch East India Company, 59–60, 127

Edo period and government, 50, 55, 105, 110, 116–17, 127, 152

"Education in Japan" (Mori Arinori), 123

education system of Japan: and American Occupation after World War II, 184–85; and English language, 191; and Japanese language and literature, 124–25, 180–82, 184–88, 198–200; and Meiji Restoration, 111, 135, 180–81; and national language ideology, 136; reform proposals for, 5–6, 198–203; and universities, 134, 137–47, 166–67, 169

Egyptian hieroglyphs, 124. See also written language

Elements of International Law (Henry Wheaton), 125

Eliot, George (Mary Ann Evans), 104

elitism and egalitarianism, 5–6, 183–84, 197–99

Encouragement of Learning, An (Gakumon no susume; Fukuzawa Yukichi), 117

England. See British colonialism

Engle, Paul, 22

English language: and colonialism, 43–44, 121–22, 172; dominance of, vii, 50, 52, 55, 64, 93, 96–97, 164–67, 196–98; and Japan, 123, 132–33, 169–72, 191, 195–98; origin of, 41; and other languages and literatures, 60–61, 160, 167–68, 202–3; as universal language, 2–5, 40–44, 78–83, 160, 202

English literature, 68, 91, 143–44

Enlightenment, 92–97

Erasmus, Desiderius, 87

Esperanto (language), 194

Essays (Francis Bacon), 139

Ethiopia, 118

Eurocentrism, 56, 97, 137

Europe and European languages, 58, 80, 87, 92, 95–96, 135–37, 168. See also specific languages and countries

existentialism, 52

external language, 72, 83; and accumulation of general knowledge, 86, 97; Chinese as, 106, 114, 124; English as, 164, 167, 169; Latin as, 75; sacred languages as, 81; and written language, 84. See also universal language

Faber, Ernst, 112

Fear and Trembling (Frygt og Bæven; Søren Kierkegaard), 95

Filipino language, 177–78

Finnegans Wake (James Joyce), 100